EMOTION-FOCUSED THERAPY FOR GENERALIZED ANXIETY

EMOTION-FOCUSED THERAPY FOR GENERALIZED ANXIETY

JEANNE C. WATSON and
LESLIE S. GREENBERG

AMERICAN PSYCHOLOGICAL ASSOCIATION • Washington, DC

Published by
American Psychological Association
750 First Street, NE
Washington, DC 20002
www.apa.org

To order
APA Order Department
P.O. Box 92984
Washington, DC 20090-2984
Tel: (800) 374-2721; Direct: (202) 336-5510
Fax: (202) 336-5502; TDD/TTY: (202) 336-6123
Online: www.apa.org/pubs/books
E-mail: order@apa.org

In the U.K., Europe, Africa, and the Middle East, copies may be ordered from
American Psychological Association
3 Henrietta Street
Covent Garden, London
WC2E 8LU England

Typeset in Goudy by Circle Graphics, Inc., Columbia, MD

Printer: Bang Printing, Brainerd, MN
Cover Designer: Naylor Design, Washington, DC

The opinions and statements published are the responsibility of the authors, and such opinions and statements do not necessarily represent the policies of the American Psychological Association.

Library of Congress Cataloging-in-Publication Data

Names: Watson, Jeanne C., author. | Greenberg, Leslie S., author. | American Psychological Association, publisher.
Title: Emotion-focused therapy for generalized anxiety / Jeanne C. Watson and Leslie S. Greenberg.
Description: First edition. | Washington, DC : American Psychological Association, [2017] | Includes bibliographical references and index.
Identifiers: LCCN 2016034042 | ISBN 9781433826788 | ISBN 143382678X
Subjects: | MESH: Anxiety Disorders—therapy | Psychotherapy—methods | Emotions
Classification: LCC RC531 | NLM WM 172 | DDC 616.85/22—dc23 LC record available at https://lccn.loc.gov/2016034042

British Library Cataloguing-in-Publication Data

A CIP record is available from the British Library.

Printed in the United States of America
First Edition

http://dx.doi.org/10.1037/0000018-000

To all those with generalized anxiety disorder—
may they find relief from their pain.

CONTENTS

ACKNOWLEDGMENTS

This book would not have been written without the support of many individuals. In particular, we would like to acknowledge our mentors, teachers, and colleagues who shared their knowledge and expertise and contributed to the development of emotion-focused therapy (EFT) as a distinctive and robust treatment approach. This book has emerged from hours of intensive observation and practice to accurately describe and understand the process of change in generalized anxiety disorder. Our students, as always, have provided inspiration and support, contributing their time and efforts to learning the approach and analyzing transcripts to inform us further about change processes in psychotherapy in general and EFT in particular. A special note of thanks is due to our clients, without whom this book could not have been written. They were courageous in seeking relief from generalized anxiety disorder and were willing to work with us to overcome their condition, so that they could look forward to living life with confidence and trust in themselves and their future.

This work requires a strong editorial team. We would like to acknowledge and thank Susan Reynolds at the American Psychological Association for her enduring patience and encouragement. Without her faith and belief in EFT, this book would not have been produced. Thanks also go to David Becker, for his input and guidance, and the team at the American Psychological Association, as well as the reviews from two anonymous colleagues whose input we drew on to strengthen this book. Their generosity of time and spirit is very much appreciated. We trust that they will be pleased with the final product.

As always, we thank our families, our partners, and our sons and daughters for their enduring support, love, and commitment as they cheered from the sidelines and provided relief from domestic chores so that we might concentrate on writing. We would like to make special mention of Brenda Greenberg, who passed away during the period that this book was being developed. We believe that she would be proud and pleased with this volume and know that our time was well spent. To all of you, please know that your love has been sustaining and invaluable during the arduous and demanding process of writing this book for publication. We trust that it will be well received and that you will agree your contributions were worth it.

EMOTION-FOCUSED THERAPY FOR GENERALIZED ANXIETY

INTRODUCTION

Generalized anxiety disorder (GAD) is a serious disorder that impairs functioning and has high social and economic costs (American Psychiatric Association, 2013; World Health Organization, 2016). Hoffman, Dukes, and Wittchen (2008) observed that GAD contributes to significant impairments in role functioning as well as decrements in quality of life. The impairment of persons with comorbid disorders is even more severe. For people with GAD, the condition negatively impacts their general health, including their physical and mental health, vitality, and social functioning, which leads to increased use of health care resources and loss of productivity due to absenteeism (Porensky et al., 2009; Revicki et al., 2012). It has been noted that the costs from health care and lost productivity exceed those of other patients. Moreover, there is the impact of intergenerational transmission, as people with GAD communicate and share their anxious worrying behavior with their offspring and other family members.

http://dx.doi.org/10.1037/0000018-001
Emotion-Focused Therapy for Generalized Anxiety, by J. C. Watson and L. S. Greenberg

GAD is the most common anxiety disorder and is underrecognized, with only 20% to 32% of patients receiving adequate treatment (Porensky et al., 2009; Revicki et al., 2012). To make matters worse, studies have found that GAD can be treatment resistant. Although approximately 50% of patients respond to short-term treatment, a large percentage either do not respond at all or relapse after treatment (Borkovec, Newman, Pincus, & Lytle, 2002; Hanrahan, Field, Jones, & Davey, 2013). As a result, numerous researchers and clinicians have called for improved and different treatments for the condition (Craske & Waters, 2005; Hofmann & Smits, 2008; Roemer & Orsillo, 2002). In this book, we provide an understanding of GAD from an emotion-focused therapy (EFT) perspective and present alternative treatment strategies that mental health practitioners can use to help clients with GAD maintain positive, long-term changes.

Until recently, EFT has focused on depression (Greenberg & Watson, 2006), trauma (Greenberg & Paivio, 1997; Paivio & Pascual-Leone, 2010), and couples therapy (Greenberg & Goldman, 2008; Greenberg & Johnson, 1988; Johnson, 2004), with no theory of anxiety or, more specifically, no theory of GAD. In EFT in general, dysfunction is seen as arising from the activation of core painful maladaptive emotion schemes of fear, sadness, and shame and the associated vulnerable self-organizations resulting from the synthesis of these schemes together with the inability to symbolize and regulate the ensuing painful affect (Greenberg, 2002, 2011; Kennedy-Moore & Watson, 1999, 2001; J. Watson, 2011). In EFT, when people experience anxiety, the self is organized as scared and vulnerable because of the activation of emotion schematic memories of harmful and painful experiences in the absence of protection and support. As a result, people do not internalize self-soothing strategies and instead develop negative ways of relating to the self and modulating emotions.

Developmentally, the experience of intense distress combined with the absence of soothing, care, protection, and support results in the inability to adequately regulate and symbolize emotional experience, leading to painful experiences being interrupted and blocked to protect the self from feared dissolution and disintegration. Without adequate protection, soothing, and succor, negative ways of regulating emotional experience and coping with challenging and distressing life circumstances are internalized. These negative ways of relating to one's experience include dismissing the experience, invalidating it, silencing the self, blaming the self for the negative experience, and rejecting the self as unworthy of being loved and supported. Thus, as a result of an intensely painful experience and in an attempt to manage feelings, there is a constriction of awareness such that individuals have difficulty representing and symbolizing their experience in consciousness. Instead, people with GAD experience a sense of *undifferentiated distress*—a vague feeling in the body at the edge of awareness. The combination of the inability to symbolize painful emotions and experiences, negative ways of treating the self, and an inability to soothe the resulting overwhelming emotions leads to a fear of dissolution and compromises the individual's affect regulation capacities. People end up worrying in an effort to protect the self from falling apart because of an inability to cope with the underlying painful feelings of fear, sadness, and shame.

GENERALIZED ANXIETY DISORDER

Estimates of the lifetime prevalence of GAD in the general population range from 1.9% to 5.4%. GAD is more common in women than in men by a ratio of 2 to 1 (Andlin-Sobocki & Wittchen, 2005; Brown, O'Leary, & Barlow, 2001). Among the elderly, estimates are even higher, with some researchers suggesting that 17% of elderly men and 21.5% of elderly woman require treatment for the disorder (Brown et al., 2001; Salzman & Lebowitz, 1991). More than half of those individuals diagnosed with GAD experience onset during childhood and adolescence, although later onset does occur after the age of 20 (Andlin-Sobocki & Wittchen, 2005).

Symptoms are often worse during periods of stress. Most people with GAD report that they have felt anxious and nervous all their lives, which underscores the important role of early life experiences in its etiology and development. Anxiety disorders, and specifically GAD, have been found to be comorbid with other Axis I disorders from the *Diagnostic and Statistical Manual of Mental Disorders, Fifth Edition* (American Psychiatric Association, 2013), including other anxiety disorders (e.g., social anxiety disorder, post-traumatic stress disorder, panic disorder), mood disorders, addictions, and eating disorders (Carter, Wittchen, Pfister, & Kessler, 2001; Craske & Waters, 2005; Kessler, Ruscio, Shear, & Wittchen, 2009). Unipolar depression is 4 times more common in GAD than is bipolar depression, with incidence being 67% and 17%, respectively (Judd et al., 1998). Overlap has also been found with Axis II disorders, including avoidant and dependent personality disorders (Mauri et al., 1992). Some researchers have suggested that given its early onset, anxiety should be viewed as temporally primary among the other disorders with which there is high comorbidity. They have suggested that early detection and treatment of anxiety might have implications for the onset of other disorders (Kessler et al., 2009).

Unlike some of the other anxiety disorders (e.g., social anxiety, phobias), GAD has no clear precipitants. It is not associated with a particular stimulus (e.g., heights, snakes) but is activated by a variety of different situations and stimuli (American Psychiatric Association, 2013; World Health Organization,

2016). The early onset of GAD suggests that it is a condition that develops early in development and may be consolidated during core developmental years. Studies looking at early childhood factors associated with GAD point to a negative early climate characterized by parental rejection and criticism, lack of parental warmth and acceptance, and a sense that family dynamics were unfair. This may be compounded by other negative life experiences and events for which people may have had insufficient protection, support, and care.

The research literature shows that not all clients respond to short-term treatments, although some clients clearly progress and their symptoms remit after several weeks (Borkovec et al., 2002; Elliott & Freire, 2010; Hanrahan et al., 2013); other individuals may require a longer length of treatment. The exact length will vary in terms of the severity of clients' early life conditions, as well as the individual capacities that clients bring to therapy (see Chapter 5, this volume). Some individuals may need time to build greater confidence in themselves and to develop an adequate understanding of what has transpired in their lives that has made them feel so vulnerable, reject their experience, and unable to regulate their emotions. As they gain a better understanding and acknowledge their experiences, they can begin to see what was so challenging and negative for them and appreciate what was lost and not received. This enables them to symbolize previously disclaimed painful experiences and identify the negative behaviors and ways of processing their experiences that were internalized as they tried to cope with intensely distressing events. This understanding points to aspects of their experience that they can change. Clients with GAD come to recognize that they do not adequately process their emotions and bodily experience, fearing that they will "disintegrate" because of the intensity of the pain. There is a recognition that they need to become more aware of their bodily experiences and emotions, experience their painful emotions, learn how to accept them, symbolize them and put them into words, and finally, with the help of the therapist, access new, more empowering emotions to transform their painful maladaptive feelings. Feeling stronger and more resilient, they are better able to modulate their distress, soothe their painful feelings, and express their emotions and needs to others.

MAIN PROCESSES IN EMOTION-FOCUSED THERAPY

EFT emphasizes the important role of the therapeutic relationship and provides suggestions and ways of working with clients to resolve how they relate to the self and others. Although therapy is a complex, multilayered interaction, we have distilled five main processes and tasks that are woven sequentially and in parallel throughout the treatment. These processes include the following: (a) providing clients with an empathic, accepting, and prizing relationship to build a stronger sense of self so that they feel more trusting of their emotional experience and perceptions, become more confident in their interactions with others, become more self-compassionate and self-nurturing, are able to tolerate and soothe their emotional experience, and modulate the expression of their emotions and needs to others; (b) working with clients to experience disclaimed painful emotions and develop an understanding of their life story or narrative to make sense of life events and their impact; (c) working with clients on identifying and changing the negative ways in which they relate to the self using two-chair tasks; (d) working with clients to transform painful maladaptive emotions by healing past emotional injuries experienced in interaction with significant others using empty-chair tasks to resolve unfinished business; and (e) working with clients to develop capacities to self-soothe using imaginal transformation and two-chair dialogues to resolve emotional suffering.

Although these processes and tasks are described as following a sequential order in treatment, they generally occur in parallel and are woven throughout the treatment process after the therapist has begun to build a positive therapeutic relationship and a positive alliance with the client in the first few sessions. So, although the therapist may focus on one of the these tasks more than the others at different times in therapy, or on additional tasks such as initially building a therapeutic alliance, developing a case formulation, or building a stronger sense of self, the process remains fluid.

Once the EFT therapist introduces chair dialogues, she or he continues to work on the relationship by providing empathic attunement, acceptance, and prizing in a sincere and congruent manner to continue to strengthen clients' sense of self and to facilitate awareness of clients' emotional experience and help clients represent it in words. Labeling their emotions, learning to regulate and modulate their intense feelings of distress, and transforming core painful maladaptive emotions enable clients to acquire the capacities to regulate and express their emotional experiences more optimally and develop more positive ways of caring for the self. Throughout therapy, as clients work to change their core painful emotions, undo their negative self-treatment, as well as to resolve their attachment injuries, they cycle in and out of tasks that focus on how they relate to the self using two-chair dialogues and how they address emotional injuries with an imagined other using empty-chair dialogues. Although working on self–self and working on self–other relationships are conceptualized as two parallel tracks, it is highly likely that to fully resolve emotional injuries with an imagined other, clients may need to have consolidated changes in how they relate to the self and their emotions so that they feel deserving and entitled to assert their needs and receive loving care and protection from others.

CASE EXAMPLE[1]

In the following case example, we provide an overview of the EFT process for GAD. Monica came to therapy after her first child was born. She and her husband had immigrated to North America from South America so he could pursue graduate studies in engineering. Five years after immigrating, they had their first child. The couple had waited to have children until Monica's husband had permanent work and they felt more settled. Before their first child was born, Monica had worked part-time with a Spanish importing company. In addition, she focused on developing and mastering her English and taking care of the home. She recalled it as a fun and carefree time. Although her husband was in school, they had sufficient money and enjoyed a relaxed lifestyle, as they made friends and put down roots in their new country. Monica had limited contact with her family of origin. Her parents had split up when she was 16 years old. Her father had remarried, and Monica did not get along with his new wife. Her mother had become angry and rejecting of her children, blaming them for her husband's desertion.

After the birth of her baby, Monica felt very stressed. She worried that she would not be a good mother, that her husband would leave her, and that she would be deserted in her new country—alone, penniless, and without support. When she first entered therapy, Monica focused on her physical symptoms of anxiety, including the feeling of tightness in her chest. She felt overwhelmed caring for her baby and constantly fretted that she could not manage. She had a sense of doom and foreboding and a fear that she was about to disintegrate. At first Monica spoke about what was transpiring in her current life. Her husband was working long hours and she often felt alone and isolated at home with the baby.

Her therapist explored the difficulty Monica had making the transition to motherhood, as well as her sadness at losing connection with her friends at work. It was difficult to stay in touch because they were still working and she found it difficult to socialize and care for the baby at the same time. Monica constantly second-guessed herself. She did not trust her judgment and sought reassurance. She would compare herself with her mother, whom she described as having been very critical and cold when she was growing up. Her mother favored her brother, whereas Monica was expected to do all the chores in the house, taking care of her mother and little brother. Her father was an ambitious man who traveled and worked long hours. He was distant and not very involved in the home.

---

[1]Client information in this book has been changed to protect confidentiality.

Building a Therapeutic Relationship and Clients' Emotional Processing Capacity

Her therapist noted that Monica was not clear about her feelings. She was easily overwhelmed and often tearful and afraid but did not know why. From the beginning her therapist focused on being empathic, accepting, and prizing of her client's experience, working with her to put it into words. In the beginning Monica found it hard to believe that her therapist was not blaming her for her difficulties, as she herself did. Slowly she came to trust that her therapist believed her and was an ally. Growing more trusting, Monica began to share more of her childhood experience of being neglected and criticized. Her therapist empathically reflected what Monica shared of her experiences, reflecting aspects of the narrative as well as Monica's feelings and experiences of her home life. Together they began to build a picture of a cold, critical, and negative climate at home; a home in which Monica felt alone, unloved, and overburdened, and where her feelings and needs were overlooked.

Working With Negative Treatment of the Self in Two-Chair Dialogues

Initially, to deal with Monica's presenting problem, the therapist introduced a *worry split*. Monica would catastrophize and imagine her baby and her husband becoming ill. She would constantly second-guess herself and worry that she had made a mistake. Noting these markers of worry, the therapist asked Monica how she made herself feel anxious and had Monica enact this in a two-chair dialogue. Monica gained a heightened sense of self as an agent acting on herself by worrying rather than being a passive victim afflicted with worry. Seeing the toll the worry took on her, Monica asked the worrier self to stop. However, the worrier self collapsed in distress, feeling sad and angry that Monica was silencing and rejecting that part of herself, leaving her alone with her feelings of loneliness and pain. The negative way she related to her experience, as well as the pain and fear of rejection from her early childhood experience, became clear. This focused the therapy, as she and her therapist began to work on these two tracks using two-chair and empty-chair dialogues.

Working in two-chair dialogues, it became clear that Monica was very self-rejecting and saw herself as responsible for making everything turn out well. She saw herself as incompetent and was critical when things did not go right. Initially, Monica minimized her mother's behavior toward her. She said she deserved her mother's criticism because Monica was careless and stupid, and her little brother needed more attention from her mother. As she shared her memories and the therapist reflected these experiences empathically, Monica began to acknowledge and recognize the fear of rejection and pain she experienced in childhood. She began to allow herself to experience her feelings and become more aware of them; she became more aware of how lonely and rejected she felt. However, before Monica was able to fully acknowledge her pain, she had to recognize that she was dismissive of her feelings and blamed herself for the way her mother treated her. Monica would tell herself that if she had been more lovable or more competent, then her mother would have loved her more. She would remind herself of how her mother's life was difficult without allowing that, as a child, she needed attention and care from her mother. The therapist would reflect these blaming statements by asking, "Do you think it was fair to blame the little girl?" or "Do you think it is fair for a child to take care of her parents?"

Working With Relational Injuries in Empty-Chair Dialogues

It was clear that Monica was immersed in her mother's perspective and had not developed her own unique view and experience of the world. An important aspect of EFT is that although the therapist shares some of his or her observations or suggests that certain behaviors are harsh, he or she does not insist that clients accept this view. Rather, the therapist is patient and accepting of clients' experience, waiting until they are willing and able to adopt a different perspective and accept their own experience without seeing themselves through the eyes of a caretaker. Once clients agree that these ways of being are problematic and express a wish to change them, then the therapist moves ahead with tasks like two-chair dialogues to resolve negative treatment of the self or empty-chair dialogues to resolve attachment injuries. Monica needed to feel strong enough to face how she had been treated as a child. She needed to feel she was able to hold her mother accountable and that she deserved more care, attention, and support than she had been given. All of this demanded that she feel deserving of having her needs met and take a stance opposed to her parents and move outside the radius of their protection.

With time, and as Monica slowly internalized her therapist's empathy, warmth, concern, and acceptance, she began to access her anger and sadness. This helped Monica acknowledge that she had been treated unfairly and that she had needed and deserved more love and protection. She saw her mother as rejecting and neglectful. This was an important shift for Monica and allowed her to attend to her own experience and needs. It took time for this perspective to coalesce as Monica oscillated between seeing herself as deserving of love and support or as deserving of her mother's blame and criticism. To work with the self-blame, the therapist introduced two-chair dialogues. As Monica became stronger and better able to process her feelings of anger and sadness and her fears of rejection, she came to validate her own experience and feel like she could stand alone.

In EFT, it is posited that as clients internalize their therapist's positive attitudes of respect, warmth, empathy, and acceptance, they begin to build a stronger sense of self and believe that they are deserving of love, protection, and support. As Monica began to acknowledge how her mother had treated her, she engaged in empty-chair dialogues with her mother to express her pain about how she had been treated and to assert what she had needed from her mother when she was a child. Once she was able to differentiate her emotions and allow herself to feel sadness and grief at what she missed, and to feel anger to protest her emotional abandonment, she was able to set boundaries with her mother. Monica was able to integrate her own needs with those of her mother's once again. She recognized that her mother had been very limited and handicapped by her own life experience. However, Monica was clear that her mother should have found other ways to address her pain and taken better care of Monica.

As this example shows, clients can cycle in and out of empty-chair dialogues and two-chair dialogues across different sessions. These processes are parallel tracks as clients move from working with negative ways of treating the self and then back to focus on the hurt experienced at the hands of another and back again to continue working toward new ways of relating to the self and others. All this work continues in the context of the therapist's remaining empathically attuned and working with clients to help them become aware of their inner experience, label it, give it words, and develop new ways to modulate and express it.

Developing Self-Soothing

In EFT for GAD, it is important that clients develop self-soothing. This occurs initially by internalizing the therapist's attitudes of empathy, acceptance, and prizing, and by learning that the clients can reduce and modulate their distress by attending to their feelings and putting these feelings into words. In addition, clients are provided with more concrete strategies and experience engaging in self-soothing using two-chair dialogues to modulate their painful feelings. An important indicator of change is when clients can effectively modulate their distress in the moment and reassure themselves when feeling distressed, thereby effectively providing comfort. This is often in the form of self-talk as well as activities and redirection of attention to more pleasant and present-focused concerns. Clients learn to interrupt the cascade of negative thoughts and instead are able to reassure themselves that they can cope, that they are not fully responsible for outcomes, and that they can turn to others for support. In the case of Monica, she developed greater confidence in herself, began to trust her perceptions and feelings more, and was able to turn to her husband for support when she was feeling overwhelmed.

She also developed ways to self-soothe, including reading and listening to music. Most important, she learned to be more compassionate toward and less demanding of herself. By the end of therapy, her anxiety had moderated considerably, she was more aware when the demanding castigating voice of her mother emerged, and she would reassure herself that there was no need to be worried. She recognized that she was "fine just the way she was" and that her husband was there to talk with her and was someone with whom she could work out her problems. By the end of therapy, she had internalized her therapist's compassion and developed different ways of self-soothing so that she felt more confident and joyful about her life.

KEY TERMS

Some key terms that are used in EFT are briefly defined as follows.

- *Emotion schemes*: The connections that form among a situation/ event/interaction, people's bodily felt sense, their emotions and feelings, their attendant action tendencies, and the meaning or interpretation that they attribute to the experience. Emotion schemes allow individuals to interpret and react to events. They give rise to action tendencies or ways of responding to our environment.
- *Emotion types*: There are four different types of emotion identified in EFT: primary adaptive, primary maladaptive, secondary, and instrumental.
- *Primary adaptive emotions*: The innate, most basic emotional responses to a given situation. These enable people to process and perceive their environment rapidly, automatically allowing for an immediate and adaptive behavioral response. For example, sadness signals a need for comfort, and inclines people to seek nurturance and solace from others.
- *Primary maladaptive emotion*: Primary emotional responses that were originally adaptive responses in harmful, neglectful, and negative environments but have become maladaptive in current contexts. For example, negative life experiences may contribute to neutral and positive stimuli becoming associated with feelings of fear, shame, and sadness as opposed to more pleasurable emotions of joy and contentment.
- *Secondary emotions*: Reactions to primary emotions. Examples include feeling and expressing anger or shame when sad. These types of emotional expressions are maladaptive in that they

prevent the full processing of primary emotions as well as access to the adaptive information provided by primary emotions.

- *Instrumental emotions*: Emotions that do not reflect an innate biological response to the environment. They are not authentic but learned responses that are enacted in interaction with the environment to elicit a specific response from another. Thus, they are used to influence and manipulate the behavior of others. For example, using the expression of anger to intimidate and force someone to submit.

- *Emotional processing*: From an EFT perspective, this is defined as approaching, attending, accepting, tolerating, regulating, symbolizing, expressing, and transforming emotion when necessary.

- *Task*: EFT uses this word to refer to specific client processes in the context of specific interventions that were developed from intense process analysis of small episodes of client and therapist interaction that indicated clients had resolved a specific problem—for example, when clients resolve a conflict between two opposing courses of action, interrupt negative self-talk, and become more compassionate and self-soothing. The main tasks covered in this book are two-chair dialogues for working with negative treatment of the self, including splits; empty-chair dialogues for unfinished business; self-soothing dialogues for emotional pain; empathic-relational work for strengthening the vulnerable self; and relational ruptures for tears in alliance.

- *Two-chair dialogue*: Self–self dialogues that are suggested by the therapist to resolve opposing sides within clients. First used and studied to resolve conflict splits, two-chair dialogues are now used to work with any negative treatment of the self, including self-criticism, self-blame, self-neglect, and worry, among others. Clients speak to an aspect of the self that is imagined in another chair. These dialogues refer to work with self–self processes. Resolving them fully requires negotiation.

- *Empty-chair dialogue*: Self–other dialogues that are suggested by the therapist for clients to express their feelings and needs to an imagined other. Clients are invited to visualize an imagined other sitting opposite them and then to express their feelings and to assert their needs to the other. The primary objective is to facilitate clients' full expression of their feelings and needs to resolve relational injuries and attachment wounds. Although there may be limited opportunity for the other to respond, a short response can provide additional information about the other. If the other's response is empathic and accepting of the client's position this is helpful and can be validated and supported, as it can be experienced as healing. However, if the other's response is negative, then the therapist is quick to name the negative behavior and shift the client back to his or her own chair. The therapist then provides an empathic response and works with clients to process and express their feelings toward the negative other more fully so as to hold the other accountable.

- *Worry split*: A two-chair dialogue, specifically to access clients' worry messages. It can differ from the usual two-chair dialogue in that vulnerability can often be experienced in both chairs. Therapists need to be aware of this so that they remain empathically attuned and responsive to both chairs.

- *Experiencing chair*: The chair in which feelings are expressed. In two-chair dialogues, a negative process (e.g., worry, self-criticism, self-blame) is activated in one chair to evoke the emotional, bodily felt response in the other chair. It is by accessing clients' primary emotional responses that they are able to access their needs and develop other ways of treating the self that are more self-enhancing and self-protective. In GAD, this process often differs from depression as the worrier self, after being told to stop and relax, may dissolve in distress because it feels that it is being dismissed and invalidated. This reveals the deeper underlying negative treatment of the self, which dismisses painful feelings in an attempt to self-protect.

- *Strengthening the self*: Building a stronger, more resilient sense of self and a positive self-organization that is characterized by feelings of self-worth, self-esteem, self-compassion, self-acceptance, and self-protection. This is a basic process in EFT that is developed through the internalization of the therapeutic relationship conditions of empathy, acceptance, prizing, and congruence along with enhanced ways of processing and regulating emotions and more positive ways of treating the self and experience.

OBJECTIVES OF THIS BOOK

One of the primary objectives of this book is to outline the treatment process in EFT for GAD. The first three chapters provide an overview of EFT and GAD. Chapter 1 articulates an emotion-focused theory of GAD. The etiology of the disorder is described, as well as the cycle of anxiety and worry in which clients routinely engage. Chapter 2 discusses the role of emotion in GAD and explores different theoretical perspectives that have been advanced to explain and conceptualize the disorder. Important EFT concepts are introduced, including emotion schemes and different types of emotions. Their relevance to an EFT conceptualization of GAD is clarified. Chapter 3 outlines the steps of treatment, including case formulation, developing a therapeutic relationship, building a stronger sense of self, working with anxiety splits, changing negative ways of treating experience, resolving emotional injuries, and developing self-compassion and self-assertion to soothe and protect the self.

The following two chapters focus on the therapeutic relationship—how it is developed and the particular qualities of the relationship that are important to healing. Chapter 4 focuses on how the therapist can facilitate the therapeutic relationship to ensure that it is positive and healing, and on how the therapist can be optimally present in the relationship. Chapter 5 explores the impact of the therapeutic relationship from the client's perspective. The different ways that the therapeutic relationship facilitates healing and support as well as changes in how clients relate to the self and others are explored.

The final chapters focus on specific tasks in EFT and ways of working with clients to treat GAD. The use of chair dialogues to resolve negative treatment of the self and emotional injuries is also discussed. Chapter 6 describes how the EFT therapist uses the worry split to help clients work directly on the worry symptoms and turn the experience of worry into something clients do rather than something that is done to them. In this process, clients either assert their need for rest from the constant pressure of the worry or access the underlying, painful feelings of fear, sadness, and shame that drive the worry process. Chapter 7 focuses on working with negative treatment of the self in two-chair dialogues. These dialogues focus on the ways that clients disregard and dismiss their painful experience and distress. As a result, they fail to symbolize their feelings clearly and are unable to soothe and care for themselves. This chapter addresses how the therapist can work with these processes so that clients can begin to develop more positive ways of relating to the self, including being more self-compassionate, self-protective, and self-nurturing.

Chapter 8 explores how the EFT therapist works with clients with GAD to resolve their underlying relational and attachment injuries using empty-chair dialogues. These dialogues focus on accessing clients' core emotion schemes developed in interactions with the imagined other. To resolve their emotional attachment injuries, clients are asked to visualize an imagined other in an empty chair, express their core pain at their negative treatment, and assert their unmet needs to the imagined other. In the process of accessing and expressing their feelings and identifying their needs, clients become more differentiated and separate from the other. In the process, they validate their feelings and perceptions and learn to be more self-protective with regard to others. To resolve these injuries fully, clients need to feel strong enough to stand independently and free of the other's influence, to protect and care for the self. Therefore, clients need to have internalized their therapist's attitudes and to have modified their negative treatment of the self to be more attentive to their feelings and deserving of their needs. This helps clients access new emotional responses to old situations. Once they feel more deserving and are able to assert their needs and grieve their losses, they become more self-compassionate and self-protective as well as more self-accepting, self-valuing, and self-caring.

The final chapter, Chapter 9, discusses how clients can develop and consolidate the capacity to self-soothe. A number of alternative strategies are presented, including ways of regulating physiological processes in the moment, as well as more transformational strategies, including seeing the self as a "wounded child." The capacity to self-soothe and feel confident in handling stress develops through the internalization of the therapist's attitudes and ways of being with clients, as well as more concrete self-soothing strategies to relieve distress in the moment. The capacity to self-soothe is the final capstone in the treatment of GAD, leaving clients with ongoing resources to counter stressful life events and take care of themselves when they feel challenged and in need of comfort and support.

This book is intended to appeal primarily to clinicians, psychologists, social workers, nurses, psychiatrists, and other mental health professionals and students who wish to learn more about EFT and specifically its application to the treatment of GAD. It offers a humanistic and experiential perspective of the disorder that provides a distinctive EFT approach to treatment. For those who work with GAD and find it treatment resistant, this book might be especially appealing, illuminating as it does the chronicity and developmental trajectory of the disorder that can make it difficult to treat in short-term therapy. The authors offer recommendations for how to work with clients who do not respond quickly, and we provide guidance to beginning therapists, as well as suggestions and alternative perspectives for more seasoned and experienced health care providers.

1

EMOTION-FOCUSED THERAPY FORMULATION OF GENERALIZED ANXIETY DISORDER

Anxiety is a condition of being alive. We are all likely to experience anxiety at some time in our lives, whether in the guise of fear, panic, tension, worry, concern, nervousness, or apprehension. The quality of our anxiety will depend on our resources and the types of situations that we encounter. Individuals would not survive were it not for the capacity of the organism to register the impact of environmental stimuli through pain, fear, hunger, thirst, cold, and heat, among others. Fear and anxiety alert the organism to danger and inform individuals of conditions that are painful and harmful to their survival and well-being.

From the moment of conception, individuals begin to interact with their environment. And once they are born, individuals will come into contact with myriad different stimuli in the process of living, needing continuous protection and nurture to survive and thrive. Infants depend on others to care for and maintain their physical and emotional well-being. Newborn

http://dx.doi.org/10.1037/0000018-002
Emotion-Focused Therapy for Generalized Anxiety, by J. C. Watson and L. S. Greenberg

babies separated from their mothers immediately start crying but settle down when soothed, and toddlers are anxious on separation from their parents but become calm and secure again when reconnected. This anxiety is regulated by the caretaker's affective attunement and soothing. Experience and interaction with significant others is important in accounting for how people come to regulate emotions, as well as their level of anxiety.

With adequate nurture and protection, infants and children develop into well-functioning and self-governing adults with the capacity to be self-protective and self-nurturing. In contrast, when physical and/or psychological survival is threatened by frightening and hostile environmental conditions and there is inadequate protection and nurture to cope with fear and pain, individuals are likely to become anxious and fearful. Individuals who have had difficult and/or traumatic experiences in childhood, characterized by threats to their emotional and physical well-being that contribute to the development of chronic and repeated attachment injuries, are more likely to grow up feeling anxious in a variety of different situations than are individuals whose upbringing was relatively free of emotional or physical challenges.

Anxiety and fear organize people to protect themselves from situations and events that threaten their physical, emotional, and psychological well-being. Most of the time anxiety recedes once individuals have been alerted and adequate action has been taken to restore their sense of well-being and safety. However, in cases where there is insufficient protection, nurturing, soothing, and support, and there is an inability to adequately process and regulate emotions, emotion schematic memories of painful experiences can be formed. If there is a chronic lack of support and nurture that becomes internalized, people will learn to cope with painful experience by tuning out, numbing, dismissing, and ignoring it, and these negative ways of coping may become habitual. As painful experiences remain out of awareness, emotion schemes are activated automatically, setting an anxious mode of processing in action. People then worry about protecting themselves from painful feelings and potentially harmful situations. When anxiety and fear become chronic, worry predominates, with painful events and emotions remaining unprocessed and identity formation compromised.

GENERALIZED ANXIETY DISORDER

Chronic anxiety characterized by excessive worry, feelings of restlessness, tiredness, irritability and tension, as well as disturbed sleep, are the symptoms of generalized anxiety disorder (GAD). GAD is one of seven distinct types of anxiety conditions listed in the *Diagnostic and Statistical Manual of*

Mental Disorders, Fifth Edition (*DSM–5*; American Psychiatric Association, 2013), which also include posttraumatic stress disorder (PTSD), specific phobias, social phobia, and obsessive–compulsive disorder. According to *DSM–5* and the *International Statistical Classification of Diseases, 10th Edition, Clinical Modification* (World Health Organization, 2016), GAD involves excessive worry and anxiety about a number of different aspects of life, including work, family, children, and physical health, among others. The worry is usually pervasive and troubling, causing significant distress in terms of functioning. It usually occurs without explicit precipitants or clearly identified triggers, although triggers are clear for some of the other anxiety disorders. Instead, people with GAD may worry about many different situations that they anticipate will evoke feelings of distress and disintegration and a concomitant sense of powerlessness and vulnerability.

THEORIES OF GENERALIZED ANXIETY DISORDER

GAD is seen to result from a confluence of genetic, biological, and psychosocial factors (Craske & Waters, 2005; Hettema, Neale, & Kendler, 2001), which has given rise to a number of different theories, including biological and psychological ones, and different ways of treating the disorder. Research has shown that genes may be partly responsible for children's degree of anxiety, with DNA and inheritance being associated with an increased likelihood of being anxious. Children with one parent who has OCD, for example, are 5 times more likely to develop the disorder than children whose parents are not affected. Studies of male mice have shown that the litters born to the males after being stressed by social isolation from peers, displayed more anxious behaviors than those litters born to the same males before they were subjected to stress. Moreover, baby mice born to males who experienced social isolation reacted more negatively to stress than baby mice born to males who had not suffered the stressful experience (Park, 2011). Other studies have shown that the neurotransmitter GABA inhibits anxiety, with anxiolytic drugs enhancing the release of GABA in the brain.

Although genetic and biological perspectives emphasize that anxiety is primarily an inherited condition, there is growing recognition that anxiety disorders are more likely to result from the interaction between genes and environment. According to this view, specific vulnerability factors interact with specific life history events to predict onset (Barlow, 2002; Craske & Waters, 2005; Damasio, 1994). In contrast to biological theories, psychological theories emphasize the role of environmental and experiential dynamics in the development of GAD.

Psychodynamic Perspectives

Sigmund Freud (1924), in his early theory, saw anxiety as caused by repression. Subsequently, in his second theory, anxiety was conceptualized as being a small dose of *signal anxiety*, which serves as a warning that steps must be taken to prevent certain ideas that would cause more traumatic anxiety becoming conscious. Psychoanalysis, as it developed, saw psychopathology, and by implication generalized anxiety, as resulting from unconscious conflicts between superego, id, and ego. Sexual and aggressive impulses at any stage of psychosexual development were seen as potentially being in conflict with the demands of the superego. The use of worry to avoid thinking about troubling issues was seen as a defense and a signal that the ego was having difficulty mediating the demands of reality, id, and superego. Psychoanalytic treatment focuses on revealing the source of the conflict and working it through in psychoanalysis. What is distinctly psychoanalytic is the view that anxiety is caused by unacceptable conscious and unconscious motives, intentions, and wishes. Debilitating anxiety, as opposed to signal anxiety, essentially results from the breakdown of defenses, whereas insight into and integration of repressed motivation is the path to a cure.

A more interpersonal, psychodynamic focus emphasizes the role of relationships in the development and maintenance of anxiety symptoms. According to psychoanalytic theorists, individuals with anxiety experienced difficult early relationships with unavailable and unresponsive caretakers. Bowlby (1973), for example, argued that separation and disturbances in parent–child bonds lead to *anxious attachment* and a vulnerability to anxiety disorders later in life. Sullivan (1953) saw anxiety as resulting from anticipated disapproval from others and Fairbairn (1952) saw anxiety as resulting from conflict between feelings of dependence and fears of being engulfed by another, leading to a loss of identity. Similarly, Bowen (1976, 1978) an analytically based family theorist, saw anxiety as resulting from impaired differentiation within the family system.

Relational psychodynamic theorists see psychopathology as coming from the failure of the environment to be responsive to the needs of the child. This arises from too little soothing and a lack of contact comfort or too much restriction of the child's needs for autonomy and separation. In contemporary relational psychodynamic views, anxiety is no longer related to defense and its breakdown but to maladaptive self–other relationship models. These models may not always be in awareness as they can develop preverbally. Although these models may have been adaptive at the time, currently they impair relational functioning. Anxiety, therefore, is related to the persistence of early patterns of relating and to the threat of being with another in a way that threatens early ties to parents. This threat is experienced when people act in ways inconsistent with internal working models of self and other. Using an attachment framework, Crits-Christoph, Crits-Christoph, Wolf-Palacio, Fichter, and Rudick (1995) developed a modified version of supportive-expressive psychotherapy (Luborsky & Mark, 1991) to treat GAD. They noted that a history of insecure or conflicted attachment relationships and/or a history of traumatic events was evident in people who developed GAD. An open trial of their model of psychodynamic psychotherapy showed promising results.

Early attachment experiences, and specifically attachment injuries, that have been repeated and chronic have been shown to be important in the development of GAD. Cassidy, Lichtenstein-Phelps, Sibrava, Thomas, and Borkovec (2009) found that individuals with GAD report less maternal love, greater maternal neglect and rejection, and more role reversal and enmeshment with their caretakers than individuals without GAD. Other research studies have found that clients with GAD worry more frequently about interpersonal concerns than other topics (Breitholtz, Johansson, & Öst, 1999; Roemer, Molina, & Borkovec, 1997) and that they report more negative early life experiences than those who worry but do not meet threshold for GAD (Rodrigues & Watson, 2015).

Cognitive Behavioral Perspectives

From a learning theory point of view, people are anxious and fearful of feelings that are associated with negative outcomes. This view focuses mostly on conscious feelings. The cognitive learning theory of the cause of psychopathology and its remediation is very different from that of psychoanalysis. In psychodynamic models, psychopathology is understood to occur as a result of excessive defenses against anxiety and guilt-producing, mixed feelings toward loved ones. Anxiety is seen as stemming from unconscious conflict in individuals' past. It is not conscious feelings but unconscious feelings of anger, fear, or sadness and unconscious anxiety and unconscious defenses that are the focus of a psychodynamic treatment model. However, in more contemporary cognitive learning theory views, worry is seen as an avoidance of thinking about difficult issues. Thus, the focus in learning theory approaches is on desensitizing clients to conscious feelings, and as a result, other feelings, such as grief, anger, or guilt over unconscious rage toward loved ones, are rarely, if ever, addressed.

Learning theory approaches to GAD have suggested that uncontrollable and unpredictable aversive events may play an important role in the development of GAD (Barlow, 2000; Mineka, 1985; Mineka & Zinbarg, 1996). Although in GAD such events are generally not seen to be as severe as those involved in PTSD, there is some evidence that people with GAD may be more likely to have a history of repeated childhood trauma than people with other anxiety disorders (Borkovec, Alcaine, & Behar, 2004). Moreover, people with GAD have been found to have a low tolerance for uncertainty (Dugas, Buhr, & Ladouceur, 2004), to be disturbed at not being able to predict the future (Roemer, Orsillo, & Barlow, 2002), and to feel constantly tense and vigilant with respect to possible future threats (Mineka & Zinbarg, 1996; Rapee, 2001).

Behavioral interventions involve a number of different ways of treating GAD. Exposure is one principle of treatment, with clients being exposed to the feelings they have learned to fear. This is expected to lead to extinction, with the anxiety fading when the feared negative outcome fails to occur. Habituation and exposure have been successful in combating some anxious behaviors (e.g., fears of snakes, heights). It is hypothesized that people can learn that if nothing dangerous follows a previously frightening stimulus, they do not have to react with fear. A modified form of exposure therapy is desensitization to anxiety provoking stimuli. This involves a gradual exposure to what is frightening, from the least scary situation or stimulus to the most threatening combined with relaxation exercises. It is expected that as people learn to extinguish and modify their anxiety reaction through cultivating a relaxation response at each stage, the body and brain will become desensitized to the feared stimulus. Another proposed way to regulate anxiety is to teach individuals to attend to their breathing (e.g., adjust shallow breathing by taking deeper breaths) and stay focused on what they are doing in the moment rather than focus on some future event.

Consistent with a learning theory perspective, cognitive behavioral perspectives posit that anxiety results from conditioning, with anxiety developing in response to external stimuli that then generalizes to other stimuli, as well as being the result of faulty cognitions (e.g., a fear of losing control or the anticipation of danger and disaster). Treatment in cognitive behavioral therapy consists of training clients in relaxation techniques, challenging negative automatic thoughts, and modifying underlying beliefs about the world as a dangerous place and the self as unable to cope (Barlow, 2000; Beck, Emery, & Greenberg, 1985). Noting that GAD is resistant to extinction (Borkovec & Ruscio, 2001), Borkovec and Inz (1990) proposed a cognitive avoidance theory of worry as an alternative to the traditional learning theory approaches. They argued that worry is a predominantly verbal-linguistic activity with relatively low levels of imagery that serves to avoid unpleasant imagery and the associated negative affect. This theory suggests that when individuals perceive threats either internal or external, somatic arousal occurs and they are motivated to escape the distressing imagery and the accompanying physical symptoms and move to conceptual verbal activity—worry. This posits that people are motivated to worry to avoid pain or, in learning theory terms, *aversive stimulation.*

Thus, worry is seen as a means of preventing exposure to distressing experiences such as memories of previous trauma, childhood adversity, or difficulties in interpersonal relationships (Borkovec, Ray, & Stöber, 1998; Borkovec et al., 2004). Borkovec et al. (2004) suggested that worry serves as a cognitive avoidance response that is self-sustaining and resistant to extinction. They suggested that worry is reinforced because the vast majority of things that people worry about never happen. Paradoxically, it has been shown that attempts to control thoughts and worry may lead to an increase in intrusive thoughts and enhanced perceptions of being unable to control them. Perceptions of uncontrollability are known to be associated with increased anxiety, and intrusive thoughts can serve as triggers for additional worry. Thus a vicious cycle of anxiety, worry, and intrusive thoughts may develop, leading to an increased sense of being unable to control worry in GAD (Mineka, 2004; Mineka et al., 2002; Zinbarg, Craske, & Barlow, 1994).

One of the perceived benefits of worry centers on peoples' beliefs that it helps to avoid catastrophe, either superstitiously or in reality, and this facilitates avoidance of deeper emotional topics that are distressing. Borkovec et al. (2004) suggested that when people with GAD worry, their emotional and physiological responses to aversive imagery are actually suppressed and that this suppression of emotional and physiological responses serves to reinforce the process of worry and increase its probability. Because worry suppresses physiological responding, it also prevents people from fully experiencing or processing the issue about which they are worrying and becoming desensitized to it. Such processing is necessary for extinction to occur. Thus, as long as the response is suppressed, the threatening meaning of the topic will be maintained. Building on the cognitive avoidance model, Newman and Llera (2011) suggested that worry serves as an affect regulation strategy by inducing negative affect to avoid acute increases in negative affect when threatening situations arise.

More recently, cognitive behavioral theories have emphasized the importance of early relationships in the development of GAD, particularly those characterized by role reversal as well as problems in affect regulation (Borkovec et al., 2004; Mennin, 2004; Newman & Llera, 2011). Mennin (2004; Mennin, Heimberg, Turk, & Fresco, 2002) suggested that worry is a result of problems with affect regulation, including (a) heightened intensity of emotions, (b) limited understanding of emotions, (c) negative responses to current emotions, and (d) unhelpful management of emotions. According to this view, GAD results from deficits in affect regulation with an over reliance on worry to manage difficult emotional experiences (Mennin, 2004; Mennin et al., 2002). These theorists suggest that worry is a way of controlling negative autonomic arousal that is triggered when individuals become anxious and are unable to label their feelings and modulate their emotions (Dugas & Robichaud, 2007; Mennin et al., 2002).

Experiential Therapy Perspectives

Early client-centered formulations saw anxiety developing as a result of incongruence (Rogers, 1959). Rogers (1959) hypothesized that incongruence makes people vulnerable to anxiety and depression because the self-structure and the needs of the organism are in conflict. Rogers suggested that anxiety occurs when the needs of the organism are in conflict with introjected conditions of worth from significant others. Fully functioning people do not need to distort experience to fit with introjected conditions of worth. Rather, they are able to be aware of and open to their experience, including their sensations, feelings, perceptions, construals, and emotions, and they are able to accurately symbolize their experience or label it in awareness, accept it, and express it in ways that are responsible for their well-being, their specific community, and society at large (Rogers, 1959; J. Watson & Watson, 2010). Gendlin (1978, 1996) focused on experiencing and saw anxiety as reflecting blocked experiencing resulting from the inability to symbolize experience in awareness.

Subsequently, other humanistic and experiential theorists, such as Wolfe (2005), posited that anxiety disorders are the result of clients' ongoing struggle with their own, subjective experience. Wolfe posited that "all painful views of the self suggest a perception and experience of the self as being unable to cope with—and therefore needing protection from—the rigors and realities of everyday living" (p. 67). Implicit in Wolfe's model is the view that anxiety is an attempt to cover up underlying self-wounds and to facilitate avoidance of painful experience. In a similar vein, Bohart (2012) posited that avoidance is self-protection, whereas Timulak and McElvaney (2015) saw the worry process as facilitating the avoidance of painful affect.

Existential theorists see anxiety as a core part of the human condition and as an unavoidable component of life. In their view, anxiety results from individuals having to face choices without clear guidelines and without knowing what the outcomes will be, and from being aware that they are ultimately responsible for the consequences of their actions (J. Watson & Schneider, 2016). Yalom (1980) suggested that four "ultimate" concerns are a source of existential anxiety. These include the inevitability of *death*; *freedom*, and its responsibility; existential *isolation*; and *meaninglessness*. Psychological dysfunction in his view results from individuals' refusal or inability to deal with the normal existential anxiety that comes from confronting these four concerns. Van Deurzen (2012) further identified the purpose of anxiety as necessary to challenge ourselves to become what we are capable of becoming. Thus, an existential view sees anxiety as stemming from the inability to cope with the challenge of living and to choose to live in a healthy and productive way.

EMOTION-FOCUSED THEORY OF ANXIETY

Maladaptive emotion schematic memories in GAD generally originate from relational injuries and problems in attachment relationships. We propose that GAD develops because of failures in attunement, as well as neglect, rejection, and harm by others that lead to the development of painful emotion schematic memories of fear, shame, and sadness and the internalization of negative ways of coping with these painful and distressing emotions. *Emotion schematic memories* (see Chapter 2, this volume) are fundamental organizations that represent specific evoking situations, children's emotional experiences, and the associated action tendencies. Emotion schemes are predominantly nonverbal, however, they can be brought into awareness as they are symbolized and represented in language.

DEVELOPMENT OF GENERALIZED ANXIETY DISORDER

Repeated exposure to threatening, painful, and negative life events, including large-T trauma and small-t trauma, without adequate protection, soothing, and nurturing compromises people's emotional processing and affect regulation capacity, as well as their identity formation. *Large-T trauma* refers to severe physical and/or sexual abuse, whereas *small-t trauma* refers to less severe interpersonal injuries that accumulate over the course of development (e.g., caretakers who are emotionally cold, withdrawn, critical, demanding, neglectful, intrusive, bullying), as well as emotional injuries that result from emotional and physical abandonment by caretakers (intentionally or unintentionally; because of illness, separation, divorce) or emotional injuries that result from other adverse and painful life experiences (e.g., witnessing conflict between parents; see Baljon & Pool, 2013; Lamagna & Gleiser, 2007; McCann & Pearlman, 1990; Prigerson, Shear, Bierhals, Zonarich, & Reynolds, 1996; Pynoos, Steinberg, & Piacentini, 1999; van der Kolk, 1996, 2005).

These painful experiences in conjunction with inadequate care and protection, and the inability to self-soothe contribute to the development of a vulnerable and wounded sense of self. If needs for connection and protection go unmet, individuals become distressed and their feelings of fear, sadness, and shame remain inadequately symbolized and soothed. Feelings of distress or undifferentiated emotional arousal are intensified as a result of inadequate protection and soothing to comfort the individual. These children feel solely responsible for their well-being. The lived experience plus the harmful situation are coded in emotion schematic memory. Thus, from an EFT perspective, an important contributor to GAD is the inability of people to process their emotions and soothe, comfort, and protect themselves when experiencing distress so as to return to a state of peace and calm.

As a result of painful and harmful experiences, negative *self-organizations* develop characterized by a sense of the self as vulnerable, wounded, and defective. The person's core self-organization, on the basis of an automatic synthesis of activated emotion schemes, is experienced as weak, unacceptable, alone, and vulnerable. There is a sense of being at risk in the world. When this organization is activated, people feel threatened and distressed. Individuals with GAD internalize the neglect and invalidation of painful feelings by others and develop negative ways of relating to the self and others to regulate their emotional experience. Not having experienced adequate support and protection to cope with their distress, individuals do not learn how to regulate and soothe their affective experience; nor are they able to process their feelings to relieve their distress and solve problems in living. Instead, they are overwhelmed by painful somatic sensations that they are unable to assuage, with the emotions in these intense states of arousal remaining unsymbolized and essentially unknown.

When individuals lack support and protection in painful and harmful situations, they feel scared, isolated, abandoned, rejected, inadequate, and/or defective. They are caught between being unsupported and helpless on the one hand and entirely responsible for their own well-being on the other; survival becomes a lonely struggle as they work to be self-reliant and provide for their own well-being and safety. They develop negative ways of coping with their painful, dreaded feelings in an attempt to protect themselves from disintegration and annihilation. This gives rise to anxiety, and a phenomenological state of being unsteady and insecure. Ignoring and silencing their primary emotions, individuals with GAD use worry to anticipate negative events to forestall and avoid those situations that might evoke feelings of distress and anguish.

Thus, according to EFT (see Figure 1.1), clients' worry and anxiety in the present is activated by specific triggers and events or the anticipation that certain situations will evoke emotion schematic memories of threatening and painful experiences with the accompanying unprocessed feelings of fear, shame, and sadness. This is followed by an activation of a vulnerable self-organization. In this state, people experience themselves as unacceptable, weak, or bad and are unable to self-soothe. In addition, they may turn against themselves, angry that they have been unable to find the protection and support that they need. All this happens out of awareness, with people aware only of a feeling of undifferentiated distress, when they attend to their bodies.

In this state, the people feel shaky, insecure, unconfident, and generally afraid and anxious, and begins to worry to protect against sensed danger in an attempt to defend against it. Their distress is intensified as they silence, ignore, and dismiss their feelings. The distress they experience is characterized as secondary, undifferentiated, high arousal with a negative valence, fueled by the unsymbolized, underlying emotions that they are unable to modulate and calm. Unaware of their core fear, sadness, or shame, and aware only of a global

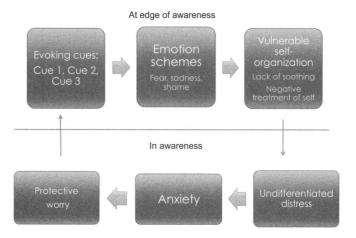

Figure 1.1. The emotion process in general anxiety disorder.

feeling of distress, individuals with GAD feel overwhelmed and fear that they will disintegrate if they acknowledge their painful, underlying feelings. Seeing themselves as solely responsible for events and situations that will activate intensely painful and dreaded feelings of abandonment, rejection, and/or loss of control, they worry to ward these feelings off.

Thus, anxiety and worry in GAD function to protect and warn people of triggers that will evoke painful experiences and the core maladaptive emotions of fear, sadness, and shame that individuals are disclaiming, discounting and dismissing, fearing that they will be unable to tolerate, soothe, and modulate the emotions effectively. The intensity of the painful emotions of fear, sadness, and shame is experienced as a threat to the integrity of the self and identity (Greenberg, 2011; J. Watson, 2011; J. Watson, 2012). Instead of feeling safe, secure, and confident in their ability to cope, people with GAD experience themselves as powerless, unsupported, and weak—at risk in their interactions with others and the world and unable to access adequate protection and succor to regulate their emotions and calm their distress. This insecure, vulnerable self-organization on the basis of core painful emotion schematic memories and negative ways of treating painful emotions is at the heart of GAD, and it is this self-organization that needs to be accessed, processed, strengthened, and transformed.

CASE EXAMPLE: DOOMED TO FAIL

The development of anxiety is illustrated with a case example. When Justin came to therapy, he was 50 years old and a successful executive who worried about his position in his company, its future, and his family. His parents, especially his father, had been very demanding and critical, insisting that he be extraordinary. When Justin entered therapy, he talked about stress and being unable to enjoy life. It soon became clear that he worried a lot about many areas of his life: professional, family, and personal. There were no clear precipitants of his worry, just an ongoing sense of vigilance. When not fully occupied, he was constantly on guard and worried. He was concerned that he might lose his position at work, be unable to stay on top of situations and issues there, or that something might go wrong at home. His feelings of anxiety were localized in his body mainly in his chest, along with constant worry and anticipation of threat.

Over time, his general vulnerable sense of self as a frightened child, feeling alone and unsupported, emerged in therapy. Justin recalled constantly feeling like he was doomed as he failed to get his father's approval. This feeling was exacerbated by his sense that his parents doted on his younger brother, who was far less competent than Justin and was not subject to the same high expectations. Justin received little warmth and understanding from either parent, both of whom traveled a lot. His sense of unfairness within the family, as well as his feelings of parental rejection, is consistent with research on the etiological factors associated with GAD (Borkovec et al., 2004; Cassidy et al., 2009; Rodrigues, 2016). In sharp contrast to his brother, Justin felt like he was a disappointment to his parents, as he failed to be extraordinary. The disappointment in his father's voice and the expression on his face were etched in Justin's memory whenever he did not excel or do as expected. This left Justin constantly vigilant for potential failure.

He harbored a lot of sadness and anger toward his parents, and his father in particular. Initially, he was afraid to experience and talk about his feelings. When Justin approached these feelings in therapy he would cut off what he was saying and go blank, aware only of a tight feeling in his chest and ongoing worry about how to prevent possible abandonment and failure. He was terrified that he would be overwhelmed by his feelings—that he would either drown in his sadness or that his rage would explode and be destructive. He was keenly aware of his worry, and the feelings of anxiety as well as the undifferentiated distress that preceded it. Therapy helped Justin connect with his core vulnerable sense of self as unsupported and alone, and with his painful underlying feelings of sadness, anger, and fear, which had remained unprocessed for most of his life.

In EFT, we propose that anxiety and worry in GAD are attempts to protect the self from being overwhelmed by painful emotions that people are unable to soothe to meet their needs effectively, silencing and dismissing the emotions instead. In this example, Justin's worry served to protect against his fears of abandonment and failure and the painful feelings that he feared would shatter him. This is in contrast to theories that see GAD as originating from intrapsychic conflict between wishes and defenses, as posited by Freud, or from guilt and fear of breaking connections to parents, as suggested by relational analysts. In EFT, it is individuals' inability to regulate their emotions as well as the negative ways that they have learned to modulate their primary painful emotions that are at the heart of worry and anxiety. Worry is seen as a misguided attempt to protect the self from overwhelming painful affect, as the distress from the activation of painful emotion schemes begins to be felt along with the inability to adequately self-soothe. Thus, worry and anxiety are seen as arising not because of conditioning or faulty beliefs, as posited by cognitive behaviorists, but as efforts to protect the self from disintegrating and falling apart, and being overwhelmed by painful emotions.

In contrast to cognitive behavioral theorists, we do not see worry as a learned mechanism for reducing arousal because verbal-linguistic activity or thought has lower levels of imagery that enables individuals to avoid the aversive stimulation of unpleasant imagery and negative affect. Although EFT shares some of this view, in seeing anxiety as avoidance of emotion, worry is an attempt by an active agent to solve a problem, to protect against disintegration from unsoothed painful affect that is being dismissed and neglected, rather than reducing aversive stimulation. This sense of painful unsoothed affect activates feelings of anxiety and undifferentiated distress in the body as a result of the absence of soothing and support and the unsymbolized underlying painful memories and emotions. At the core is the fear of disintegration from painful emotions with worry, an attempt to protect oneself from painful emotions and fragmentation.

From an EFT perspective, people are seen as goal-directed, active agents, striving to regulate their emotions, and needing attachments and identity validation to enable them to flourish and grow to maintain their emotional, physical, and psychological well-being. They are not merely conditioned by reward and punishment. From this perspective, worry is a misguided attempt to regulate affect. Individuals with GAD do not know how to cope with their distress and the overwhelming feelings that contribute to a fear of disintegration. They fear that if they pay attention to their emotions, they will be overwhelmed, unable to cope, shatter, and disintegrate. Therefore, individuals with GAD worry to preserve their self-organizations and function effectively. Their attention is focused outside as they try to control and avoid the outcomes of future events to protect themselves from situations that will evoke intense undifferentiated distress and the associated painful emotions they felt as children and that have not been adequately processed. From this perspective, worry reflects a proactive coping strategy: intelligent behavior.

DEVELOPMENT OF A VULNERABLE SENSE OF SELF

The development of a vulnerable sense of self is rooted in core maladaptive emotion schemes of fear, shame, and sadness and is characterized by maladaptive action tendencies and negative self-organizations. These negative self-organizations consist of negative self-concepts, a sense that the self is helpless and without control over events, as well as negative ways of relating to the self and others and inadequately processed experiences. Thus individuals develop a heightened attention to situations that will evoke feelings of pain and helplessness. Their primary means of protection is worry, as they attempt to anticipate and avoid situations that evoke the painful feelings of vulnerability and woundedness. As such, anxiety serves as a constant reminder of the pain that has not been attended to and is inadequately processed and soothed.

Identity Formation and Negative Self-Organizations

EFT theorists postulate a psychological need for self-coherence, self-esteem, and mastery for survival and well-being, in addition to a need for attachment, connection, and protection (Greenberg & Goldman, 2008; Greenberg & Watson, 2006). During development, some experiencing becomes conscious, resulting in the formation of a sense of self. The self is focused on maintaining coherence and developing a sense of mastery and control to protect its identity (Bakan, 1966; Kohut, 1984; Rogers, 1959). Failure to satisfy this need for mastery and identity inevitably results in difficulties and a sense of being damaged and distressed.

Identity formation encompasses the assertion of preferences, agency, or differentiation and includes a motivation for individuals to explore and master their environments. This formulation differs from Freud's (1922/1961) view of aggressive drives or from a motivational view of needs for autonomy (Murray, 1938), as identity formation happens in constant interaction with others. The opposite pole of identity or differentiation has been variously called dependence, enmeshment, powerlessness, low self-esteem, annihilation, disintegration, or invalidation. We refer to this complexly evolved human tendency to be agentic as reflecting a need for identity validation (Greenberg & Goldman, 2008) and the differentiation of the self and experience (J. Watson, 2011; J. Watson & Greenberg, 1996).

The internal affective stream generated by emotion schemes provides the building blocks for people's basic self-organization. Emotion schemes are dynamically synthesized into self-organizations, which when activated in specific situations can result in a conscious experience of feeling shy, confident, or worried (Greenberg, 2011). These self-organizations form in interaction with the environment as individuals develop beliefs and a sense of self as a result of how they are treated and viewed by others. As specific self-states are activated and symbolized in words, self-understanding forms, which in turn is molded into beliefs, self-representations, and narratives about the self and the world. Identity unites who individuals were in the past with who they are becoming in the present, and also shapes who they will become in the future.

As Stern (1985) showed, infants in the first years of life rapidly develop a sense of coherence, affectivity, agency, and continuity. This is greatly facilitated by caretakers' affect attunement and mirroring (Legerstee, 2013; Legerstee, Markova, & Fisher, 2007). The self strengthens as its affects and intentions are recognized and it begins to self-regulate. Processes to regulate the self as well as interactions with others are two separate but interconnected strands of affect regulation and identity formation that develop simultaneously. Just as the body needs oxygen, the self needs empathic attunement and validation to regulate self-esteem (Kohut, 1984; Rogers, 1959). The self grows stronger and a coherent identity develops when its agentic strivings are recognized, understood, and validated by others. With increasing mastery and self-confidence developing in interaction with the environment, the self continues to develop capacities to self-regulate and self-soothe.

A vulnerable sense of self, as opposed to being confident and resilient, develops when individuals are overwhelmed by threatening and painful events without adequate support and protection or the capacity to soothe and calm themselves that would allow them to respond in adaptive and self-protective ways. Unable to calm themselves, individuals feel helpless and weak. A vulnerable sense of the self and compromised capacities to self-soothe may develop in the context of under- or overprotection. As we have noted, in some cases vulnerability and lack of confidence have their roots in experiences of neglect, rejection, and abuse in early childhood and the absence of protection or care. In nonresponsive environments, it is difficult to acquire a sense of competence and self-worth, which develops when individuals' needs are responded to and met. Responsive caretaking results in people feeling that they can have an effect on people and the events around them (Legerstee, 2013). They feel seen, cared for, and important. The identity injuries that develop as a result of not being seen or responded to can lead to individuals feeling ashamed of their needs, undeserving of attention and support, unimportant, and unlovable. These feelings compromise a person's sense of self-esteem—his or her sense of mastery—and sense of being able to cope with situations and events. Feeling anxious about their ability to cope with the demands of life, they develop a negative problem orientation (Rodrigues, 2016; Rodrigues & Watson, 2015).

When individuals are neglected, unprotected, or unsupported by caretakers, they may assume responsibility for their own well-being by staying close to and becoming enmeshed with their caretakers to maintain proximity and meet their attachment needs. In situations like this, role reversal may occur at the expense of the individual's own identity formation and agency, especially if caretakers are perceived as weak and helpless or too strong and overpowering.

In contrast to the impact of nonresponsive caretakers, those characterized as overly protective can contribute to a vulnerable sense of self. Research has shown that overprotection puts individuals at risk for developing a number of different disorders, including GAD (Craske & Waters, 2005).

When caretakers overly protect individuals, enmeshed relationships develop that require them to forfeit their needs in the service of others' needs for control and mastery. This is similar to what happens with role reversal or parentification. However, in these latter processes people are required to extend beyond their capacities for self-regulation, while with overprotection they are required to submerge them. Individuals in relationships characterized by overprotection do not develop adequate skills to care for themselves, nor do they acquire a sense of mastery and competence. Instead, they feel weak and dependent on others for succor and protection. Being overly protected, they fail to develop the capacity to self-soothe when faced with challenges and distressing situations. They rely on others to minister to their needs and calm and ease their fears. Their agency becomes restricted, contributing to the development of negative self-organizations as they succumb to feelings of shame, weakness, and helplessness. Some support for the role of parental overprotection in the development of GAD was found recently in a community sample, where it, along with maternal rejection and a responsibility for the welfare of others at an early age, was predictive of GAD and worry (Rodrigues, 2016; Rodrigues & Watson, 2015).

Negative Treatment of the Self and Regulating Emotion

The development of maladaptive emotion schemes means that individuals with GAD are unable to regulate their affective experience or adequately label and process their emotions. The abilities to regulate affect and symbolize and reflect on emotions are essential to individuals' well-being and to a sense of the self as capable and competent to cope and interact optimally with others. If individuals have experienced attentive, responsive, and caring others, they learn how to attend to their experience, symbolize it accurately, label it, modulate it, and express it in ways that meet their needs. Effective expression of their needs increases the likelihood of their being heard and responded to by others. Infants with responsive caretakers learn that when they are hungry or afraid, they will be held, fed, and comforted. In contrast, infants with caretakers who are neglectful, rejecting, or uncaring learn from an early age to feel ashamed of their needs, to try to silence them and find alternative ways to meet them (e.g., disowning them or becoming quiet and withdrawn; Bowlby, 1988).

We propose that instead of learning to protect and comfort themselves when distressed, individuals in unresponsive and hostile environments develop negative ways of treating or relating to their experiences as they try to regulate and cope with overwhelming feelings of anguish. Their emotional processing capacities are compromised as they are unable to soothe and acknowledge their distress, and the action tendencies in core primary emotions become distorted and transformed (Greenberg & Watson, 2006; J. Watson, 2011). These negative ways of relating to their experience reveal negative attitudes toward the self, including lack of self-acceptance and a sense of not being valued and prized. All of which contribute to the sense of the self as vulnerable and wounded.

Research supports the view that people diagnosed with GAD have emotion regulation difficulties (Borkovec, 1994; Brown, O'Leary, & Barlow, 2001; Cassidy et al., 2009; Dugas & Robichaud, 2007; Mennin et al., 2002; Mennin, Heimberg, Turk, & Fresco, 2005; Rodrigues & Watson, 2015; N. Watson, Watson, & McMullen, 2014). They have more difficulty experiencing intense emotions; they have more difficulty identifying, labeling, and describing their emotions; they have a greater dislike of negative emotion; they are more intolerant of uncertainty (Dugas & Robichaud, 2007); and they are less able to self-soothe after becoming distressed (Craske & Waters, 2005). The interruption or impairment of emotional processing is thought to occur in interaction with their environments.

Support for the important role that the absence of responsive caregiving plays in the development of anxiety comes from the work of attachment theorists. Differences have been observed in infants with responsive caretakers and those with caretakers who are intermittently available or unavailable. In responsive environments, infants and children learn how to process emotions, modulate levels of arousal, and modulate expression of emotion so that they can meet their needs and interact with others in satisfying ways (Cassidy et al., 2009; Gottman & Declaire, 1997; King & Mallinckrodt, 2000). Caretakers are the primary affect regulators. However, infants and children in unresponsive and deprived environments where caretakers fail to provide adequate affect regulation and protection have difficulty acquiring and mastering the skills of effective affect regulation resulting in impaired emotional processing.

Consistent with theories of anxiety that link the development of a vulnerable self as a result of early childhood experiences and impaired attachment relations to impaired affect regulation strategies (Greenberg & Goldman, 2008; J. Watson, Goldman, & Greenberg, 2007; J. Watson & Lilova, 2009; J. Watson & Watson, 2010; Wolfe & Sigl, 1998), findings from community samples show that anxiously and/or avoidantly attached individuals lack emotional clarity, do not accept their emotions, and have limited access to emotion regulation strategies (Lecce, 2008; Lecce & Watson, 2007; N. Watson et al., 2014). In addition, attachment avoidance was related to lack of emotional awareness. Thus, anxious individuals do not know what they are feeling or how to identify and express their needs to have them met in ways to protect and soothe themselves and transform their emotions and feelings. Not only are individuals unable to differentiate their painful emotions to know what they are feeling, but they also acquire maladaptive ways of relating to their experience as a result of negative responses from their environment that contribute to their distress.

Individuals internalize how others respond to them to regulate and modulate emotional experience. When painful emotions are met with protective, caring, and nurturing responses, individuals learn how to attend to and symbolize their experience and to use it as a guide to meet their needs. However, when painful emotions are silenced, neglected, dismissed, and denied, these negative responses become internalized and are used to regulate and modulate emotional experience. This means that painful emotions remain unprocessed as individuals lack the means to adequately soothe and protect themselves and the action tendencies implicit in their primary emotions become distorted so that they are unable to effectively meet their needs.

By internalizing negative ways of responding to their painful emotions, individuals continue the cycle of inadequate protection and succor. Their inability to respond to their own pain with comfort and support further fuels anxiety. Dismissal and negation of painful feelings are attempts to feel strong and disassociate from parts of the self that are experienced as weak, contemptible, and unacceptable to others. Individuals with GAD do not know how to listen to, attend to, soothe, or regulate their painful feelings. Rather, they continue to avoid, dismiss, and deny their feelings, responding to their pain as others have responded to it. Unable to calm or soothe themselves, they cannot be guided by their primary feelings to problem solve, protect themselves, and enhance their well-being.

The failure to attend to their distress with care and support when it has been triggered by potentially threatening and harmful situations or events generates anxiety and further exacerbates worry. They fear that if they experience their emotions in the present, they will be overwhelmed and the self will disintegrate because the capacity to self-soothe and effectively calm the self is lacking. This becomes self-perpetuating as the negative ways of coping with painful feelings continue to be activated so that emotional experience is inadequately processed and soothed in an ongoing cycle. Instead of attending to their inner experience, their attention is focused externally, as they try to anticipate and control outcomes in the future. Individuals with GAD remain vigilant to avoid situations that will evoke painful feelings of powerlessness and vulnerability. They are unable to seek support from others, seeing themselves as burdens and as undeserving of care and attention.

Negative ways of coping with distress and painful experiences are maladaptive and ineffective in the long term because they fail to ensure adequate care for the self or to provide for the development of a sense of mastery and competence in the world. Effective emotional processing and regulation is compromised as adaptive action tendencies have been distorted. Over time, worry becomes debilitating, exhausting individuals and depleting resources. Moreover, when stressed and coping mechanisms are challenged, individuals may experience more intense anxiety and increased distress and anguish.

This can be illustrated in the case example of Debbie, a client with GAD. She recalled that as a toddler, she experienced intense, painful feelings of fear and aloneness because her mother's attention was constantly diverted to the needs of her baby brother, who was weak and in poor health. As a result, she developed a fear of being left alone, developing a sense that she was invisible and had been discarded, along with a sense that she was not important. This formed the basis of Debbie's vulnerable self-organization, which resulted from a synthesis of emotion schematic memories of fear and shame as a result of the experiences of emotional neglect and abandonment. To deal with her sense of being forgotten, Debbie learned to follow her mother around and assist with caring for her baby brother. However, in doing so, Debbie's needs and feelings were overlooked, ignored, and silenced. She learned to cope with feelings of vulnerability and fear by channeling them into caring for others.

As a consequence, Debbie never learned to regulate her affect, process her own feelings, or seek and receive adequate attention, validation, and comfort when feeling distressed. Instead, she continued to focus on the needs of others—putting their needs ahead of her own. She remained disconnected from her own feelings of vulnerability and distress, and was unable to access her needs in a congruent manner that would allow her to respect herself and others. Being unable to tolerate and symbolize her experience accurately in the moment, she was left with a continual undercurrent of anxiety that intensified and flared up when she felt stressed or excluded, along with a deep sense of shame.

Inadequate Symbolization of Experience

An important aspect of maladaptive emotion schemes is that emotion schematic memories are inadequately processed and painful stimuli are not properly encoded. Intense emotion and negative ways of treating the self and relating to experience can prevent individuals from representing their experiences accurately in conscious awareness. This, in turn, exacerbates the sense of the self as vulnerable. Individuals who do not accurately represent their experiences and emotions are at risk in terms of understanding the impact of their environment and are unable to represent their feelings and identify their needs, thereby compromising their psychological and physical well-being and survival. In EFT, we posit that anxiety arises because individuals are not attending to aspects of their experience that require attention. Lack of symbolization characterizes aspects of the situation that trigger anxiety as well as the person's emotional responses to the situation. This results in some experiences and emotions not being adequately accepted, tolerated, and symbolized in awareness with the result that the essential needs for comfort, solace, and support are not met.

As we noted earlier, individuals with GAD are not aware of the specific trigger that is associated with the onset of their anxiety symptoms. Rather, the anxiety is observed to be free floating and marked by worry. In GAD, the triggers are amorphous and can be activated by any situation, event, internal state or cue that is viewed as potentially harmful and that will lead to feelings of distress. For example, Justin, in the previous case example, after posting a letter in a mailbox, would worry that there was something in the envelope that shouldn't be there, and continued to worry about possible negative consequences that might follow. The absence of specific triggers makes GAD more like panic than other anxiety disorders, which have identifiable precipitants. For example, in social anxiety, the trigger is fear of criticism from others or being ridiculed in social situations, with attendant feelings of shame. In phobias, anxiety is triggered by various stimuli (e.g., heights, snakes, spiders) that are seen as dangerous and harmful. In PTSD, there are usually known traumatic events, and specific stimuli that have been inadequately processed that trigger individuals' reactions of anxiety and fear (e.g., loud noises, angry voices). In GAD, a variety of different evoking cues can activate core schemes on the basis of emotion schematic memories of fear, sadness and shame that went unsoothed. These organize implicitly into a vulnerable self-organization with the negative ways that people have internalized to deal with their feelings contributing to a state of undifferentiated distress. When people enter a vulnerable state and sense their feelings of distress, they begin to feel anxious and worry.

The absence of a clearly symbolized and articulated trigger for anxiety in GAD and the painful emotional responses it produces may be attributed to the fact that the threatening, distressing experiences that occurred either pre-verbally or at later stages of development are so intense that effective cognitive and emotional processing was interrupted (Korte, Koolhaas, Wingfield, & McEwen, 2005; McGaugh, 2002; Weinstock, 2009). Research has shown that individuals with GAD have impaired attention and difficulty discriminating among specific stimuli that might elicit fear responses. As a result, they have difficulty discerning cause-and-effect relationships. It has been suggested that impaired discernment among different stimuli and situations contributes to overgeneralization as opposed to more specific responding to explicit cues (Craske & Waters, 2005). In addition, recent research in memory consolidation suggests that it may be compromised under stress, with the activation of negative emotions (Korte et al., 2005; McGaugh & Roozendaal, 2002).

Therefore, if conditions are experienced as very threatening, or when cognitive processing is more limited, the organism may be unable to consciously symbolize the threatening situation so that the specific trigger or stimulus that contributed to the painful emotions can be clearly known and apprehended. The stimuli associated with the person's emotion schemes become overly generalized, easily activating emotion schematic memories of other earlier situations of fear and vulnerability. Innocuous stimuli that bear some resemblance to or have some features in common with earlier threatening situations in which people experienced intense distress are responded to with fear and anguish. Learning to discriminate among different stimuli is a biological need that is vital to the organism's functioning and ongoing survival. If full symbolization of the situation is interrupted or inhibited, the organism will continue to act with alarm to situations that evoke similar feelings of distress and fear. Thus, the overgeneralization of some features of negative and/or threatening life experiences to different situations requires that the details, impact, and meaning of the situation be adequately processed and symbolized so that the threat can be known and individuals can respond more adaptively. People need to adequately symbolize their experience, emotional responses, and action tendencies to be informed and organized by them.

An example of the overgeneralization and lack of specificity with respect to the triggers of anxiety is illustrated by the following case example. Jessie was a client who experienced periods of intense anxiety and worry about her physical safety, which perplexed her. As she explored her anxiety with the therapist, she noted that it arose at different times during the day, including when she was at work, driving, or sitting in her apartment. During one session, as the therapist explored one specific situation in which she had felt anxious and worried at work using systematic evocative unfolding, she realized that she had started to become anxious at her desk when her attention lapsed and she had been daydreaming.

After this realization, Jessie recalled an incident that had occurred 3 years previously. She had been sleeping over at her aunt's house and had just drifted off to sleep on the sofa when she awoke to find a friend of her cousin's sexually assaulting her. She interrupted the attack and extricated herself from the situation. However, she did not share or express her distress and her emotions to anyone in an attempt to protect her aunt and her cousin. As she continued to explore the situation with the therapist, she realized that this incident was the source of her anxiety and that she became anxious when her attention lapsed (e.g., while daydreaming, falling asleep, engaging in activity that took her full attention) and left her feeling vulnerable and at risk.

In the next few sessions, as she processed the incident further, Jessie realized that she felt helpless and powerless as she continued to socialize in the same group as her cousin and the person who assaulted her. She did not want to lose her friends, nor did she wish to expose or shame her cousin. After she engaged in an empty chair exercise, during which she confronted the person who assaulted her, she was able to access and clearly symbolize her fear and a newly experienced sense of empowered anger. Jessie realized that even though the person who assaulted her was still part of her social circle she could still take action and report the incident to the police. She noted, too, that if he was inappropriate again or if he harmed one of her friends, they would be able to report him to the police and protect each other. This experience and clear symbolization of her need for boundary protection and her felt sense of protective anger made her feel more powerful. She felt less at his mercy and less as if he had the power to hurt her. Subsequently, her anxiety subsided so that she was able to resume her daily activities with no further symptoms.

Current threatening events, high stress, or loss of control can all precipitate anxiety. Unexpected life events have been found to be significant precursors of GAD. When people with negative and insecure self-organizations face current threats, stress, or loss of control, their core anxious self-organizations are activated, leaving them feeling shaky and vulnerable. In EFT, symptoms of GAD and worry are seen as *protective acts*, by an active agent, against being overwhelmed by intense feelings of distress generated by situations that activate an insecure and wounded sense of self. In our view, worry is more than avoidance of painful emotion because the pain is aversive; rather, it is an attempt to protect and prepare individuals for negative outcomes and situations in the future that will evoke painful emotions of fear, helplessness, aloneness, powerlessness, and neglect. Unable to soothe their emotions, individuals fear that the feelings will overwhelm them and lead to their disintegration and fragmentation. Thus, anxiety and worry serve to warn people of certain actions or events that will evoke anguish and suffering, maintain their self-coherence, and draw attention to unmet needs and painful experiences that require processing.

EMOTION-FOCUSED THERAPY TREATMENT FOR GENERALIZED ANXIETY DISORDER

To effectively treat GAD, painful emotions of fear, sadness, and shame from neglect and harm need to be processed and more adaptive emotions schemes and more positive ways of relating to distress and painful feelings need to be developed. To undo worry, the EFT therapist needs to help clients change their negative treatment of the self and how they relate to their experience and reprocess their maladaptive emotion schemes. Individuals with GAD need to acquire different ways of processing and regulating their emotional experience so as to maintain a sense of coherence. This requires that they come to value and accept themselves and their feelings. They need to use their adaptive feelings and needs as guides to protect themselves and maintain their well-being. Confronting intense, painful feelings requires new ways of relating to the self and others. People with GAD need to feel deserving of attention and care, and they need to access protective anger as well as greater self-compassion and self-acceptance.

Once individuals feel able to protect themselves and are more self-accepting and self-compassionate, they will begin to feel stronger and less fearful that they will disintegrate. They develop a sense of confidence and trust in their perceptions and emotions and in their ability to cope so that they no longer fear that they will be overwhelmed or destroyed by intense feelings of pain or anguish. Better able to soothe their painful feelings, they can avert a sense of disintegration and distress, attend to their needs for protection and nurture, and preserve their identities.

The EFT therapist works with clients with GAD to strengthen their sense of self and develop self-acceptance, self-compassion, and greater self-protection, as they facilitate their emotional processing. EFT is designed to facilitate clients' development of more positive self-organizations and the acquisition of effective affect regulation skills, including access to emotional experience; enhanced capacities for labeling, tolerating, modulating, and transforming emotion; increased tolerance of negative emotion; and improved capacities for self-soothing and self-assertion (Elliott, Watson, Goldman, & Greenberg, 2004; Greenberg, Rice, & Elliott, 1993; Greenberg & Watson, 2006). Clients are encouraged to access more adaptive action tendencies to better meet their needs. The course of treatment is described more fully in Chapter 3 of this volume.

General support for an emotion-focused approach in the treatment of GAD has been provided by a number of studies. Berg, Sandell, and Sandahl (2009) showed that psychotherapy that focuses on clients' affective and bodily experience was more effective in treating individuals with GAD than treatment as usual. Moreover, the clients in this study reported that supportive reflective interventions as well as the practice of emotionally expressive interventions were very helpful. Further support for this approach comes from a substantial proportion of clients with comorbid diagnoses of depression and GAD, who were successfully treated with EFT (Goldman, Greenberg, & Angus, 2006; Greenberg & Watson, 1998; J. Watson, Gordon, Stermac, Kalogerakos, & Steckley, 2003) as well as two current sets of repeated intensive single case studies of EFT for anxiety in GAD that are showing successful outcomes (Saedi-Chekan & Watson, 2015; Timulak & McElvaney, 2015) and two group studies of social anxiety (Elliott, 2013; Shahar, 2014). In addition to these studies of efficacy, EFT is grounded in decades of research that has analyzed microprocesses in psychotherapy to illuminate the process of change and develop models of client–therapist interactions that facilitate change (Elliott et al., 2004; Greenberg & Paivio, 1997; Greenberg et al., 1993; Greenberg & Watson, 2006). This work provides a strong empirical foundation for the approach. In the next chapter, we discuss the role of emotion in GAD.

2

THE ROLE OF EMOTION IN GENERALIZED ANXIETY DISORDER

Emotions provide adaptive information and associated action tendencies that help orient people in complex environments (Damasio, 1994; Greenberg, 2011, 2015; Greenberg & Safran, 1987; J. Watson & Greenberg, 1996). Anxiety from an emotion-focused therapy (EFT) perspective reflects impaired emotional processing and the interruption of the experience and expression of painful emotions that result from repeated exposure to harmful and threatening situations without adequate protection and support. The intense feelings of distress that have been experienced in threatening environments characterized by neglect, abandonment, isolation, or harm without protection and soothing prevent the underlying primary emotions of fear, sadness, and shame from being adequately processed, soothed, or modulated, leading to the development of a vulnerable self-organization.

As a result of repeated attachment and identity injuries, emotional reactions in generalized anxiety disorder (GAD) can be triggered by various stimuli that may or may not be objectively threatening. This may be because

http://dx.doi.org/10.1037/0000018-003

individuals were not able to precisely discriminate among numerous different cues in their environments, which helps establish cause-and-effect relationships, as discussed in Chapter 1 of this volume. These triggers activate maladaptive schemes, and the resulting emotions are not processed or regulated. Lack of support and protection when vulnerable often produces feelings of weakness, rejection, deficiency, unworthiness, sadness, and shame, all of which contribute to the development of a self that is organized as vulnerable and unable to cope. As time goes on, the experience of painful feelings (e.g., fear, isolation, rejection) is exacerbated for people with GAD because they do not feel that they have the resources to cope with their feelings and are not able to access adequate protection, soothing, and support to modulate their distress in the face of threatening situations.

From an EFT perspective, people with GAD have difficulty processing their feelings, including symbolizing, labeling, and expressing them, as well as modulating their levels of arousal, and thus are unable to cope effectively (Kennedy-Moore & Watson, 1999, 2001). EFT posits that GAD is characterized by the activation of maladaptive emotions, a lack of clarity about emotions, an inability to label and name emotions, and a suppression of positive emotions that allow for protection and self-soothing. It is the interruption of primary emotions (e.g., fear, sadness, shame) that is most centrally linked to GAD. According to this view, anxiety results from deep feelings of fear of harm and abandonment, as well as sadness and shame at rejection and neglect, which people with GAD have learned to dismiss, neglect, or silence, developing a deep sense of sadness and shame about their feelings and needs as a result.

EFT does not conceive of this lack of awareness as repression of motivation or emotion as in psychodynamic theory, but rather that people's emotional experience is unformulated and suppressed; it has been symbolized inadequately and thus is not clearly known or labeled so that it could be used to guide behavior. Instead, it is disclaimed, dismissed, and invalidated so that it cannot be accepted, experienced, and processed. As such, it remains unassimilated. In EFT, emotional experience that is disowned is seen as potentially leading to dysfunction because the emotion is not allowed to be experienced, used as information, and transformed, if necessary, to support adaptive action. According to this view, it is important for painful feelings to be processed so that their attendant needs can be identified, expressed, and responded to and so that more positive feeling states that change people's self-organization can emerge.

EMOTIONAL PAIN

In our view, painful feelings are at the heart of GAD, but what is meant by *emotional pain*? In a qualitative study of clients' subjective experience of pain, Bolger (1999; Greenberg & Bolger, 2001) found that at the center of emotional pain was a feeling of being broken or shattered. In descriptions of their pain, clients often referred to their bodies, and the deep, dark places therein where there was a visceral experience of damage. People spoke about it in words such as, "it is like a part of me being torn away and left bleeding," it is like "feeling ripped apart," or it is like "my heart being broken." Some people compared it to a relationship in which the bond was broken or shattered. Thus, psychological pain, like physical pain, is experienced in the body, and participants reported that it is their sense of disintegrating or fragmenting that is so frightening.

Prototypically physical pain occurs when a painful stimulus impinges on the exterior of the body, with the automatic response being to move away from the destructive force. If the experience results in injury, it needs to be healed. Similarly, if emotional pain is not responded to appropriately, then it often remains unhealed, leading to a sense of the self as damaged and defective as well as helpless and powerless. Until emotional pain is properly processed, it remains live and easily triggered. Unprocessed and neglected pain cannot be properly expressed or addressed, nor can individuals meet their needs to be protected, loved, validated, and supported. People may feel powerless to stop the sensation of feeling shattered, and without protection, they feel helpless. Emotional pain in which the self feels damaged is different from grief, which is a biologically based response to loss (e.g., of a person, place, or thing). In contrast, emotional pain results from a sense that the self has been damaged. When the self is damaged, a need that feels important to survival has gone unmet, with attendant feelings of helplessness and powerlessness and concern that the need will never be met in the future.

As we noted in Chapter 1 of this volume, GAD is seen as stemming from an insecure or vulnerable sense of self that develops as a result of attachment and identity injuries from infancy. When people's sense of resiliency and their ability to cope are compromised by attachment and identity injuries across the lifespan, feelings of loneliness, fear, sadness, defectiveness, incompetence, and shame can result. People with GAD fear they will fragment and be overwhelmed by intense feelings that will shatter their self-concept. Therefore, an important objective in EFT is to work with clients to own their unacknowledged painful emotional experiences, and to overcome their fears of being overwhelmed and disintegrating. Feelings of loneliness and isolation that are not integrated can be as destructive as disowning feelings of pain at being physically injured. Once individuals are able to face their painful feelings and needs, these feelings and needs can be symbolized in awareness and assimilated to guide protective and life-sustaining actions (e.g., protective anger, self-compassion, self-soothing) or transformed by the experience of new emotions. This change in emotional experience contributes to a more integrated and coherent sense of self (Greenberg, 2011).

EFT emphasizes the importance of the therapist's being empathic, accepting, and congruent while working with clients to process their pain. As clients process their pain with a responsive other, they learn alternative ways of coping with painful feelings, including being more nurturing, accepting, and protective of themselves. Clients learn what they need and how to provide for themselves, as well as how to access new adaptive emotions. This results in a renewed sense of agency, self-assertion, and self-compassion, which contribute to clients' feeling more resilient and more confident in their ability to cope. Feeling stronger, they are less likely to be easily triggered and overwhelmed by negative and difficult events and situations.

EMOTION AND THE BODY

Organismic experience consists of all the ways humans experience themselves and their environments through their bodies. Some of this organismic experience becomes formulated as emotions, which represent the internal complexity on the basis of a synthesis of emotion schemes that can be attended to and form our self-organizations. Knowledge of others, the world, and ourselves comes, in part, from senses like hearing, vision, and touch as well as construals, feelings, and emotions. Thus, organismic experience is made up of inner and outer experience as people apprehend what is occurring in their environments through their senses, react to that experience with emotions and or feelings, and come to know and understand its impact on them (J. Watson, 2011).

Other sources of knowledge reside within the body, including interoception and proprioception, which provide information on the basis of somatosensory stimuli. *Interoception* is the way of sensing stimuli arising from within the body, and especially in the viscera. People learn in childhood that they only have five senses to experience the world and themselves within the world, and comprehending that their very first experience of being in the world comes from another sense requires a reorientation. However, it is important to recognize that every tissue, muscle, and joint of the body transmits neural signals upward through the central nervous system to give a sense of internal experience. The processing of such neural signals though interoception is a basic element of how the central nervous system "senses" the self in the world and is the means through which physiological balance is maintained. In addition, *proprioception*—the ability to sense the position, location, orientation, and movement of the body and its parts—is another aspect of receiving internal body information. These forms of somatosensory stimuli create a subjective sense of being in the world through a mixture of physiological, subcortical, and cortical processes. The *experiential awareness* of the sensations and processes initiated at a physiological body-based level is thus an important source of information about people's current state or self-organization. Cultivating experiential awareness of internal sensations and the physical body is necessary in order to support clients' gaining emotional awareness and developing the ability to feel with greater clarity and depth.

Experiential theorists, among others, have identified the organism and its regulating capacities as essential to survival, and see emotion as being at the heart of this regulatory process (Damasio, 1994; Greenberg & Safran, 1987; Rogers, 1959). Emotions are brain representations of body states that provide a reading of individuals' internal environment and how it is being affected from without, as it processes information from the senses (Damasio, 1994). At an elemental level, interoception initiates processes that keep the physiology of the body balanced and productive. It also helps determine emotional experience and subjective awareness, ultimately influencing cognition and behavior. With the safety of the therapeutic relationship as a backdrop, psychotherapy can affect patients' physiology and characteristic responses to their internal and external world, creating significant change on multiple levels.

Although much regulation occurs out of awareness and is never directly known, other types of regulation are in awareness and governed by instinctual responses to various body states. Instinctual regulation occurs in the brain stem and hypothalamus, with some help from the limbic system. Although the first two areas are not modifiable, the limbic system can be changed by experience. The more complex the environment and the more complex the organism, the greater is the need for modification and more conscious self-regulation in order for the organism to survive. According to emotion theorists, this is where the conscious apprehension of feelings and emotions comes into play: to help humans adapt to and cope with complex social and physical environments (Damasio, 1994; Frijda, 1986; Greenberg & Safran, 1987). Emotions provide individuals with information to guide their behavior and communicate their needs to others.

EFT theorists see body representations as dynamic, ongoing syntheses of what is happening in the body moment-by-moment, as a result of specific neural and chemical changes (Damasio, 1994; Greenberg, 2011; Greenberg & Safran, 1987). Much of the information that humans acquire through their senses is processed out of awareness and activates emotion schemes that promote efficient and effective action. In this way, different experiences are recognized, understood, and acted on appropriately to enhance survival. To do this, some of that experience becomes conscious so that it can be known and acted on to change behavior. By focusing on their inner experience and feelings, people are able to make sense of their experience and come to know and understand its impact on them.

In EFT, it is recognized that clients are not always conscious of their inner experience. In fact, one of the changes observed in good outcome cases or with people who are able to engage successfully in psychotherapy is that they became more aware of their inner experience and better able to represent and name their feelings and identify their needs in order to guide their behavior (Greenberg & Malcolm, 2002; Rogers, 1961; J. Watson, McMullen, Prosser, & Bedard, 2011). They learn to be more congruent in their expression of their feelings, such that their inner experience matches what they are communicating and needing. By becoming aware of their inner experience and feelings, people are no longer driven blindly by their emotions, but rather they are able to use their emotions to inform them of the impact of events and to guide their behavior and future actions, and they are able to transform emotions when they are maladaptive. According to this perspective, healthy functioning is a capacity to be aware of inner emotional experience moment-to-moment and to use that awareness to guide actions for living that are satisfying and enhancing (Gendlin, 1978, 1996; Greenberg, Rice, & Elliott, 1993; Rogers, 1959; J. Watson & Watson, 2010), and to use the awareness to identify maladaptive emotions and unmet needs to access and experience new emotions.

EMOTION SCHEMES

Emotions are natural responses to environmental events. Emotion theorists suggest that humans come into the world predisposed to react to certain stimuli as threatening, whereas other reactions to stimuli are acquired as a function of experience (Damasio, 1994; Frijda, 1986). Damasio (1994) posited that emotions are triggered by the innate dispositional characteristics of different stimuli (e.g., size, motion, sound), as well as by specific body states (e.g., hunger, thirst, pain, exhaustion), to enhance survival. In our view, it is some of these innate dispositional characteristics of stimuli that trigger fears related to the development of phobias (e.g., heights, snakes, spiders; J. Watson, 2011). In addition to these innate predispositions, some connections between various stimuli and emotions become customized as individuals interact with their environments. Damasio (1994) termed these connections *dispositional representations*.

For example, seeing someone looking hurt and wounded has distinct meanings for different people. One person might see the expression as manipulative, whereas another might freeze in fear, and yet another might feel compassion and try to help. As individuals experience the world, they learn to connect their feelings with specific stimuli. For example, people may feel comforted by an outstretched hand because previously they had received care and relief from being touched. This is in contrast to others who may view an outstretched hand with fear and apprehension because previously they have been beaten and physically abused.

The capacity to form dispositional tendencies contributes to the development of emotion schemes (Elliott, Watson, Goldman, & Greenberg, 2004; Greenberg et al., 1993; Pascual-Leone, 1987; Piaget, 1972; J. Watson, 2011). The connections that are formed among the bodily felt sense, the situation, the feelings, and the meaning that is attributed to experience underlie the formation of emotion schemes. Emotion schemes allow individuals to interpret and react to events. Another benefit is that feelings can be generalized to other stimuli and situations without individuals having to have direct experience with them (Damasio, 1994; Frijda, 1986; Greenberg, 2002, 2011). This enables individuals to anticipate and plan ahead to predict the probability of certain stimuli being present in different situations (Damasio, 1994). In our view, anxiety disorders result from the formation of connections between primary emotions and environmental stimuli that individuals have encountered in threatening environments. Thus, innate preprogrammed stimuli that elicit primary emotions of fear and alarm contribute to the development of phobias. Whereas learned connections between threatening, harmful, and negative stimuli that may not be adequately processed in conscious awareness give rise to emotion schemes that are associated with GAD.

Emotions can be experienced on two levels: (a) an immediate, sensory level of emotion, involving the experience of primary emotion related to a current situation; and (b) a more complex, emotion-schematic level of emotional experience on the basis of past experience (Greenberg, 2011; J. Watson, 2011). EFT uses the term *emotion scheme* to refer to a multicomponent construct comprising affective, cognitive, motivational, action, and relational processes that develop over time as a result of experience (Greenberg, 2002; Greenberg et al., 1993; Greenberg & Safran, 1987). Emotion schemes do not necessarily act alone to create a response; rather, they are synthesized to configure a response to a situation with the help of other mental operations, such as attention and executive processes, which can either boost or interrupt the application of specific schemes (Greenberg & Pascual-Leone, 1995, 2001; Pascual-Leone, 1991). The dialectical synthesis of activated schemes and other processes results in people's current self-organization. Stable self-structures and trait-like characteristics, such as being anxiously organized, appear as specific states that are regularly recreated as people interact with their environments and are triggered by stimuli that are in some ways associated with, or echo, previously unprocessed experiences.

In GAD, self-organizations or inner states of worry are continually constructed and reconstructed (Greenberg & Pascual-Leone, 1995, 2001; J. Watson & Greenberg, 1996; Whelton & Greenberg, 2001). A vulnerable state of self in GAD is not generated by a single emotion scheme or a single level of processing but by the tacit synthesis of multiple schemes that may produce a vulnerable self-organization at a specific point in time. Thus, a worried self-organization may manifest more stridently in a specific situation as a result of the dialectical synthesis of many factors; for example, not sleeping well results in a person feeling tired, which is followed by a difficult interaction with a family member while getting ready for work, and then topped off by especially intense rush hour traffic causing the person to feel stressed as his timely arrival for an early morning meeting at work has been compromised. The impact of all of these experiences may contribute to the salience of a specific self-organization—either worried or calm.

Emotion schemes are also understood to facilitate interpretation and anticipation of events (Greenberg, 2002). Where strong emotions are evoked in a particular situation, they will be stored in memory. This means that, on an automatic level, emotional meaning may be ascribed to current experiences and stimuli that resonate with ones previously experienced. Current stimuli act as triggers of previously experienced emotional states (J. Watson, 2011). Although emotion schemes generally promote more efficient processing of information and response formation, they can also be maladaptive (Greenberg, 2002). *Adaptive emotion schemes* are flexible and open to transformation as new experiences are encountered. In contrast, *maladaptive emotion schemes* are resistant to change. As emotion schemes orient individuals toward aspects of their experiencing, they may serve to confirm preexisting emotion schemes that in turn promote behaviors that continue to confirm the schemes (Greenberg et al., 1993).

Maladaptive emotion schemes may develop for a number of reasons. In EFT, we posit that the self can become organized around painful emotional experiences to form maladaptive emotional schemes to cope with difficult events and feelings (Greenberg, 2011). These schemes may lie dormant; however, problems can occur if they are evoked when people face challenging life events (Greenberg, 2011). Elements of earlier situations that were not clearly discriminated may activate emotion schemes of fear and vulnerability. This results in a number of different stimuli and contextual cues from earlier situations being extrapolated to the current situation and evoking emotion schemes of harm and pain from past situations and experiences (Damasio, 1994; Greenberg, 2011; J. Watson, 2011). The degree to which this will result in dysfunction depends on a number of factors from the past, including the intensity of the past experience and how often the triggering events occurred, as well as factors that are relevant to the present, including temperamental and organic factors, physiological factors, and a person's general mood or situation at the time of challenge (Greenberg, 2011).

Although it is possible that biological factors may be implicated in the development of maladaptive emotion schemes, in EFT we emphasize the view of maladaptive emotion schemes as being learned (Greenberg, 2011; J. Watson, 2011). If an emotional experience or expression is responded to negatively, or if people encounter harmful and painful events and there is inadequate protection, care, or nurturing at the time, then maladaptive emotion schemes may form as a result (Greenberg, 2011; J. Watson, 2011). For example, if abused by a caretaker, a child's primary source of safety is also his primary source of fear. The child must therefore learn to cope with the distressing emotions associated with the abuse, as well as cope with a hostile, negative, and unprotective caregiver. Although fear is an adaptive response to such a situation, it can become problematic if it is perpetuated in relationships with others who are genuinely and consistently caring.

TYPES OF EMOTION

Although emotion theorists recognize that certain emotions are innate, it is in interaction with the environment that individuals' emotions become differentiated and emotion schemes are formed. In EFT, we distinguish among four distinct categories of emotional experience and expression: primary adaptive, primary maladaptive, secondary, and instrumental (Greenberg & Safran, 1987). These categories are described briefly in the following paragraphs.

Primary adaptive emotions refer to the innate, most basic emotional response to specific situations. These are seen as helping people rapidly process and interpret their environment, and to allow for an immediate, and adaptive, behavioral response. For example, sadness signals a need for comfort and inclines people to seek nurture and solace from others. The impetus to try to meet people's needs on the basis of different emotional states is referred to as an *action tendency*. It is action tendencies that mediate individuals' emotional experiences and needs with their environment. Examples of primary emotions include anger in response to violation, fear in response to danger, and sadness in response to loss. The information derived from these emotions is seen as crucial to guide goal setting, maintain relationships, and facilitate decision making.

Primary maladaptive emotions refer to primary emotional responses that were originally adaptive as a result of harmful, neglectful, or negative environments but are maladaptive in current contexts. They reflect the distortion of primary emotions such that specific internal states (e.g., the feeling of becoming closer or more connected to another person) are experienced as negative. Negative life experiences contribute to neutral stimuli becoming associated with feelings of fear, shame, and sadness as opposed to more pleasurable emotions of joy and contentment. Research has shown that these maladaptive connections affect individuals' neurochemical states; for example, clients diagnosed with borderline personality disorder show an increase in levels of oxytocin and distress, as opposed to comfort and calm, when they experience closeness with another person (Bartz et al., 2011).

Thus, emotional responding and corresponding biological states may become dysfunctional when individuals experience negative or traumatic events and their emotions remain unprocessed, contributing to the development of maladaptive emotion schemes (Greenberg, 2002). As mentioned in Chapter 1 of this volume, when individuals become distressed as a result of emotions not being responded to appropriately, emotional processing may become interrupted, blocking the normal flow of emotional experiencing. A number of sequelae follow from this. First, the connections that are formed between the stimuli associated with the threatening event and the primary emotions can result in an overgeneralization of those stimuli when experienced in different, more benign circumstances. They are filtered through the lens of the past emotional experience that was threatening. When this happens, painful feelings of fear, isolation, abandonment, or harm can be triggered by innocuous stimuli in the present. In these situations, the resulting emotions do not provide information that promotes adaptive responding in the present, where the feared stimulus is not an indication of danger or harm. Moreover, the primary maladaptive emotions that are triggered are experienced as overwhelming or distressing and may contribute to interpersonal problems. Three of the most frequently observed maladaptive emotions in GAD are sadness, shame, and fear.

Secondary emotions are reactions to primary emotions (Greenberg et al., 1993; Greenberg & Safran, 1987). Examples include feeling and expressing anger or shame when sad, as well as undifferentiated distress. These types of emotional expression are maladaptive in that they prevent the full processing of primary emotions as well as access to the adaptive information these emotions provide. Moreover, the expression of secondary emotions creates difficulties interpersonally as people are unable to get their needs met; for example, people who need comfort to address feelings of sadness may push others away with expressions of anger instead of bringing them close. Not only do secondary emotions distort individuals' action tendencies, but they are confusing for others to whom the feelings are being expressed.

Finally, *instrumental emotions* (Greenberg et al., 1993) are those emotions that do not constitute a biological response to the environment. Rather, they are learned responses that are expressed to influence and manipulate the behavior of others. Instrumental emotions can be learned unconsciously, or they may be consciously acquired and used to achieve certain objectives (e.g., using the expression of anger as a means to gain power, expressing sadness and vulnerability to elicit sympathy).

EMOTION AND ANXIETY

In EFT, anxiety is the holistic, bodily felt sense of the self as vulnerable and unprotected. We distinguish between *fear*, which is viewed as a transient response to a specific stimulus that dissipates when the danger has lapsed, and *anxiety*, which is a chronic response to interrupted emotional processing. Fear is understood to be an immediate precursor to adaptive action tendencies: As the sympathetic nervous system is aroused, people feels a rush of adrenaline, become more alert, and focus attention on the immediate situation in preparation for the flee, fight, or freeze response. There is also a distinction made between primary maladaptive fear and primary maladaptive anxiety. The former is a phobic reaction to a stimulus, which may be a feeling, thought, or memory, usually associated with a single traumatic event or stimulus. In this case the fear would have been adaptive to the original situation, but it continues to be inappropriately activated, and over time may become anxiety. For example, individuals may respond with fear at the sound of a car engine after a life-threatening accident or to the sound of shattering glass following an assault. These stimuli may evoke the experience of pain and the sense of powerlessness experienced in the earlier traumatic situation, and individuals may deal with this by avoiding situations where those stimuli could be encountered (e.g., busy streets, restaurants). In GAD, anxiety is chronic and free floating so that it is not attached to any specific stimulus. Instead, individuals worry in an attempt to prepare and respond to anticipated negative consequences in a range of different situations.

Primary maladaptive anxiety is generated by the activation of a core insecure or vulnerable self-organization that has developed over time. To understand the emotions that are activated, it can be helpful to understand clients' attachment history combined with in-session indicators of uncertainty, timidity, hypersensitivity, hypervigilance, and self-consciousness. An anxious self-organization is sometimes indicated by an anxious-avoidant attachment pattern (Bowlby, 1973) whereby people either cling to significant others, becoming fearful when separated, or give up seeking attachment and withdraw from others, becoming self-sufficient. An insecure attachment style is usually the result of repeated attachment injuries that cause people to lose trust either in their capacity to protect and care for themselves or, alternatively, in the capacity of caregivers and other attachment figures to respond appropriately to protect and support them.

As emotion schemes are formed, people come to act in habitual ways in response to their construction or interpretation of their internal state and different stimuli, thereby developing more enduring self-organizations. As a result, specific stimuli may be experienced repeatedly either as enhancing and positive or threatening and aversive. If experiences are negative and overwhelming, individuals may feel so threatened and vulnerable that they are unable to cope. This sense of being helpless and overwhelmed can be experienced as anxiety. Therefore, emotion schemes generate self-organizations and characteristic ways of acting that mediate between individuals and their environments. The focus of anxiety can be interpersonal (e.g., fear of being intimate with someone as it may lead to rejection) or intrapersonal (e.g., shame and rejection directed at the self). Chronic or problematic anxiety can also occur in environments characterized by unpredictability or ones in which people lack control.

PRINCIPLES OF EMOTIONAL CHANGE

Emotional processing is essential to survival (Damasio, 1994, 1999; Elliott et al., 2004; Greenberg, 2002; Greenberg & Watson, 2006; LeDoux, 1996). The primary focus in EFT is to facilitate optimal emotional processing and a reorganization of the self (J. Watson, 2011, 2015). Dysfunctional emotional processing in GAD is seen to result from blocks to emotional processing that impede people's capacity to lead full and satisfying lives. In EFT, change is seen to come about through the processing of emotion in new ways and the development of stronger more positive self-organizations that are reflected in new narratives of the self and others. From an EFT perspective, transformation occurs through changes in how clients process and express their emotions. Clients in EFT become more accepting and aware of their emotional experience and learn to express, regulate, reflect on, and transform it in the context of an empathically attuned relationship with their therapist who facilitates these processes. A positive relationship with the therapist provides clients with corrective emotional experiences from which they can learn greater self-compassion and self-acceptance, as well as to become more assertive and self-protective to ensure their safety and well-being.

Awareness

Increasing awareness of primary emotion is fundamental to processing emotion. Once people know what they feel, they can reconnect to their needs, becoming motivated to meet them. Recently, a series of studies showed that naming a feeling in words helps decrease amygdala arousal (Lieberman et al., 2007) and that exposure plus labeling affective states, compared with exposure alone, led to more snake touching and lower physiological arousal for people with fear of snakes and a greater reduction in physiological arousal for people with anxiety about public speaking (Niles, Craske, Lieberman, & Hur, 2015). Increased emotional awareness is therapeutic in a variety of ways. Becoming aware of and symbolizing core emotional experience in words reduces physiological arousal, provides access to the adaptive need in the emotion, and points to the action tendency. Awareness of emotions also helps to define what the problem is and what needs are not being met. Having accepted an emotion rather than avoided it, clients are able to improve their coping with the assistance of their therapist. Clients make sense of what their emotions are telling them, and this helps them to identify their goals and recognize their needs and concerns, as well as the necessary actions to take. In this way, emotion is used to inform and to move people to action.

Awareness and Avoidance of Feelings

Heightened awareness of emotional experience and access to emotional memory structures and accompanying pathogenic beliefs and action tendencies formed as a result of traumatic experiences are important to facilitate change in individuals with GAD. In EFT, we posit that anxiety is a sign that aspects of experience are not receiving attention. It serves as an indicator that some experiences are being disowned, the action tendencies are being disclaimed, and essential needs are not being met. Likely, there is some dreaded emotion that is not being allowed, accepted, and processed. Emotions become unacceptable for a variety of reasons; because of their spontaneous nature, they are not easily in people's control. They may be seen as dangerous partly because people have had negative prior experiences with emotion and its expression. People may have learned to block feelings rather than attend to them, because their emotions and needs were not responded to or because their feelings were punished or resulted in other negative consequences, such as rejection. In some cases, this is not because the feelings themselves are painful but because the consequences of feeling the feelings are painful. In other cases, the feelings themselves are painful and feeling them is experienced as unbearable because people do not know how to soothe and modulate their feelings. Alternatively, they may fear that allowing and expressing their feelings will disrupt their functioning and sense of self-organization such that they might fragment.

A central concept in many theories of GAD is that of the avoidance of emotion and the hypothesis that worry serves to avoid pain. This raises three questions: (a) What is avoidance and how does it occur? (b) What is being avoided? and (c) Why do people avoid? (Greenberg, 2011). It is important to note that not all lack of awareness of emotion is avoidance (Kennedy-Moore & Watson, 2001). Emotions can remain unsymbolized in awareness by means of a variety of mechanisms. First, inattention to feeling states and emotions is not necessarily deliberate. People may not attend to emotion out of a learned habit of never having paid attention to their emotions. Another variant of this is *emotion illiteracy*—or not having words for emotions or being highly undifferentiated about emotion. This can be the case with people who were brought up in an environment in which denied feelings resulted in a basic problem of learning and are not an indication of a deliberate attempt to avoid emotional experience. Rather, emotions are not seen or thought to be important. In other instances, the feeling may not be fully formed, and what is being prevented is its symbolization and labeling. Here people are not yet aware of what they are feeling because its formation has been headed off at the pass. When this happens, people need to pay attention to and allow the feeling to form by a process of inner focusing and construction. Another form of not knowing what one is feeling stems from the complexity of emotional experience, which can lead to confusion about what is felt. Here it is the multiplicity of feelings that is confusing, and to make sense of their experience, people may need to explore and clarify what they are feeling.

In contrast to these states of not knowing, some people may be unaware of what they are feeling because they are avoiding a feeling. They may automatically suppress feelings of shame or fear, for example, to avoid them. In these cases, the feelings are formed and sensed but are ignored or disowned as not belonging to the self. Thus, people may not be conscious that they are avoiding their feelings. In another class of unacknowledged feelings, people may intentionally, not automatically, block their experience of emotion by not attending to their feelings or interrupting them by some other means out of a sense of experienced discomfort. This process may vary in degrees of awareness from being a fully aware intentional process, to a partially aware one, to the totally unaware process previously described. This process of interrupting the experience of emotion generally is signaled by anxiety. Freud posited that anxiety signals danger of the unacceptable from the impulse world below and leads to repression. Rogers (1959) suggested that bodily felt experience that was contrary to the self-concept was subceived and denied to awareness by a process that Porges (2011a, 2011b) recently labeled *neuroception*. In EFT, we see that anxiety can be an indication that individuals are not attending to their emotional experience but instead are dismissing, disowning, and disclaiming the emotions and their implicit action tendencies or otherwise failing to attend to it in the present, forfeiting an important compass to orient them to their needs.

To promote clients' awareness of their emotional experience, EFT focuses them on their bodily reactions and feelings. The therapist works with clients to find the labels for their emotions and feelings and to express and tolerate their emotional experience, as well as to develop ways of self-soothing to modulate their arousal and find new ways of expressing and meeting their needs. In EFT for GAD, it is not awareness of the anxiety that is change producing, clients are only too aware of this secondary symptomatic experience. It is the underlying fear and sadness from attachment injuries of neglect and harm, as well as shame from maltreatment, that needs to be brought into awareness and labeled. As clients become aware of the underlying feelings and begin to label them, their anxiety decreases. By labeling their feelings, they begin to create meaning and have easier access to unmet needs, and they can develop and access more self-validating internal resources and responses. Awareness also leads to finer discriminations among the stimuli in the originating situations, so that the triggers can become known. Knowing the triggers of their anxiety and understanding their emotional meaning enables clients to react with less intensity and to work to meet their needs in the present and in the future.

Expression

Expression involves the act of making your feelings known by speech, writing, or some other means, like gestures (e.g., shrugging, eyes expressing deep sadness). Expression means showing, conveying, or communicating. It produces interoceptive cues that are coded by the brain automatically and registered by mirror neurons (Decety & Jackson, 2004; Ferrari, Gallese, Rizzolatti, & Fogassi, 2003; Gallese, 2005; Rizzolatti, 2005). It can be thought of as a type of embodied symbolizing in action. The role of emotional expression and arousal and the degree to which it can be useful in therapy and in life depend on what emotion is expressed, about what issue, how it is expressed, by whom, to whom, when and under what conditions, and in what way it is followed by other experiences of affect and meaning. There can be no universal rule about the effectiveness of emotional expression, and a distinction between expression in therapy (to reexperience and rework past problematic experience) and expression in life needs to be kept clear.

In clients with GAD, there is a strong tendency to try to protect the self by worrying about situations that will evoke painful emotions. So clients are encouraged not to avoid painful emotions but to approach them by attending to their bodily experience, often in small steps. This may involve changing explicit beliefs (e.g., crying is weak; shame of feelings and fear that the therapist will be rejecting) that may govern the client's avoidance of talking about her feelings. Often clients with GAD, like other clients who have experienced deep pain, may need a lot of support to face their fear of dissolution (Greenberg & Bolger, 2001). Anxious clients need to allow and tolerate being in live contact with their emotions.

The two steps of learning how to approach and tolerate emotions are consistent with notions of exposure. There is a long line of evidence for the effectiveness of exposure to previously avoided feelings (Foa & Jaycox, 1999). From an EFT perspective, however, approach, arousal, and tolerance of emotional experience, although necessary, is not sufficient for change. Exposure just doesn't get the job done. Imagine exposing oneself to the feeling of shame at being worthless, the feeling of being like garbage, or the feeling of being alone and unloved. If clients overcome these fears and face feeling this felt sense of defectiveness or aloneness, they may be able to tolerate feeling defective or alone, but more is needed to produce change, including how clients relate to emotional experiences and how they feel about themselves in the process.

Optimal emotional processing, in our view, involves the transformation of old emotions by new emotions and an integration of cognition and affect to create new meaning (Greenberg, 2002; Greenberg & Pascual-Leone, 1995; Greenberg & Safran, 1987). Once contact with painful emotional experience is achieved, it is important for clients to receive a corrective emotional experience by reacting with a new emotion to the old cues and cognitively orienting to the painful emotion as information, that can be explored and reflected on to make sense of it. Thus, clients who feel angry may become more assertive and self-protective or experience self-compassion and grief in response to situations that previously evoked core fear or shame. It is important to note that in EFT the emotions that people are being exposed to are not the symptomatic emotions of anxiety that are modified in behavioral interventions, but are the primary emotions of basic fear, shame, or sadness underlying the symptoms usually addressed in exposure treatments.

Regulation

The third principle of emotional processing involves the regulation and modulation of emotion. An important issue in any treatment is what emotions are to be modulated and how are they to be regulated. In GAD, the emotions that require modulation are either the secondary symptomatic anxiety that creates feelings of despair and hopelessness or the primary maladaptive emotions such as shame, worthlessness, and anxiety rooted in basic fear and panic. Maladaptive emotions of core shame and feelings of shaky vulnerability require regulation to enable clients to create a working distance from them, instead of being overwhelmed by them. Emotion needs to be regulated when distress is so high that the emotion no longer informs adaptive action.

In EFT, affect regulation is seen as a core motive and people are seen as being motivated to seek relief from unpleasant emotions and seek out pleasant emotions. Some emotions feel good, whereas others do not. People clearly seek calm, joy, pride, excitement, interest, and pleasure. Equally, people seek to avoid pain, shame, anxiety, and fear. Ironically, though, sometimes people may choose not to seek pleasant emotions to meet some other need. Emotions were designed evolutionarily to promote survival, and part of this design is the motivation to change negative states. This affect regulation tendency aids survival and growth. Much action and interaction thus is driven by felt satisfaction (e.g., joy when relationships allow needs to be met or excitement when goals are attained) and by felt dissatisfaction (e.g., loneliness when relationships falter or shame and anxiety from failure).

In our view organismic, including emotional and physical, experience is important as people confront anxiety. Organismic experience guides people as to what is good and bad, and they develop and maintain their identities on the basis of a sense of competence because of how their actions make them feel. It is important to note that although people primarily seek to feel positive emotions, negative emotions are highly functional. People also regulate their emotions with the aim of achieving their goals, not simply to seek pleasure and avoid pain. For example, some people may endure suffering to achieve a goal (e.g., dying for a higher ideal) and some may work to maintain anxiety (e.g., to ensure they study for tests), yet others seek out the experience of fear (e.g., riding roller coasters). Surgeons or soldiers will sweat and strain for hours, not to achieve pleasure in the moment but rather to feel the pride and satisfaction of a life saved or the relief of an enemy destroyed. Thus, short-term displeasure or pain is sought out and endured to attain long-term satisfaction. Much of human behavior is motivated and reinforced by felt gratification, but this is not to suggest that humans strive only for instant gratification. People may endure pain that is perceived to be functional and consistent with their objectives (e.g., working toward a goal that is anticipated to bring approval and recognition). In addition, the positive feelings people seek are not all based on pleasure. Therefore, we do not propose a hedonistic view of functioning. Instead, we see people as capable of second order valuing that allows them to choose among different situations on the basis of their goals and values (J. Watson & Greenberg, 1996).

People's goals, therefore, consist of more than "feeling good." At times, under certain circumstances, they will seek negative emotions, tolerate pain, embrace anger, or sacrifice themselves in the service of higher order feelings of virtue or love. Instead of seeing the pursuit of hedonism (seeking pleasure and avoiding pain) as a primary motivation, we propose that people are motivated to regulate their emotions to adapt and survive. Specific emotions lead to specific needs and actions tendencies that enhance survival. And learning to regulate distress and intense emotion contributes to a sense of competence and mastery. People are motivated to seek meaning as well as to regulate affect (Greenberg, 2011, 2015). The search for meaning is a drive all people share. One way they do this is by developing narratives about their experience to provide meaning and understanding for their actions and experience. People constantly try to make sense of their feelings. In addition, meaning creation itself brings positive feelings and even pleasure and enhances people's sense of competency and mastery in the world.

Anxiety disorders are seen as a symptom of underlying emotional states that individuals are trying to regulate and understand (Greenberg, 2011). Healthy emotion regulation requires that individuals are guided by their emotions but not coerced and dominated by them. Regulating emotions in this way is a key developmental task. An inability to regulate emotions constitutes a form of dysfunction. To deal with chronic anxiety and painful emotions in GAD, the EFT therapist focuses on facilitating clients' access to their painful emotions as well as the ways that they have learned to respond to them and cope with their experience (J. Watson, 2011). The therapist works with clients to develop alternative ways of responding to the self and to process painful emotional experiences so that they can access and experience positive emotions of pride, joy, and self-assertion. By developing alternative strategies for regulating and processing their emotional experience, individuals are able to generate alternative actions as well as new emotional experiences.

Learning to Self-Soothe

Negative ways of relating to emotional experience and difficulties in regulating emotions are often accompanied by an underdeveloped capacity to self-soothe. The capacity to modulate distress and self-soothe is developed in interaction with others, as well as with the accretion of positive experiences that do not overwhelm people's sense of being able to cope, but rather enable them to develop a sense of mastery and confidence. The internalization of self-soothing is forged with adequate support from the environment as well as the development of physical, cognitive, and emotional competence. As people grow and master different situations, they learn to trust themselves more, are able to reassure themselves when distressed, and rely on others when they need help. There is an optimal balance between challenging our capacities so that we grow and having sufficient support so that we are not distressed and overwhelmed by difficult and challenging experiences.

Developmental neuroscientists suggest that protective, nurturing adults help children develop a sense of competence and mastery by providing supportive and challenging environments (Legerstee, 2013). According to these theorists, lack of support from caregivers and the external environment results in inadequate connections forming between the amygdala and the cortex, contributing to difficulties in modulating distress as well as problem solving. In environments that overtax their abilities, children may not learn how to self-soothe when they are distressed, or how to adequately problem solve and find solutions. Moreover, they may not be comforted and calmed by reassurance from others, lacking positive experiences on which to draw to support the belief that things will work out or that they will be able to cope with feeling overwhelmed and distressed. Instead, they worry in an attempt to protect the vulnerable self against the activation of painful emotions and the absence of more effective affect-regulating strategies.

Self-soothing involves, among other things, diaphragmatic breathing and relaxation, as well as the development of self-empathy, self-compassion, self-acceptance, and calming self-talk. Self-soothing also comes interpersonally in the form of others demonstrating empathic attunement to one's affect and through acceptance and validation by another. In EFT for GAD, the therapist helps clients contain and regulate emotional experience by providing a validating, empathically attuned environment. Over time, this way of being is internalized and clients develop implicit self-soothing strategies, so that they develop the ability to regulate their feelings automatically without deliberate effort.

Reflection

In addition to recognizing emotions and symbolizing them in words, promoting further reflection on emotional experience, helping people make narrative sense of their experience, and promoting its assimilation into their ongoing self-narratives is an important change process. Reflecting on their emotional experience tells people who they are. It helps them make sense of their experience and forms the basis of new narratives to explain their experience and themselves (Goldman, Greenberg, & Pos, 2005; Greenberg & Angus, 2004; Greenberg & Pascual-Leone, 1997; Pennebaker, 1995; J. Watson & Rennie, 1994).

Exploration of emotional experience and reflection on what is experienced is an important process of change in GAD. Reflection helps to make sense of our bodily arousal. In this process, feelings, needs, self-experience, thoughts, and aims are all clarified and organized and come to form part of our narratives in which different parts of the self and their relationships are identified. People, for example, may come to see how a catastrophizing voice leads to feelings of anxiety, which can help them to recognize their agency in the creation of their symptoms and how they might be changed. The meanings of situations that have evoked anxiety are comprehended and patterns in relationships are recognized. To develop a new outlook on what is important involves a fundamental change in attitude that can lead to profound changes. For example, reflecting on a near death experience can lead to profound changes in people's approach to life, like providing the impetus to overcome an addiction, rediscover spirituality, or become more honest and appreciative with others.

Reflection promotes understanding of the way in which the self is psychologically constructed and constituted. The narratives that people construct provide a *cognitive organizing process*, a type of temporal Gestalt, where the meaning of specific life events and actions is determined not by the characteristics or abilities they exhibit but by their relationship to the unified story with a particular plot or theme. Life narratives render the experiences and memories of clients into meaningful coherent stories. They provide a sense of self and identity that can be known and shared with others.

Transformation

The most important way of dealing with emotion in therapy involves the transformation of emotion by emotion. This applies most specifically to using adaptive emotions to transform primary maladaptive emotions, such as fear, sadness, loneliness, abandonment, and shame (Greenberg, 2002). We suggest that maladaptive emotional states are best transformed by undoing them through activating other, more adaptive emotional states. Spinoza (1967) was the first to note that emotion is needed to change emotion. He proposed that "an emotion cannot be restrained nor removed unless by an opposed and stronger emotion" (p. 195). Although thinking usually changes thoughts, only feeling can change primary emotions. In EFT, an important goal is to arrive at maladaptive emotions to make them accessible to transformation. In time, the coactivation of more adaptive emotions, along with or in response to the maladaptive emotion, helps to transform it.

The process of changing emotion with emotion goes beyond ideas of catharsis, completion and letting go, exposure, extinction, or habituation, in that the maladaptive feeling is not purged, nor does it simply attenuate as a result of people feeling it. Rather, another feeling is used to transform or undo it. Although dysregulated, secondary emotions such as panic and the anxiety of obsessive compulsiveness may be overcome by exposure, in many situations in therapy, primary maladaptive emotions, such as the shame of feeling worthless, the anxiety of basic insecurity and the sadness of aloneness, are best transformed by other emotions. Thus, change in previously avoided primary maladaptive emotions is brought about by the activation of an incompatible, more adaptive experience, such as empowering anger and pride, healing grief, or compassion for the self, that undoes the old response rather than attenuate it. This involves more than simply feeling or facing feelings leading it to their diminishment. Rather, primary maladaptive emotion is transformed by activating the approach tendencies (e.g., in anger, to set boundaries to protect the self; in sadness, to reach out to seek comfort from others; Moons, Eisenberger, & Taylor, 2010).

It appears that happy feelings can transform bad ones, not in a deliberate manner, for example, by trying to look on the bright side or by replacement, but by evoking meaningfully embodied alternative experiences of the self in the world that undo the physiology and experience of negative feelings.

This principle, however, applies not only to positive emotions changing negative ones but also to maladaptive emotions being changed by activating dialectically opposed adaptive emotions (Greenberg, 2002). Thus, in therapy, maladaptive fear of abandonment or annihilation, once evoked, can be transformed into security by the activation of more empowering, boundary-setting emotions of adaptive anger or disgust, or by evoking the softer soothing feelings of sadness and the need for comfort. Maladaptive shame can be transformed by accessing anger at violation and self-compassion and by accessing pride and self-worth. Thus, the tendency to shrink into the ground in shame can be transformed by the thrusting forward tendency in newly accessed assertive anger at violation. Withdrawal emotions from one side of the brain are replaced with approach emotions from another part of the brain or vice-versa (Davidson, 2000a, 2000b). Once the alternative emotion has been accessed, it transforms the original state, and a new state is forged. Often a period of regulation or calming of the maladaptive emotion in need of change is required before an opposing emotion can be activated.

How does the therapist help his or her clients access new emotions to change their maladaptive emotions? A number of ways have been outlined (Elliott et al., 2004; Greenberg, 2002, 2015). Focusing on what is needed and thereby mobilizing a new emotion is a key means of actuating a new emotion (Greenberg, 2015). The newly accessed, alternate feelings are resources in the personality that help change the maladaptive state. For example, bringing out implicit adaptive anger in anxious clients can help change maladaptive fear of abandonment or the shame of invalidation. When the tendency to run away in fear is combined with anger's tendency to thrust forward, this leads to a new relational position of holding the abuser accountable for wrongdoing, while feeling deserving of protection, rather than guilty and unsafe. It also is essential to symbolize, explore, and differentiate the primary maladaptive emotion, in this case fear, and regulate it by breathing and calming, before cultivating access to the new more adaptive emotion, in this case anger.

Other methods of accessing new emotions involve using enactment and imagery to evoke them, remembering a time an emotion was felt, changing how clients view things, or even the therapist expressing an emotion for clients (Greenberg, 2002). Once accessed, these new emotional resources begin to undo the psychoaffective motor program previously determining clients' mode of processing. New emotional states enable people to challenge the validity of perceptions of the self and others that are connected to maladaptive emotion, thereby weakening its hold on them.

In our view, enduring emotional change occurs by generating a new emotional response not through a process of insight or understanding alone. EFT, as we have said, works on the basic principle that people must first arrive at a place before they can leave it. Maladaptive emotion schematic memories of past childhood losses and traumas are activated in the therapy session to change these by memory reconstruction. Introducing new experience in the present into currently activated memories of past events has been shown to lead to memory transformation by the assimilation of new material into past memories (Nadel, Hupbach, Gomez, & Newman-Smith, 2012). By being activated in the present, the old memories are restructured by the new experience of being in the context of a safe relationship and by activating more adaptive emotional responses to the old situation, as well as new adult resources and new understanding. The memories are reconsolidated in a new way by incorporating these new elements. Although the past cannot be changed, the experience of it can be changed.

Corrective Emotional Experience

Finally, a key way of changing an emotion is to have a new lived experience that changes an old feeling. New lived experience with others provides a corrective emotional experience. Experiences that provide interpersonal soothing, disconfirm pathogenic beliefs, or offer new success experience can correct patterns set down in earlier times. Thus, an experience in which clients face shame in a therapeutic context and experience acceptance, rather than the expected disgust or denigration from their therapist, has the power to change the feeling of shame. Corrective emotional experiences in EFT occur predominantly in the therapeutic relationship, although positive interactions and experiences in the world are also helpful and encouraged.

Individuals with GAD do not know how to cope with their distress and overwhelming feelings of disintegration. Having internalized negative ways of relating to their feelings, individuals do not have the tools to tolerate and effectively listen to, attend to, and soothe their painful feelings. Instead, they tend to avoid, dismiss, and deny them. In this way, people are responding to their pain as others responded to it, and as they have learned to do so in interaction with their environments as described in Chapter 1 of this volume. Intense distress and negative ways of coping inhibit the adequate processing of painful feelings, leaving individuals with a sense that they will disintegrate and fall apart. Their anxiety is often accompanied by a deep sense of shame, especially when developing children's feelings and needs have not been seen or validated but instead have been ignored and dismissed, leaving individuals feeling vulnerable, overwhelmed, and unsupported. As a result, they may develop a sense of themselves as inadequate, defective, unworthy, and unlovable.

The goal in EFT is for clients, with the help of more favorable circumstances in therapy, to experience a sense of mastery as they face and reexperience emotions that were ignored and dismissed in the past for fear of disintegration as a result of neglect and rejection. When this happens, clients can undergo corrective emotional experiences with their therapist that repair the traumatic influence of previous relational experiences. Corrective interpersonal emotional experiences occur generally throughout the therapeutic process, whenever the patient experiences the therapist as someone who is attuned to and validates the client's inner world. Therapy offers new opportunities for affect regulation with a helpful other, new self-experience through being in contact with the other, and being mirrored and accepted by the other, as well as through new experiences that promote the activation of alternate adaptive emotion schemes that can potentiate new emergent self-organizations. Overall, a genuine relationship between client and therapist, with its constancy, is a corrective emotional experience.

Clients in therapy thus can reexperience and process events differently than they did originally, because they experience the relationship with their therapist in a different way than they experienced their formative relationships as children with caretakers. Now clients can express vulnerability or anger with their therapist without being punished; they can assert themselves without being censured. The undeniable reality of this experience allows clients to experience that they are no longer powerless children facing powerful adults.

CONCLUSION

The core ingredient in the treatment of GAD is the process of accessing and transforming core maladaptive emotion schemes formed earlier in life. This produces changes by enhancing emotional processing in clients with GAD. We propose that GAD reflects deficits in individuals' capacities to process their emotions; therefore, in EFT, clients learn to become aware, tolerate, label, modulate, and express their feelings to become less anxious and more confident in their interactions with the world. There is a focus on experiences of fear, shame, anger, and sadness as a result of attachment and identity injuries suffered early in life. The EFT therapist supports clients as they access their unmet needs and their negative ways of treating their experience to transform their emotions and move forward with optimism, confident in their ability to cope. In the next chapter, we discuss the treatment sequence in more detail.

3

TREATMENT FRAMEWORK

In this chapter, we lay out an overall treatment framework for generalized anxiety disorder (GAD). Previous texts have specified a set of principles for the conduct of treatment in general (Elliott, Watson, Goldman, & Greenberg, 2004; Greenberg, Rice, & Elliott, 1993). The two major treatment principles articulated in these texts, facilitating a therapeutic relationship and promoting therapeutic work, remain the bedrock of the approach. Here we apply these to the treatment of GAD. We then outline the sequence of steps that are followed in treatment that we have found effective in working with clients with anxiety in general and GAD in particular.

The treatment sequence in GAD involves (a) creating a safe relationship that contributes to the development of a stronger sense of self and the internalization of positive ways of treating the self; (b) strengthening clients' vulnerable self by developing their confidence in their capacity to trust inner resources, including their perceptions and feelings; (c) working on the process of anxiety generation using two-chair dialogues between a worrier, the anxiety

http://dx.doi.org/10.1037/0000018-004
Emotion-Focused Therapy for Generalized Anxiety, by J. C. Watson and L. S. Greenberg
Copyright © 2017 by the American Psychological Association. All rights reserved.

creator, and the experiencing self to create a sense of the self as an agent rather than a victim of anxiety; (d) dealing with the negative ways of treating the self and the self-interruption of experience that prevent access to more adaptive ways of responding and to need satisfaction; (e) resolving the unfinished business and the underlying attachment- and identity-related painful emotions that led to the vulnerable self-organization and to access assertive anger; and (f) developing self-acceptance and self-compassion for the vulnerable self, as well as the capacity to self-soothe to consolidate a stronger sense of self and greater confidence in clients' capacities to cope and feel a greater sense of mastery in their environments.

MAJOR TREATMENT PRINCIPLES IN EMOTION-FOCUSED THERAPY

Greenberg and colleagues (1993) specified three subprinciples under the main principle of facilitating a therapeutic relationship: presence and empathic attunement, bonding, and task collaboration. They also specified three subprinciples under the principle of promoting task-specific work: differential processing, growth and choice, and task completion.

Facilitating a Therapeutic Relationship

In emotion-focused therapy (EFT), a constant way of being for the therapist is to be present and curious about clients and their experiences. This stance is a precondition for *empathic attunement* to the client's immediate experience in the session, emphasizing moment-by-moment attunement to her or his shifting affective experience. Empathic attunement focuses on the therapist's way of being or experiential state and the therapist's perceptual processing capacity, including attending to and observing clients' affective experience. Clients' affective experience provides a guide—it is with this that the therapist remains in contact and it is his or her understanding of this that he or she shares with the clients.

The second relational subprinciple, *bonding*, emphasizes that to develop a secure and trusting relational bond, clients must be able to receive their therapist's expressions of understanding and experience their therapist as genuine and accepting. Thus, it is expected that throughout the treatment the therapist will communicate the Rogerian conditions of empathy, acceptance, and positive regard in a genuine manner (J. Watson & Greenberg, 1994). This principle refers to the feelings of trust, respect, and feeling valued that develop in clients as they internalize their therapist's attitude and work together to achieve their goals.

Task collaboration, the third relational principle, emphasizes moment-by-moment and overall collaboration on the goals and tasks of therapy (Bordin, 1979; Horvath & Greenberg, 1989; J. Watson & Greenberg, 1998). To establish agreement on goals and the perceived relevance of different tasks (e.g., two-chair dialogues), the therapist may offer clients information about anxiety, or offer rationales for the importance of allowing and accepting emotion. The goal of these explanations is to help clients develop a general understanding of the importance of working with the emotions that underlie their anxiety. Alternatively, to further develop collaboration, the therapist also provides rationales for specific therapeutic activities (e.g., two-chair and empty-chair work).

Promoting Task-Specific Work

The second main principle of treatment, promoting task-specific work, is facilitated by differential processing, growth and choice, and task completion (Greenberg et al., 1993). A central feature of EFT is that productive emotional processing involves working differentially with different emotional states at different times. *Differential processing* covers different modes of emotional processing as well as working on key therapeutic tasks, each of which involves specific processes. *Different modes of emotional processing* include deepening experience and emotional arousal, by having clients attend to immediate bodily experience and felt meaning, elaborating the stimulus situation, facilitating awareness and symbolization of immediate emotional experience, expressing wants or needs, and reflecting on experience to create meaning. For example, when clients present unfinished business related to attachment injuries, the therapist might suggest an empty-chair dialogue with an imagined other, whereas when clients are unclear about his or her feelings and not attending to his or her bodily felt sense, the therapist might propose focusing on becoming aware and symbolizing a bodily felt sense.

Growth and choice is seen to promote the work of therapy and privileges clients' self-determination. Here the therapist supports clients' potential and motivation for self-determination, mature interdependence, mastery, and self-development. Growth is promoted first through a process of listening carefully for clients' strengths and internal resources, as well as by helping clients explore the growing edges of their experiences and encouraging them to focus on possibilities. For example, the therapist might hear and reflect on an emerging sense of anger and self-assertion implicit in an anxious client's feeling of helplessness. The therapist can work with clients to access these feelings more fully to address attachment wounds. In our view, clients are able to take more risks in therapy when they feel safe and comfortable.

Task completion promotes the resolution of specific change episodes and facilitates the therapeutic work. This principle emphasizes that therapist and client work toward resolving or completing specific tasks. This requires that the therapist pay attention to themes and offer the client opportunities to move to the next stage of a task so as to complete it, if it is consistent with the client's current states and goals. However, when clients shift to another state or the task is experienced as contrary to clients' goals, the therapist returns to following the moment-by-moment process to become more attuned to those states and goals. Adopting these principles leads to a style that smoothly combines following and guiding clients' moment-by-moment experience (J. Watson & Greenberg, 1998).

In the most general terms, EFT is built on being responsive to clients' experiences. At the same time, the EFT therapist also assumes that it is useful to guide clients' emotional processing in different ways at different times. The optimal situation in this approach is an active collaboration between client and therapist, with neither feeling led nor followed by the other. Instead, the ideal is an easy sense of cooperation and coexploration. Nevertheless, when disjunction or disagreement occurs, clients are viewed as the experts on their own experience, and the therapist always defers to the clients. Thus, therapist interventions are offered in a nonimposing, tentative manner, as conjectures, suggestions, experiments, or offers, rather than as expert pronouncements, lectures, or statements of truth (J. Watson, 2002, 2015). In this way, the therapist can be seen as an emotion coach (Greenberg, 2002, 2015) working to help clients access the painful emotions that their worry is protecting against. She or he promotes awareness and acceptance of emotional experience and coaches clients in new ways of processing emotion. Following provides acceptance, whereas guiding introduces novelty and the possibility of change. Guidance by the therapist provides direction for exploration, not by suggesting what content clients should focus on, nor by interpreting the meaning of their experience, but by guiding the type of processing in which they engage.

Working with anxious clients to become aware of their underlying painful emotions involves helping them to label their emotions verbally. Initially, the focus is on emotions related to their experience of anxiety and emotions from the immediate past, but as therapy progresses clients will begin to label feelings from their more distant past, as well as current feelings that are being felt in the immediate present. This involves accessing painful primary maladaptive emotions, facilitating new ways of processing these emotions, and guiding clients to find ways of soothing or regulating their emotions. In addition, working with anxious clients involves facilitating the utilization of adaptive emotions, usually anger, sadness, and self-compassion, to help transform maladaptive emotions (e.g., fear from feeling disconnected or unprotected, sadness from feeling lonely because of abandonment, or shame from feeling worthless or humiliated).

In our view, for enduring change to occur, people cannot simply be taught new skills for dealing with anxiety but, rather, need to access the underlying determinants of their anxiety and experience new emotions to change old painful emotion schemes. For example, accessing protective anger at having been unfairly treated or feeling grief and sadness for what was lost or missed in childhood may be very helpful in overcoming the sense of anxious help-lessness, weakness, insecurity, or shame that so often underlies their anxiety. However, explicitly teaching people that this is what they should do is not the goal. Instead, the therapist needs to facilitate access to new emotions by asking clients as their narratives unfold, at the right time, in the right way, what it is they need and feel as a result of what they have endured or what they have not received as their needs went unmet.

In addition to the general relationship and work principles previously outlined, three other important principles have been identified to guide treatment (Goldman & Greenberg, 2014): emotional change (see Chapter 2, this volume), case formulation, and marker-guided interventions. A *case formulation* is a set of working hypotheses about the client's core painful emotion, which includes the therapist's conjectures about what the emotion is, what caused it, and identification of the thoughts and behaviors that sustain it (Goldman & Greenberg, 2014). This formulation serves as a clinical map for intervention. Although case formulation is revised throughout the process as it consolidates, it is generally consistent across treatment as an overarching conceptualization.

CASE FORMULATION

A context-sensitive approach to EFT case formulation has been developed to help promote the development of a focus for brief treatments (Goldman & Greenberg, 2014; Greenberg & Goldman, 2008). Case formulation relies on process diagnosis, development of a focus, and theme development rather than person or syndrome diagnosis. In a process-oriented approach to treatment, case formulation is an ongoing process, as sensitive to the moment and the in-session context as it is to an understanding of the person as a case. The therapist keeps his or her fingers on the client's emotional pulse at all times as he or she formulates what is happening and listens for what painful emotions seem key to the client's suffering. A process-oriented approach to formulation is adopted, to maintain a respectful, egalitarian type of relationship and because it sees people as active agents who are in flux, constantly creating meaning.

People are viewed as dynamic self-organizing systems entering different self-organizations at different times. The state people are in at the moment and the current narrative are more determining of their current experience and possibility than any conceptualization of a more enduring pattern, attachment style, or reified self-concept that may be constructed early in treatment. Therefore, in a process diagnostic approach, there is a continual focus on clients' current states of mind and current cognitive–affective problem states. The EFT therapist's main focus in formulation is to follow their clients' pain because this acts as a compass that will guide the therapy to the core emotion schemes underlying clients' symptoms of anxiety. In addition, it is the formulation of core markers of current emotional concerns that guide interventions rather than a picture of people's enduring personality or a pattern of experience and behavior across situations.

Although case formulation tends to remain more or less stable throughout treatment, specific marker-guided interventions are chosen on the basis of the moment-by-moment experience with clients in session. Once the therapist has created a safe environment by being present, empathic, accepting, and validating, then he or she must listen for clients' markers of underlying processing difficulties. Then the therapist offers interventions that match the difficulty to try to resolve it. The emergence of clients' in-session problem states are seen as markers of opportunities for differential interventions best suited to help facilitate productive work on that state at that point in the process. This is a form of process diagnosis.

To understand clients, the therapist makes EFT formulations as he or she follows what is most painful or most poignant in clients' narratives, rather than listening to content and forming a conceptual model of underlying causes. Formulation in EFT, first and foremost, involves following clients' *pain compass* to guide them and the therapist to the core problem. It is the client's pain that directs the therapist's and the client's attention in therapy. The client's pain highlights those experiences that need to be explored further so that they can be processed and transformed. As the therapist follows this pain, he or she privileges process (e.g., how clients treat their experience and emotions) over the content of their stories. The steps of formulation have been outlined in detail by Greenberg and Goldman (2008) and Goldman and Greenberg (2014) and are described briefly next. The first phase of case formulation involves unfolding the narrative and observing clients' emotional processing styles, including (a) listening to clients' presenting problems, (b) identifying poignant and painful experiences, (c) attending to and observing clients' emotional processing styles, and (d) unfolding the emotion-based narrative.

The process of formulation begins at the first meeting or even with the initial phone contact when the therapist starts to develop an understanding of the client's presenting anxiety and other problems. From the beginning, the therapist listens for poignancy and pain. For example, a therapist might hear the following from a client:

> A friend's child just went through chemotherapy. She says now [her son] is okay, thank God. But, I was thinking [how] he is the same age as my son and I said wow what would I do [in that situation]? I don't know if I could survive [if something happened to my son]. I would die. [Thinking about it is] always like an empty thing, like an empty pain. It's [a kind of] sadness and I thought what will happen to [my son]? [What if he can't] find a job here? Where are we going to live in a one-bedroom apartment together? I don't know.

As the client's problems and related stories unfold, the therapist asks himself what is most poignant in the story and what is most painful for the client. The client's pain compass directs the therapist's attention (J. Watson, 2002). This identification of the chronic enduring pain underlying the client's anxiety sets the goal for treatment: to resolve the client's underlying pain. In this example, the client's fear of loss and feelings of aloneness and abandonment became the focus of treatment.

Clients' emotion-based narratives of their lives, and their history, are developed, to aid formulation. The EFT therapist listens to clients' stories, paying particular attention to the emotional tone that pervades them. Clients' stories reveal what they feel, and about whom they feel it, along with their implicit needs or concerns, that may or may not have been addressed. As clients unfold their stories, their therapist observes various elements of their emotional processing style (Elliott et al., 2004). The therapist attends to and assesses the clients' manner of emotional processing. Early on, the therapist notes whether anxious clients' emotions are overregulated or underregulated and whether they are panicky or controlled. The therapist is attentive to whether his or her clients are describing their symptoms and expressing secondary anxiety rather than their primary, underlying emotions. Anxious clients often have an externalizing processing style, talking about what happened in situations rather than what they feel or what it means to them. Identifying clients' processing style is a key element in case formulation because it informs the therapist about how to intervene. To make these assessments of emotional processing, the therapist observes his or her clients' nonverbal expressions, including facial expressions, tones of voice and vocal quality (i.e., how things are said; Rice & Kerr, 1986; J. Watson, 2002), emotional arousal (Warwar & Greenberg, 1999; J. Watson & Prosser, 2002), and depth of experiencing (Klein, Mathieu-Coughlan, & Kiesler, 1986). The therapist's case formulations then move on to the cocreation, with the client, of a focus for the treatment that identifies the core painful emotion schemes in the narrative.

There are six major aspects to identifying the core emotion schemes in the case formulation process (Goldman & Greenberg, 2014). These elements of the formulation process outlined as follows and are represented in the acronym MENSIT: markers, emotion (core schemes), needs, secondary emotions, interruptions, and themes. The therapist listens for markers of clients' in-session emotional problem states, such as anxiety splits, unfinished business, and self-interruption processes. Marker-guided interventions help access underlying feelings to reveal the core painful emotion schemes, which usually involve fear, shame, and sadness. Core needs for connection and recognition, and the secondary emotions that obscure clients' core emotion schemes, are identified as they arise. Any interruptive processes, such as self-silencing or self-neglect, that block access to experiencing core painful states and clients' sense of entitlement to their needs, also are identified. Over time themes emerge, such as sadness at loss, fear of abandonment, or shame of inadequacy. Using MENSIT as a guide to the different aspects that are important to processing and resolving clients' difficulties can help therapist and client coconstruct a narrative that ties the client's presenting problems, triggering stimuli, and behavioral avoidances and consequences of ways of coping, with their core painful emotion schemes.

Having formulated the client's painful emotions, the therapist continues to make process formulations over time. He or she focuses on more moment-by-moment formulations, identifying current client states and ongoing markers related to clients' core issues and micromarkers within tasks. In addition, as new meanings emerge, the therapist assesses how clients' new emerging narratives connect back to their presenting problems to assess the degree of change and their readiness for termination of therapy (Goldman & Greenberg, 2014).

CASE EXAMPLE: CASE FORMULATION FOR GENERAL ANXIETY DISORDER

Jennifer is a 28-year-old woman who lives with her boyfriend and is currently attending college. She is the eldest of three siblings, one of whom experiences chronic health issues. She came to therapy because she was experiencing high levels of anxiety and had been depressed previously. At the beginning of therapy, she described her anxiety as building up over the past few years. It was characterized by rumination, constant worry and apprehension, somatic symptoms, and occasional panic attacks. She presented with worry, saying she worries about everything, especially her school work. She noted that she often felt shaky and fragile. As she presented her story, although she focused on external details primarily, she showed some capacity for focusing internally on her experience. She described her mother as insensitive and her father as mostly absent. She reported that she was anxious as a child in school and was afraid of her teachers. Her treatment of herself was harsh and critical. This led her to devalue herself and her needs, and she was intolerant of her own vulnerability.

The first markers that emerged were worry and catastrophizing, which the therapist saw as opportunities for two-chair dialogues. The core emotions from which Jennifer protected herself for fear of disintegration were feelings of being rejected, of being lonely and unloved, and of feeling worthless. Her main need was to be cared for and accepted. In an unfinished business dialogue with her parents, she said, "I just need to feel that unconditional love that you should have for me." She had adopted a strategy of disallowing her feelings, disclaiming that she experienced any pain, which led to feeling nonspecific secondary anxiety and worry as she tried to protect against situations (e.g., being alone) that would activate these core painful feelings. The themes of the treatment were her tendency to protect herself from possible disasters and ultimately from rejection. In Session 3, the therapist summarized their work:

> As we have discussed it seems your worry protects you from those terrible feelings of being alone and unloved which as you have seen come a lot from your mother's neglect and preoccupation with her own life. So it seems like your coping strategy is to avoid these painful feelings of sadness and fear of being rejected, so you critically monitor yourself at all times always needing to be on top of things so something unexpected won't happen and you won't be rejected and left alone without support. This leaves you feeling anxious but also prevents real contact with others.

Here the therapist, guided by the client's painful feelings of sadness and rejection, framed the worry and pointed the way to chair tasks. After the earlier sessions, which focused on worry and self-criticism using two-chair tasks, different markers for empty-chair dialogues and unfinished business with Jennifer's disapproving and rejecting mother emerged. After a number of unfinished business dialogues with her mother, Jennifer was able to establish a stronger and clearer boundary with her. She expressed anger at her mother's inability to support and protect her. This led to a more empowered sense of self, which was validated by the therapist.

MARKER-GUIDED INTERVENTIONS

A defining feature of our approach is that interventions are *marker guided*. Research has demonstrated that in therapy, clients enter specific problematic emotional processing states that are identifiable by in-session statements and behaviors that mark underlying affective problems and that these afford opportunities for particular types of effective intervention (Elliott et al., 2004; Greenberg et al., 1993). Client markers indicate not only clients' states and the types of interventions to use but also their current readiness to work on these problems. The therapist identifies markers of different types of problematic emotional processing problems and intervene in specific ways to resolve these problems.

Process diagnosis is privileged over person diagnosis. This is done mainly by having clear descriptions of client markers of emotional processing difficulties that indicate that clients are in particular problem states that are amenable to particular types of intervention. For example, the marker of a *self-critical split*, in which one part of the self (the critical self) is criticizing another part (the experiencer), in an emotionally involved manner, indicates that clients are currently struggling to resolve this problem and that these processes are currently active and, therefore, accessible. Therapist interventions create a particular task environment designed to facilitate particular types of client performances that have been found to be helpful in resolving these types of problems, such as integration and self-acceptance for self-criticism (Greenberg et al., 1993).

Each of the different EFT tasks, such as unfolding problematic reactions and two-chair dialogues for self-criticism, has been studied extensively and the key components of resolution and the specific forms that resolution takes have been specified (Elliott et al., 2004; Greenberg et al., 1993). These models of the actual process of change act as maps to guide the interventions. Often it is only through intervening with these exploratory and emotion-arousing tasks in process-sensitive ways that clients' experience is deepened, enabling them to get to their core pain and emotion schemes.

AN EMOTION-FOCUSED PSYCHOTHERAPY TREATMENT MANUAL FOR GENERALIZED ANXIETY DISORDER

GAD, as we have said, is characterized by worry as a protection against painful underlying emotions that have not been processed or adequately soothed. Often these are core feelings of sadness at being alone, isolated, or neglected, feelings of fear at being unprotected from violence or abuse, or feelings of shame at humiliation and powerlessness. These painful emotions stem from unresolved attachment- and identity-related injuries and from past traumas that have resulted in a vulnerable insecure sense of self. Clients with GAD, in our experience, also have difficulty experiencing and expressing anger and being assertive with others and generally lack the ability to self-soothe. All these processes need to be addressed in therapy.

Once a safe working environment and a working alliance have been established to work on clients' emotional awareness, and an initial focus on aspects of clients' experience that are generating their anxiety has been formed, the treatment proceeds to the evocation and exploration of emotionally painful material in the vulnerable self. This is what most clearly characterizes EFT.

In this work, it is crucial that clients experience their emotions in the session, so that focal concerns are felt experientially and not just known intellectually. To promote experience, clients' internal and external supports for making contact with their experience, and their capacity to contain and process what is contacted must be assessed. If supports are insufficient, the therapist works to help clients develop the resources and capacities necessary to process their experience.

EFT works on the basic principle that to change, people cannot leave a place until they have arrived. Clients, therefore, need to reclaim disowned experience before they can change it or be changed by it. In this process, it is not that people simply discover things they did not know but rather that they experience in a bodily felt manner aspects of themselves they have not consciously felt or may have previously disclaimed (Greenberg & van Balen, 1998; J. Watson, 2002). The therapist helps clients to experience their emotions and actively remember what they are talking about so that they can become aware of their feelings and the impact of events (J. Watson & Greenberg, 1998). In this way, the message or significance of their feelings can be clearly experienced with impact and used, transformed, or reflected on to create new meaning.

As clients leave the place they arrived at, the emphasis shifts to transformation through the construction of alternative ways of responding emotionally. This is done by accessing new internal resources in the form of adaptive emotional responses and by making sense of experience in new ways. This shift occurs once the emotional experience at the core of the problem has been evoked in the session, reclaimed, and its origins or generators explored. In the transformation process, the therapist offers his or her process expertise to focus clients on ways of accessing new adaptive emotional responses to transform maladaptive ones and facilitate the construction of new meaning. It is particularly helpful for the therapist to help clients with GAD to develop self-soothing capacities as they attain greater self-compassion and self-acceptance, in addition to accessing their self-sustaining internal resources of empowering anger and grief for what they never received in the way of support and nurture.

In addition to generating new experience through their emotions, clients need to construct new narratives. In this way, a new lived story as well as a new told story emerges. It is at this point that the dialectical process of making sense of newly synthesized experience, a central process of change in EFT, is most evident in consolidating change. New meaning is consolidated and new explanations and narratives that help make sense of changes in peoples' experience of themselves and the world, are generated.

EFT is not complete without the following fundamental processes: the sequence of forming a trusting bond and increasing emotional awareness to strengthen the self; evoking a painful experience previously disowned, rather than simply talking about it; developing new emotional responses, including anger, grief, and self-soothing; and creating new meaning. Throughout treatment, clients are seen as agents who are experts on their own experience. The therapist is seen as offering process expertise that can help to guide the process and facilitate movement toward their clients' goals. The EFT therapist offers his or her expertise as a process facilitator with knowledge of how to help people arrive at and process what they feel at their core. The goal is to help people experience their core painful emotions underlying their presenting anxiety. This involves accessing internal and external supports to promote contact with a previously disclaimed experience and on helping clients not to interrupt and prevent their experience from entering their awareness.

Steps of Treatment

The seven steps of treatment of GAD are outlined as follows. They tend to occur in this sequence, although many steps overlap and there is always a circling back and forth and moving forward and backward. The steps include developing and maintaining an empathic, caring relationship; strengthening the vulnerable self; working through the anxiety split; undoing negative self-treatment and self-interruption; resolving emotional injuries; and client self-soothing and consolidation of a new narrative (Elliott, 2013; J. Watson, 2012).

The Genuinely Empathic, Caring Therapeutic Relationship

An EFT psychotherapist begins and continues the treatment of any disorder or condition grounded in an empathic relationship. The empathic relationship is viewed as contributing directly to a reduction in clients' anxieties by helping them feel safe. This allows space for the development of clients' narratives to locate their anxiety issues in their life stories and creates an opportunity for clients to access their dreaded feelings. The therapeutic relationship is highly important in the treatment of GAD as it contributes to building the vulnerable self so that clients can develop a stronger sense of self and internalize positive ways of treating themselves and their experience (J. Watson, 2002, 2015; J. Watson, Steckley, & McMullen, 2014). Positive therapeutic relationships also facilitate the development and enhancement of emotional processing and affect regulation capacities (Paivio & Laurent, 2001; J. Watson, 2002). It is important for the therapist to be fully present with his or her clients to encourage them to be more present with themselves and their experience. This is particularly important for anxious clients who often avoid their present experience.

Strengthening the Vulnerable Self, Increasing Awareness of Emotion,
and Developing More Positive Affect Regulation Strategies

This step in the treatment includes clients' developing more coherent life stories to make sense of their experience; developing a sense of agency and greater confidence in themselves; acquiring enhanced affect regulation capacities and a sense of mastery, along with a belief that they can cope; and developing positive introjects and self-talk to create more positive self-concepts. In positive relationships with their therapist, clients internalize their therapist's attitude. They become more accepting of themselves and their subjective experience; they learn to value their experience, including emotions and perceptions; they learn to trust themselves; and they develop more supportive and protective ways of caring for themselves. As clients develop their life narratives, they begin to see cause-and-effect relationships. They see events and situations more clearly and begin to become aware of their impact.

The therapist works with clients to overcome their difficulties with emotion regulation, including increasing attention, awareness, and acceptance of primary emotion. In this process, clients, with the help of the therapist's empathic attunement to affect, first need to learn to value their feelings and the information contained therein. One of the ways that this is achieved is by the therapist validating clients' experience and perceptions. When clients' experiences are witnessed and validated, they begin to develop confidence in their perceptions and experience of the world. This strengthens the self. With the help of focusing they are able to turn attention to their bodily felt sense (Gendlin, 1996) and are encouraged to attend to, label, and accept their feelings. This helps in developing affect regulation, which is essential for coping with intense feelings of anxiety and fear and to assist people to develop stronger less vulnerable senses of self (J. Watson, Steckley, & McMullen, 2014). Another key aspect of productive emotional processing is emotion regulation. The activated emotional experience has to be sufficiently regulated so that it is not overwhelming. The therapist thus helps clients to develop and maintain a working distance from the emotion (Gendlin, 1996) and to cognitively orient toward it as information, thus allowing for an integration of cognition and affect. Dysregulation is often because of failures early in life in the dyadic regulation of affect (Schore, 2003; Stern, 1985). Internal security develops by feeling that one exists in the minds and hearts of others, and the security of being able to self-soothe develops by internalization of the soothing functions of protective others (Schore, 2003; Sroufe, 1996; Stern, 1985). In EFT, the therapist helps clients contain and regulate emotional experience by providing a soothing environment and important behaviors to regulate their affective experience. Over time this is internalized and helps clients develop implicit self-soothing and self-compassion so that they are able to regulate feelings automatically without deliberate effort.

Working Through the Anxiety Split

An *anxiety split* is a way of construing the internal process of anxiety generation using EFT's theory of different parts of the self or internal voices. The anxiety worked with here is seen as secondary anxiety, which is the symptom of more core underlying insecurity or shame that is being masked by the secondary anxiety. This is one of the first chair dialogues in the treatment that is suggested to help in symptom management and in facilitating access to the client's underlying core fears. In this form of two-chair dialogue, one part of the self is characterized as the anxiety producer who worries the self by catastrophizing about possible negative outcomes and events that might occur in the future. This aspect of the self is partially driven by a protective concern for the self.

The presenting problem is the symptom of worry and the attendant anxiety, which is seen as a secondary reactive emotional response. The worry serves the function of protecting against people's more primary underlying painful, insecure sense of self. Intervening with the symptom at this level is relatively superficial but is consistent with clients' phenomenology and is a good way to begin to establish collaboration. Anxious clients want help with their anxiety and need the therapist to focus on their presenting concern. Beginning this way is experience near, staying with what clients are aware of and attending to it in the moment, and that helps to form a positive therapeutic alliance. Clients experience anxiety as something that happens to them and working with their worry process enables them to transform their sense of anxiety from something that happens to them to something they are doing to themselves. It is important that they identify their agency in generating their anxiety for the treatment to progress. The self then reacts by becoming anxious, and the dialogue is then carried through as described in Chapter 6 of this volume. Working with a worry split differs from working with conflict splits and negative treatment of the self that manifest in depression. As we discussed in Chapter 1, in GAD, earlier developmental fault lines emerge so that there is often pain expressed in both chairs, and the therapist needs to be prepared to address this and offer empathic holding to each side.

Two-Chair Work for Undoing Negative Treatment of the Self

Clients with GAD engage in a particular form of negative treatment of the self, which leads them to dismiss, block, silence, and reject perceptions and feelings. This interruptive process may also entail dealing with the shame of having feelings and needs. People, as adults or children, feel shame at not being wanted, and this often leads to blaming the self for not being good enough to be loved and cared for. This occurs in two different ways. In one form, the worrier self can sometimes dissolve into a puddle of distress about the painful emotions they experienced as a child without adequate support and care. They often express feeling inadequate and helpless to deal with the adult demands made on them as a child. Examples include a client who, as a little boy, felt ashamed, useless, and bad for not being able to ease his mother's pain; another client felt that she was totally disposable; and another client saw herself as "a half-formed fetus left in slime." The second form of negative self-treatment is holding the self responsible and blaming it for the bad treatment received. These clients come to regard their needs as unimportant. When GAD is experienced as part of an early developmental cycle and there are few positive experiences to draw on to internalize, some children see themselves as responsible for others' behavior. Part of the resolution of the unfinished business process involves clients' recognizing that it was not their fault; that they were not to blame but that a parent or significant caretaker was weak, bad, alcoholic, sick, inadequate, etc.; and that children deserve to have their needs met.

When self-blame and anger at not having received the care and protection that the clients needed emerges in two-chair work, the process is dealt with by a combination of two-chair dialogues with coercive and blaming aspects of the self, as well as the enactment of self-interruption, which reflects neglect and disregard for feelings. Self-critical/blaming splits occur when one aspect of the self is critical and blaming toward another aspect (e.g., blaming the self for being such a difficult, unhappy child). A client might say of herself, "It is your fault he punished you; you were always difficult, whining, and complaining. [It is] no wonder you were always so isolated. Nobody liked you." Self-critical splits like this offer an opportunity for *two-chair work*. In this work, two parts of the self (the critical self and the self who is being criticized) are put into live contact with each other. Criticisms and negative thoughts, and the feelings and needs experienced in response to this negative self-organization, are explored and communicated in a real dialogue to achieve a softening of the critical self, which promotes and accesses greater self-compassion and self-acceptance, resulting in an integration between the two selves.

Self-interruptive splits, on the other hand, arise when one part of the self interrupts or constricts emotional experience and expression and dismisses or silences feelings in the other part. For example, a client expresses her interruption and neglect of her experience as follows: "I just tighten up and suck back the tears; [there is] no way am I going to cry." Silencing the self is highly prevalent in clients with GAD, as their feelings and needs have gone unmet and were dismissed, invalidated, or ignored in hostile, painful, and negative environments. As a result, some of these clients do not feel entitled to self-expression, and this can be exacerbated when they bear the burden of responsibility for their own and others' welfare.

In the *two-chair enactment* (Greenberg et al., 1993), the interrupting/silencing self is made explicit. This is a dialogue between an agent, who does something to the self, which is in contrast with self-critical splits in which the critical part is negatively evaluating the self. As clients engage in chair work, they become aware of how they silence and interrupt themselves and their feelings. They are guided to enact the ways they do it, whether physically (with gestures of choking or shutting down the voice) or verbally ("shut up, don't feel, be quiet, you can't survive this"), so that they can experience themselves as an agent in the process of shutting down. Once they are aware of this process they are encouraged to react to and challenge the interruptive part of the self. Resolution involves expression of the previously blocked experience reflecting greater compassion and acceptance of themselves and entitlement to their emotions and needs.

Empty-Chair Work to Resolve Emotional Injuries

GAD is typically grounded in early attachment injuries, including abandonment, neglect, abuse, humiliation, intrusion, and rejection by primary caregivers or siblings/peers. This leads to a sense of vulnerability and a fear- or shame-based organization in which people feel weak, insecure, helpless, worthless, inadequate, and powerless. After working on the anxiety split the therapy moves over to the deeper source of the symptomatic anxiety which lies in the emotional injuries that have left the self fragmented, fragile, and insecure. Here lies the deep painful feelings of insecurity, shame, and sadness and a terrifying sense of aloneness, a lack of support and feeling hyperresponsible or bad. This unfinished business is worked on by means of *empty-chair dialogues* with an imagined other who harmed clients and failed to provide adequate support, connection, validation, and protection. These dialogues involve imagining the other who injured them and recalling past painful situations to transform their relationships with the self and the other. Clients access the core pain of the vulnerable self and what they need to heal. An important part of the healing process is for clients to access protective and assertive anger to hold others accountable, and to experience healing grief for what was never provided, and ultimately to soothe the insecure self.

In the empty-chair dialogue, and sometimes in two-chair dialogues, the ability to access and express anger in clients with GAD is very important. Anger, which provides an action tendency to puff up and thrust oneself forward to protect one's boundaries, is an approach emotion. It acts as a change process by undoing the withdrawal tendencies in anxiety, fear, and insecurity. Thus, accessing and expressing anger in empty-chair or two-chair dialogues seems helpful in overcoming anxiety. However, it may not be possible for clients to fully resolve or engage in empty-chair dialogues as long as they continue to treat their experiences negatively. Clients who continue to deny, ignore, or dismiss their experience may first need to acquire greater self-compassion and a stronger sense of self to access protective anger and fully resolve their attachment-related injuries with others. Accessing compassion for the wounded self is transformative of the core self and helps clients deal with the symptoms of anxiety.

Emotional Transformation: Accessing Anger and Compassionate Self-Soothing

Promoting clients' abilities to receive and be compassionate to their emerging painful emotional experience is an important step toward tolerating emotion and developing self-soothing. The ability to self-soothe develops initially through internalizing the soothing functions of protective others (Sroufe, 1996; Stern, 1985) and, in therapy, through a positive therapeutic relationship in which clients feel understood, accepted, and entitled to their feelings and needs. Over time these attitudes are internalized and help clients develop the capacity for implicit self-soothing, as well as the capacity to regulate their feelings automatically without deliberate effort. Emotion can be down-regulated by soothing at a variety of different levels of processing. Physiological soothing involves activation of the parasympathetic nervous system to regulate heart rate, breathing, and other sympathetic functions that speed up under stress. Coping self-soothing, like breathing and relaxation exercises, can be used to down-regulate anxiety. In addition, there is transformational self-soothing. In this process, clients become aware of and respond to their underlying anguish. As they acquire greater self-compassion and self-acceptance, they are more able to soothe the wounded self and learn to be more aware of, label, and use their emotions to better meet their needs personally and interpersonally.

In a self-soothing dialogue, the focus is on helping clients find ways of soothing the underlying painful emotions of fear of harm and disconnection, sadness at loss, or shame at invalidation by supplying comfort or validation. These capacities need to be acquired if clients did not have a caretaker to meet their needs for protection and care so that they can seek out comfort and validation in the present and future. The strengthened self is able to view the wounded self as hurt and in need of protection and care. It is able to decenter and, metaphorically speaking, respond as an adult to its own wounded child and provide solace and soothing. With the capacity to self-soothe, people are now able to regulate their own anxiety by evoking compassion and acceptance for their abandoned or neglected self. Self-soothing essentially involves a process of evoking compassion for the insecure inadequate self (Greenberg,

2015; J. Watson, 2006). Moreover, for clients with GAD who have assumed too much responsibility, the statement that they are not to blame can be quite soothing. It allows them to relax and stop worrying about the outcome of events or their impact on others.

Finally, new meaning is consolidated as clients reflect on experience to make sense of it and develop a new narrative of how the transformational experience they have been through fits or changes their identity. The new lived experience is consolidated in a new story. Clients construct alternative meanings, develop a narrative of resilience, greater self-acceptance, and entitlement, and explore the implications of this new self-validating view. The goals are now to clarify an experientially based story about their selves, their past, and their future, on the basis of a sense of self-worth and strength and to promote actions to enable clients to thrive based on these new realizations.

Homework

Homework can be useful in promoting and consolidating transformation. It is used in EFT principally to promote emotion awareness, regulation, reflection, and transformation of emotion. The main purpose of homework in experiential therapy is to consolidate and reinforce in-session changes that have taken place through extra-sessional practice. Practice enhances learning (Goldfried & Davidson, 1994), so once a person has become aware of something such as awareness of a new feeling or of a critical voice, she or he can be asked to practice being aware of this during the week. People who have gone through a significant transformation in a session, like the softening of a critical voice or mobilizing to meet an unmet need, can be asked to practice being compassionate to themselves or asserting their needs during the week to fully integrate these changes.

Treatment Sequence

Hughes, Timulak, and McElvaney (2013; see also Hughes, 2013), in an intensive analysis of three GAD clients in EFT, found a sequence characterizing the progression of therapy over time. Generally, anxiety markers arose fairly early in treatment. These involved catastrophizing statements, negative expectations that caused heightened or obsessional concern, should statements, if–then statements expressing regret and/or external restraints, expressions of feeling like a failure, and statements expressing worries that appeared disproportionate to actual dangers threatening the client. The clients expressed a lack of control and frustration that their worries were disruptive to their daily functioning. The markers of maladaptive worry were either revealed quickly or more slowly over time as it became apparent that some clients worried about numerous issues.

Clients who improved progressed from talking about their symptoms of worry and anxiety to speaking about experiencing painful emotions, which they tried to avoid. These feelings surrounded events that held residual pain for them. They indicated that these were topics they tried not to think about because of the painful feelings the topics evoked. The clients observed that it was difficult to speak about their pain and were reluctant to sit with and explore painful experiences and emotions. Instead, they attempted to avoid their painful experience by switching topics or going into more immediate concerns or worries.

As therapy progressed, the clients were able to better tolerate exploring their painful experiences. They were able to sit with and experience the painful feelings in the moment, without being overwhelmed by them, and were able to differentiate more specific emotions and meanings from the undifferentiated painful experience. They explored feelings of sadness, loneliness, fear, and shame and were actively engaged with the content of their painful experiences. This led clients to begin to discuss the underlying determinants and events that triggered the painful emotions.

Once clients began to process their painful emotions, they expressed a past unmet need or needs. This unmet need in many ways was at the heart of the matter and contributed to the experience of pain and distress. Clients who improved were able to reown previously unacknowledged and unmet interpersonal needs from childhood or other past situations (e.g., significant others failed to fulfill their need to feel safe and secure). After experiencing themselves as deserving to have the unmet need met, clients expressed adaptive, boundary-setting, assertive anger and held others accountable for wrongs done to them. This freed them up to be more self-assertive in their current life circumstances. There also was a softening of a previously harsh critical voice regarding past misgivings and clients' abilities. Clients became more accepting and demonstrated increased feelings of self-worth. They expressed an appreciation for their personal abilities and achievements, as well as their limitations, and generally showed greater strength and self-compassion, with much less self-criticism and blame.

The clients then progressed to self-soothing. This took different forms, including remorse and empathy from imagined others, soothing from the adult self, recalling memories of positive experiences from childhood, or forgiving others for their failures. By the end of treatment, clients demonstrated a greater sense of mastery, control, and agency over emotional experience in general, and more specifically over their worry and painful emotional experiences. Clients worried less and looked toward to the future with new vigor.

They were more optimistic about their ability to manage their life goals and displayed greater comfort with an unknowable future.

As we can see, the EFT therapist is aware of clients' process and follows them in terms of which tasks are most salient at any given time. For some clients, the most important task initially may be to represent what has happened to them. These clients may not have developed a life narrative that adequately represents or takes account of what they have experienced. For some clients with GAD, their narratives may be interrupted, or distorted because of how others have represented what has happened; and sometimes, as a result of severe distress and painful experiences, their narratives may be chaotic. The EFT therapist is patient and respectful of clients' process and allows them time to sift through the events in their lives so the feelings can come into focus, be seen clearly, named, and acknowledged. This process may require that clients adopt a different perspective. Clients with GAD may have adopted the perspective of their caretakers or significant others. Once the narrative is clearer, these clients are better able to see how they have been injured and to recognize the negative behaviors that they have internalized to modulate their emotions and perceptions.

The EFT therapist recognizes and respects that clients must feel strong enough to view their worlds through different lenses and feel able to tolerate the implications for themselves and their relationships with other people. Once clients agree that their ways of being are problematic and express a wish to change, the EFT therapist moves ahead with tasks like two-chair work to resolve negative treatment of the self or empty-chair dialogues to resolve attachment injuries. As task markers emerge in the sessions, the therapist can introduce chair dialogues to facilitate clients' awareness of what is happening and what has been internalized. It is not expected that the dialogues will proceed smoothly to resolution the first time they are introduced. Rather, as the process unfolds and clients become stuck, the therapist can see what work the clients need to do. Working on a two-chair or empty-chair dialogue can help to illuminate whether clients are having difficulty being aware of and labeling their emotions, whether they need to represent what happened to them more fully, or whether they continue to feel undeserving of having their needs met. Thus, clients may be stuck in terms of their emotional processing, narrative construction, or developing a stronger sense of self.

Notwithstanding that clients cycle through different tasks, the EFT therapist works to maintain some stability of focus while engaged in two-chair or empty-chair dialogues to facilitate resolution and avoid the process becoming chaotic. However, this is a very delicate balance between leading and following. If it is clear that the task does not fit, or if another task becomes more salient, the therapist follows the client and may suggest shifting to another task or letting the task go in the session and resume reflecting on the client's experience to bring the focus in the session back in line with the client's process. However, it is important for the therapist to keep track of the client's process and not randomly cycle through different ways of working. The different tasks are resolved in the context of a relationship with the therapist characterized by ongoing empathic attunement, acceptance, warmth, and genuineness. The therapist is responsive and follows the client as he or she remains fully present with them and continues to reflect their feelings and narratives. In addition, the therapist works with clients in chair dialogues to access and express pain and develop self-soothing and self-care to resolve their painful life experiences and become more self-confident and self-accepting, so that they can go on to lead lives free of anxiety and the stifling, self-neglect of their experience.

CASE EXAMPLE

The following clinical example illustrates an EFT approach to GAD. The steps of treatment previously outlined are highlighted, including the development of an empathic, accepting relationship; strengthening the self and attending to emotions; working with the anxiety split; undoing negative self-treatment; resolving emotional injuries; transforming emotion; and developing self-soothing. The role of the therapist's empathy and acceptance in the development of a stronger sense of self as well as the client's exploration and transformation of her emotional experience are demonstrated. We show how emotion transforms emotion, how the client accesses her fear and shame, and how she works with the therapist to transform these emotions with anger and sadness to access feelings of pride and joy.

The client is a woman in her early 50s who sought therapy for GAD. She has been married and divorced several times. Initially, she presented as independent and aloof. She found it difficult to connect with others and had trouble forming and maintaining relationships, outside of those she had with her four children. At intake, she reported that she experienced intense anxiety as well as strong feelings of loneliness. She sometimes was so agitated that she felt she was "climbing the walls," and was "cut off" from what was happening around her. She had been physically and emotionally abused as a child, and her experience, including her perceptions and feelings, had been constantly invalidated. She had been continually told that she was "crazy" and "stupid," and that she was exaggerating when she was upset. These negative messages had become internalized and guided how she related to her own experience. She recalled that she had been so scared and anxious at times that she felt separated from the world, feeling that she was "living in a glass corridor," with only brief moments of feeling like she was participating spontaneously and easily. As a result of the childhood abuse, fear, anxiety, and shame were her predominant feelings growing up.

As an adult, the client continued to fear her parents, who had dominated her life, and she was often confused about her own perceptions and emotional experience. She learned early on to dismiss and silence her perceptions and feelings, and was thus unable to use them as a guide. She was afraid of close interpersonal contact and repudiated her own experience of weakness and neediness. She had learned to cope by withdrawing into self-sufficiency and by neglecting, discounting, and disclaiming painful memories and emotions. This left her alienated and alone, as well as disoriented and out of touch with her feelings and needs. She was unable to use her feelings as a guide to protect and nurture herself. She observed that fear and anxiety, particularly ongoing fear of her parents, had dominated her life. Her major goal in therapy was to find some relief from her anxiety and to be free of her parents' influence. She wanted to be more self-accepting and self-compassionate and to trust what she was experiencing so that she could connect with others and maintain relationships.

Forming an Empathic Relationship and Becoming Aware of Emotion

The treatment focused on working with the client to address her pain and sadness related to the physical and emotional abuse and lack of love she had experienced. Initially the focus was on providing interpersonal safety and developing a positive relationship with her therapist.

At the beginning, she found it difficult to acknowledge that she had been hurt. She said she would never let her parents know she needed anything from them or that they had hurt her. It was difficult to open up and allow herself to express weakness. The therapist helped her to acknowledge her intense vulnerability and needs for protection and support by repeatedly validating her feelings, attending to her internal experience of pain and sadness, and working with her to symbolize that experience in awareness. The first three sessions were focused on establishing an empathic bond, and the focus then turned to working with the client's primary fear of her abusive parents. This fear had been originally adaptive in that it had helped to keep her out of harm's way some of the time by minimizing her contact with them. However, currently she found it maladaptive because it continued to dominate her relationship with her parents as well as with others with whom she became close. Interventions were aimed at accessing the client's emotion schemes about her childhood and experiencing and reprocessing her fear as well as developing a stronger sense of self based on validating her perceptions and story of abuse, understanding her emotions, and developing the capacity to process and modulate them in new ways.

Strengthening the Self

The positive relational experience with the therapist, including a sense of being accepted, supported, and understood, began to build a stronger sense of self as she shared her story of abuse and began to have her perceptions and feelings acknowledged and validated. This was important, as the client's perceptions and feelings had been discounted. She had been accused of exaggerating and had been told that her feelings were crazy. She needed to have her story heard so that she could begin to acknowledge the pain and work to transform her feelings and regain trust in herself. Once her feelings of fear and sadness were validated, the client began to allow and accept her previously painful emotional experience and memories regarding her attachment injuries. She had learned, through parental invalidation and ridicule, to distrust her internal experience and, in particular, to avoid painful experiences associated with unmet attachment needs. In therapy, she began to acknowledge these painful experiences and accept them as part of her core self-structure.

Working With the Anxiety Split

Early on, her therapist suggested that they work with how she made herself anxious. She would tell herself to hide or she would be beaten and that she needed to be careful or something bad could happen. The client reexperienced how she had learned to keep quiet and disappear. She articulated her sense that she could not escape, that there was no protection. She experienced how her fear overwhelmed and overpowered all her other experiences. She realized that she blocked her sadness and pain. She recalled being beaten and left alone with no support. She had no one to turn to, no protection or safe place, and was unable to speak about her plight. The client recalled that, as a child, she would frequently dream about being left alone, abandoned, utterly unable to protect herself. The therapist's empathic responses (e.g., "So life was just full of fear, just trying not to be seen so you wouldn't provoke an attack" and "You never knew when it would come; you were just so afraid and alone in your fear") highlighted primary fear and sadness as core parts of the client's construction of herself and the world, as well as the ways in which she interrupted her emotional experience.

Working With Negative Treatment of Self

The client came to see that she contributed to her anxiety and would constantly silence her feelings of vulnerability and neediness. She had learned to cope by withdrawing into self-sufficiency, and by neglecting, discounting, and disclaiming painful memories and emotions. Many sessions focused on exploring her internalized messages of worthlessness and her fears about being weak and needy. Approximately midway through the 20-session treatment, the client addressed her fears of dependency, weakness, and vulnerability. By means of this process, adaptive information from her primary emotions and needs were integrated into her current constructions of reality. In addition, coaching interventions and memory evocation helped her to access core maladaptive fear and shame structures related to her childhood abuse and maltreatment so that the originally self-protective emotional responses, associated beliefs, and negative behaviors that she had developed, and that were no longer adaptive to current contexts, were transformed. As she became more compassionate toward the child who had been wounded, and more accepting of her experience, she succeeded in getting past her maladaptive fears to contact how deeply she had been hurt. At this point the therapy turned to addressing the client's attachment injuries to try to heal these wounds.

Resolving Emotional Injuries

The client concentrated on resolving her unmet dependency needs as a child, plus her chronic difficulty in forming lasting attachments in adult life. A major focus of therapy was the client's ongoing fear of her parents, particularly her father. In one session, she described a recent visit to her country of origin to see her parents, only to find that she was still terrified of them as an adult. Seeing her father, who was now using a walking stick, terrified her as she feared he would hit her with it. The therapist validated how scary that must have felt and how deeply ingrained her fear was so that it was an automatic response. Her therapist acknowledged her struggle to be free of the fear and anxiety. Together, they agreed to focus on overcoming her fear and to work on developing self-empowerment as a goal of therapy.

The evocation of emotional memories that were critical in the development of the client's vulnerable anxious self-organization was important in the treatment. One of her earliest memories was of her father forcing her to watch him drown a litter of puppies. This was to "teach her a lesson about life," and the client believed that her father enjoyed it. During the exploration of the memory, the client accessed a core self-organization, which included her suppressed screams of horror at this experience. As she vividly recalled this scene in therapy, the therapist guided her attention to the expression of disgust in her mouth while she was feeling afraid. This mobilized the subdominant, adaptive emotion of anger as a resource that helped her access more assertive and protective feelings. The therapist helped the client evoke and explore other memories of her father's violence and threatening sexuality. Imagining herself back in her family home brought the traumatic scenes alive and helped the client to access her core emotion schemes and some of her coping responses, like that of "slinking away like a dog" to try to disappear and make herself invisible.

Like many clients who have been abused, she expressed a desire to distance herself from her parents, to sever ties to gain control of her life. Simultaneously, the client wanted to have the courage to face her parents unafraid, and to overcome her fear. The therapist responded to this desire by saying that "the best thing would be that they not have so much power over you." The client responded that although they had real power when she was child, now that she was an adult her parents' power was in her mind. To this the therapist responded, "Something [in your head] keeps you tied, victimized?" This led the client to focus on how her internal processes gave power to her parents and resulted in her current experience of fear and disempowerment. This was a first step toward her feeling some control.

The client also felt that she should confront her parents directly. It was the desire to do this, rather than actual behavioral confrontation in the real world, that the therapist, at this point, acknowledged and supported. Although clients are not explicitly discouraged from such confrontations, they are more likely to be successful in doing this after exploring and clarifying issues and developing a stronger sense of self. The desire to confront parents is a healthy adaptive response and is supported by encouraging clients to "speak your truth" in the session. Here the client found it helpful to write a letter to her parents, but she did not send it. The therapist in the fifth session helped the client confront her father in her imagination using an empty-chair dialogue. The client imagined her father sitting in front of her, and this evoked disgust and fear. As in childhood, her fear initially overpowered all other emotions and made engaging in an enacted dialogue with him very difficult. The therapist, however, helped the client stay with the process and regain control, and maintain a safe distance by putting her imagined father across the room and directing only crucial, self-empowering statements (e.g., anger) at him. The expression and exploration of her vulnerability, particularly her feelings of fear and sadness took place not to the imagined father but in an affirming and safe dialogue with the therapist.

These imaginary confrontations with the father evoked fear in the client, as well as painful memories of childhood beatings, of being told she was bad, and of being aware of nothing but her desperate need to escape. The therapist responded supportively to the client's overwhelming fear and powerlessness at the time and asked how she felt now as she thought about herself as a little child going through that and what she had needed. This directed attention to her internal experience and helped her access her primary anger at being treated so cruelly. Access to her primary adaptive emotion of anger mobilized her self-protective responses, and she began to stand up for herself saying to her imagined father, "I don't really think I was bad; you are bad." The therapist was attuned to and supported the emergence of these self-empowering challenges to the client's old views of herself and her father. The client was encouraged to direct these statements to her imagined father in the empty-chair dialogue and to intensify her expressions of assertive, self-protective anger, and experience. To support this, the therapist encouraged the client to say the self-assertive statements again in a strong clear voice, and attended to the client's internal experience by asking her to turn inside to see how it felt to say the statements. Each time, as the client turned inward to get a sense of what she was feeling, the therapist would focus her on accessing her needs for safety and protection by asking, "What did you need?"

Soothing and Transformation

An important focus of the therapy was working with the client to overcome her core maladaptive fear as she accessed her sadness at being hurt and anger at being abused. The client's maladaptive fear and shame was related to the maltreatment she received as a child, as were the negative ways of treating her experience that she had internalized. The therapist's questions and interventions helped the client restructure her fear scheme. As her anger replaced her fear, and with her therapist supporting her newfound sense of power, the client began to be more aware of her strengths. She became more self-assertive and self-validating and better able to soothe herself when she felt vulnerable or painful feelings emerged. She was able to change her way of relating to her experience and become more self-compassionate and self-accepting. By the end of therapy, she was able to be more self-assertive and self-soothing when confronted with difficult and challenging situations.

CONCLUSION

The treatment goal in GAD is to access and restructure the underlying maladaptive emotion schemes (Greenberg, 2011). In working with the client's anxiety in the session, it must be determined first whether he or she is experiencing primary anxiety or secondary anxiety. Primary maladaptive anxiety involves a core vulnerable, insecure self—a sense of basic insecurity—that leaves the self feeling ineffective and unprotected. On the other hand, secondary anxiety involves insecurity regarding a specific internal experience that threatens to overwhelm (e.g., anxiety about anger or sadness, catastrophic expectations, anticipated fear of failure). Secondary anxiety is marked by future-oriented expectations or imagined dangers, and prototypic "what if" statements, accompanied by a helpless response, such as worrying about being rejected, failing, or being incompetent (Greenberg & Paivio, 1997).

In EFT, after providing a secure relational base and strengthening the vulnerable self, the treatment involves first heightening clients' awareness of what they are doing to themselves to create the secondary anxiety (i.e., scaring themselves). This serves to highlight clients' agency so that they can feel empowered to change the process. Their awareness of how they contribute to creating their experience of anxiety is highlighted, and the catastrophic expectations that generate their anxiety are specified. Specifically, clients' awareness is heightened through the use of two-chair dialogues, whereby they sit in one chair and express the concerns of the worry critic; clients also sit in a self chair to determine the reaction of the self to these verbalizations. This is similar to a self-critical split, except that now one side is scaring the other side rather than being condemning or critical. A longer term part of this process is to determine the core maladaptive emotion scheme(s) resulting from the attachment and identity injuries to which anxiety is the secondary response. In the next two chapters of this volume, we focus on developing the therapeutic relationship before discussing each of the chair tasks in greater depth.

4

THE THERAPEUTIC RELATIONSHIP

The development and maintenance of a healing therapeutic relationship, characterized by presence, understanding, caring, warmth, attunement to affect, and genuineness, is one of the foundational principles of emotion-focused therapy (EFT). This relationship emphasizes a way of working with clients that combines acceptance, understanding, and a willingness to trust clients as the experts on their experience, whereas the therapist remains responsive, offering guidance and structure to facilitate clients' emotional processing and the development of new ways of being. A good therapeutic relationship provides a context for clients to address emotional and psychological pain and learn new ways to protect and care for themselves so that they can thrive. In EFT, it is recognized that the relationship serves an affect-regulation function, with the positive ways that the therapist interacts with clients being internalized over time. The EFT therapist is attuned to clients' emotional experience and works with them to process it.

http://dx.doi.org/10.1037/0000018-005
Emotion-Focused Therapy for Generalized Anxiety, by J. C. Watson and L. S. Greenberg

In this chapter, we describe the therapist's contributions to the therapeutic relationship and the development of positive alliances, as well as how the therapist can enhance his or her responsiveness to clients. We continue to elaborate on the therapeutic relationship and how it contributes to change in Chapter 5.

THERAPEUTIC PRESENCE

Recent research has identified therapeutic presence as a core therapeutic stance that contributes to the development of a healing relationship (Geller & Greenberg, 2012; Pos, Geller, & Oghene, 2011; J. Watson & Geller, 2005). Rogers (1957) suggested that the conditions of empathy, positive regard or acceptance, and congruence were part of a therapeutic way of being—a way of being fully present with another. In EFT, this presence is seen as a precondition of the Rogerian relationship conditions.

Therapeutic presence is defined as the therapist's ability to be fully immersed in the moment, without judgment or expectation, with and for clients (Geller & Greenberg, 2012). When the therapist is fully in the moment with clients, his or her receptive presence sends a message that clients are going to be heard, met, felt, and understood, which elicits a sense of safety. Current neuroscience research is beginning to reveal the neurological underpinnings of client safety through the therapist's presence and affective attunement. In his polyvagal theory, Porges (2011a, 2011b) explained that when clients feel met and connected with the therapist, their brain neuroceives a state of safety. *Neuroception* is used to describe how neural circuits discern safety, danger, or life-threatening situations outside the realm of conscious awareness. The neuroception of safety creates feelings of security in clients, which allows them to trust the therapist and be open to engaging in the work of therapy.

To provide the kind of presence that facilitates clients' neuroception of safety requires an awareness of their moment-by-moment emotional reactions, as well as the thoughts and perceptions that are occurring within the client, within the therapist, and between the two of them. To attend to all this information, the therapist needs to let go of his or her own specific concerns and be fully present in the session. This means that she or he must empty her- or himself and be open to clients—clearing a space inside so as to be able to listen clearly in the moment to the narratives and problems that clients bring to therapy. When fully present, the therapist attends to the client's face and listens to the client's voice—he or she focuses on their narratives with full attention, fully absorbed in the moment.

With the therapist's undivided and focused attention, clients begin to feel valued and safe, and they are better able to discern their own concerns and difficulties. When the therapist gives clients his or her full attention, he or she is able to resonate fully with their feelings and their experience of events to provide the necessary level of empathic responding, acceptance, and prizing (Geller & Greenberg, 2012; J. Watson & Greenberg, 2009). Buber (1957) described these as *I–thou moments*: moments that people share as they attend to and experience the same emotional event at the same time, knowing that others are coexperiencing it with them. The sharing of experience in this way creates a strong bond, a sense of togetherness that breaks a sense of existential isolation and promotes trust and openness.

ACCEPTANCE AND WARMTH

The EFT therapist knows that it is essential for clients to feel accepted and prized, if they are to confront and share painful and possibly shameful aspects of their experience. A relational context in which clients feel safe and able to explore and symbolize their experience without judgment is fundamental to healing. By internalizing an accepting and nonjudgmental other, clients come to accept themselves and their experience. These conditions provide the bedrock of support as clients face their fears and accept themselves to overcome their anxiety. As they learn to trust their perceptions and feelings, as well as their own needs, clients become better able to hold others accountable for not being there for them in times of distress, for hurting them, for being too domineering or suffocating, or for otherwise neglecting them. In healing and safe therapeutic relationships, clients are able to grow stronger and more resilient. The internalization of the therapist's nonjudgmental attitude promotes self-acceptance that, together with a growing ability to trust themselves, makes clients better able to cope with challenging situations and be less fearful in the world.

Experiential theorists and practitioners have long recognized acceptance as an active ingredient of change (Bozarth, 2001; Rogers, 1959). When the therapist is accepting and nonjudgmental, he or she allows clients the freedom to experience and reveal who they are and what they feel. Feeling accepted and prized by another reduces interpersonal anxiety; people do not have to worry about others' judgments or reactions. There is a greater tolerance of intrapersonal anxiety with clients who are able to attend to and accept their own feelings. Acceptance by another builds self-esteem and greater trust in the self, along with a belief that the self can cope and has the resources to master life's challenges. Changes in how clients view themselves and their experiences are essential to reversing and counteracting the sense of vulnerability in generalized anxiety disorder (GAD). By learning to trust their experience, discovering their competence, and becoming self-accepting, clients are released from a sense of vulnerability and fear of harm.

If the therapist is to be truly accepting, it is important that he or she disinvest from outcomes. When the therapist focuses on what clients need to change or how they need to behave differently, then the therapist risks becoming judgmental and critical of the client. Anxious clients need a safe place to experience their painful emotions of fear, sadness, and shame. They need time to allow and accept these emotions. In this process, clients need a witness to what has harmed them, and to have their perceptions and feelings about events validated by another. In this way, clients learn to trust their own organismic responses and perceptions and give voice to aspects of their experience that may have been dismissed or disclaimed. In a relationship with an accepting, genuine, and understanding other, clients develop the capacity for self-soothing. They learn to be reassured so that they can soothe themselves when anxious and distressed.

Clients with GAD usually do not have experience of being reassured and soothed. Often their feelings have been suppressed or disregarded. They may have had to assume responsibility for themselves in the face of threat or danger, without the support of others. Thus, they did not learn and internalize ways of self-soothing to assuage their anguish. As a result, reassuring statements like "things will be all right" and "not to worry—you will manage" do not ring true. To believe these statements, clients with GAD have to develop self-acceptance and greater confidence in their capacity to cope and survive without worrying or assuming full responsibility for the outcomes of events. They need to believe that they can protect themselves and rely on others for support before they are able to take in words of comfort and soothing.

The EFT therapist helps clients with GAD believe in themselves and develop trust and confidence in words of comfort and solace so they can modulate their anxiety and remain calm when things do not go as planned. The therapist does this by being responsively attuned, valuing, and accepting of clients and their experience, and these skills are further developed as clients engage in chair dialogues. Chapter 9 of this volume explores some of the ways in which the EFT therapist actively works with clients to cultivate the capacity to self-soothe. If clients are to stop worrying, they need to be able to accept themselves as they are and feel confident that they will be able to cope without constant vigilance and preparedness. This requires that they accept their limitations and not assume that they must be responsible for things going well. They need to be able to rely more on others. Most of all, they need to allow for the fact that they are humans with weaknesses but that they still warrant love and respect from the self and others.

Rogers (1959) emphasized the importance of the therapist's positive regard for clients, which is seen as an essential component of building an empathic healing relationship. More recent studies have shown that the quality of the relationship between the empathizer and the recipient of empathy is very important in determining whether or not individuals will empathize with another (de Vignemont & Singer, 2006). Being received warmly and feeling valued is vital to developing self-esteem, confidence in and comfort with the self, as well as to enhancing the bond between therapist and client. The EFT therapist works at maintaining positive feelings for clients to guard against the loss of empathy as a result of negative feelings. The therapist may find this challenging at times when clients feel despondent about being able to change or express frustration with the treatment. It is important for the therapist to seek support from others at these times to remain empathic, valuing, and accepting of clients.

EMPATHY

In addition to demonstrating acceptance in a congruent and sincere way, the EFT therapist actively works to convey empathic understanding and remain empathically attuned to clients' moment-to-moment processes in the session. Her or his focus is on tracking clients' emotional experiencing to unravel their emotional logic and to work together to make sense of clients' feelings and actions. The EFT therapist trusts that clients' emotional experiencing is the silken thread that will lead them in and out of the minotaur's labyrinth. Empathic attunement requires not only full attention but also full acceptance of clients' inner worlds (J. Watson & Prosser, 2002).

In his initial formulation, Rogers (1967) suggested that the relationship conditions needed to be experienced and shared with clients, who in turn must be able to receive them. Subsequently, Barrett-Lennard (1993, 1997) posited an interpersonal cycle for empathy that includes three phases: resonance, expression, and reception. According to this view, the empathic therapist needs to *resonate* to what clients are saying; he or she needs to take it in fully, savor it, and distill its essence. Then he or she needs to *express* his or her understanding in a way that is helpful for clients. Finally, clients need to *receive* and appreciate the therapist's empathy. This may not be easy for some clients initially, as they may not trust that the therapist understands or accepts them, or, alternatively, clients may feel ashamed to reveal their feelings of vulnerability and fear. But as they work with the therapist over time, clients will come to feel accepted, especially if they experience the therapist as congruent and sincere.

CONGRUENCE

Congruence or sincerity is essential for the other conditions to take root and be credible. Rogers (1951, 1959) defined congruence as the capacity for the therapist to be aware of his or her own thoughts and feelings in the moment when he or she is with clients. Lietaer (1993) subsequently differentiated authenticity into two components: transparency and congruence. *Transparency* refers to the therapist's self-disclosures within the session, whereas *congruence* refers to his or her covert feelings and thoughts. It is recognized that it may not always be possible for the therapist to share his or her feelings with clients, especially as he or she strives to maintain positive alliances and empathize with them. The EFT therapist self-discloses if he or she feels that it is in clients' interests and in the service of the relationship. To be seen as reliable and as an expert, the therapist needs to be experienced as sincere and trustworthy. The therapist can instill trust and confidence in clients by being congruent, and clients can then rely on the therapist for accurate feedback, as well as understanding and support.

Congruent responses need to be embedded within the therapist's conditions and communicated nonjudgmentally. Special care must be taken when sharing negative feelings, as this may be destructive (e.g., sharing feelings in an attacking, blaming manner; Henry, Schacht, & Strupp, 1990; J. Watson & Kalogerakos, 2010). To be facilitative and healing, congruence must be qualified by a number of other attitudes and commitments (Greenberg & Geller, 2001). It is important that the EFT therapist be genuine in a facilitative way. This means that he or she is congruent and transparent in a disciplined manner and does not just blurt out whatever he or she feels or thinks. To be transparent in a facilitative manner, the therapist first needs to be aware of his or her deepest level of experience. This may take time and disciplined reflection. Next, the therapist needs to be clear about his or her intention for sharing the experience, making sure that it is for the good of the client or the relationship and not only for the therapist's own satisfaction. It is also important for therapists to be sensitive to the timing of disclosure, sensing whether clients are open and able to receive feedback or whether they are too vulnerable. Disciplined transparency on the part of the therapist requires him or her to be optimally attuned to the client's needs and states at different points in the session and over the course of therapy. When he or she does share his or her feelings with clients, the EFT therapist ensures that what is expressed is a core or primary feeling rather than a secondary emotion, and hence is careful not to request caretaking from clients and upset the balance of the therapeutic relationship (J. Watson, 2015).

Another concept that clarifies transparency is *comprehensiveness*, which requires that the therapist express not only the central or focal aspect of what is being felt but also the meta-experience, and that she or he devote attention to the process that is occurring in the session. Thus, feeling irritated or bored in the session may not require the therapist to express these feelings but to use this information to attend to what is happening. The therapist might note that his or her attention was wondering and reflect on why. If the therapist observes that a client has been meandering or intellectualizing, he or she might observe this and ask what is happening or suggest that the client focus internally on their organismic experience to see where they wish to direct their attention. For the therapist to share that he or she is bored would not be good for the relationship. Instead, the therapist needs to communicate his or her concerns about what is happening in the interaction and how this may be getting in the way for clients. The objective is to share the information to improve connection and repair ruptures (Safran & Muran, 2000). Thus, to be optimally congruent and transparent, the therapist needs to be aware of the full complexity of the interaction to facilitate the client's process.

The interpersonal process between client and therapist can be illuminated by examining interactions in terms of the structural analysis of social behavior, a circumplex grid of interpersonal interaction, on the basis of the two major dimensions of dominance/control and closeness/affiliation (Benjamin, 1996). This grid outlines a set of complementary responses that can potentially pull for each other. For example, attack can pull for defense, and affirmation can pull for disclosure or revelation. The therapist who is trying to be congruent in a facilitative manner needs to be careful not to react in a complementary fashion to a client's negative interpersonal behaviors and respond negatively in turn (e.g., becoming defensive and angry when attacked). Instead, the therapist needs to try to respond in a noncomplementary fashion so as to try to elicit more therapeutically productive processes and responses from clients. Ideally, the therapist's responses facilitate clients' disclosure and the clear expression of their experience.

Thus, when clients express negative emotions about the therapist or therapy, it can be optimal to follow with an empathic understanding response. For example, when they complain or tell the therapist that he or she is failing to help alleviate their distress, a negative response from the therapist would be, "That is not fair and makes me angry. You are not cooperating or doing the things that I am suggesting." Even if this has some truth, it would be better for the therapist to respond to the client's frustration with an empathic reflection: "It seems to you that I am not helping and that the therapy is not working, and this makes you feel very frustrated with me right now." Here the therapist lets the client know that he or she has heard the client's frustration and hopes his or her response will open up the conversation to explore what is not working. Even if the therapist feels angry and unjustly blamed, it would not necessarily be productive to focus on those feelings at that moment given the client's distress. If the therapist feels unable to modulate his or her feelings, it would be important to seek supervision to explore what is happening in the relationship with the client. Once this is clearer, the therapist would be in a better position to come back to explore the relevant issues in a transparent way with the client.

The therapist who does not react to the negative pull of clients' statements, but instead responds in a way that pulls for a more constructive response from clients, can overcome a blame–withdraw cycle. Disclosing or affirming responses from the therapist has a high probability of leading to changes in interactions between therapist and client, by redirecting and reengaging the client in disclosure and exploration with a focus on the client instead of on the therapist. When dealing with difficult feelings about clients, therapists can follow a sequence of steps to assist them in working congruently and effectively. First, therapists need to be aware of what they are feeling (e.g., threatened or angry when being attacked). These feelings need to be symbolized in awareness. The next step is to communicate in a nonblaming, nonescalatory manner. Here according to Benjamin's (1996) circumplex model, responses perceived by clients as openly disclosing and revealing are more likely to facilitate friendly listening, whereas empathic understanding will more likely facilitate open expression. For the therapist, the interpersonal stances of disclosing and empathic listening are crucial for transparency to be facilitative.

When working with clients with GAD, the EFT therapist may feel impatient as clients focus on their physical symptoms and not on their feelings. The tendency for clients with GAD to worry and become abstract in their presentation of their concerns as the therapist tries to remain alert and vigilant can leave the latter feeling blocked and helpless. However, if the therapist can be patient, trust the process, and persevere by refocusing clients on their inner experience, clients will come to see the value of their feelings in time. The therapist may also have to provide a rationale to clients about focusing on feelings and being more attentive to bodily and organismic processes. As clients begin to attend to their bodily felt experience, and clients see that a primary impediment to conquering their anxiety is the dismissal of their pain, they realize that they need to be more accepting of and attentive to their feelings. The therapist's congruence, empathy, and acceptance of clients and their experience not only engender trust but communicate that clients are valuable and deserving of care and attention.

EXPRESSING THE THERAPEUTIC ATTITUDES

The EFT therapist is consistently warm, receptive, involved, attentive, concerned, and responsively attuned to clients (Malin & Pos, 2015; Mlotek, 2013; J. Watson & Prosser, 2002; Wing, 2010). She or he tries to distill the emotional meaning of clients' utterances, being carefully attuned and responsive to shifts, and follows the client's lead, even as he or she makes suggestions and proffers conjectures, careful at all times to communicate that clients are the experts on their experience. The therapist's vocal quality is natural, soft, and tentative, and he or she expresses him- or herself clearly (Bernholtz &

Watson, 2011; Rice, 1965; J. Watson & Prosser, 2002) and reflects clients' experiences. The more clearly a message is communicated, the more prized, understood, and accepted clients feel (Bohart & Greenberg, 1997). Truly empathic, prizing, and accepting, the therapist understands the client's goals for therapy overall, as well as moment-by-moment in the session as they try to grasp the live edges of the client's narratives. When clients are experiencing painful or intense feelings of vulnerability in a session, or are revealing cut-off, silenced aspects of their experience, they are especially in need of support, prizing, acceptance, and empathic attunement from the therapist (Elliott, Watson, Goldman, & Greenberg, 2004).

One of the most important ways that the EFT therapist facilitates the development and maintenance of a healing therapeutic relationship and facilitates changes in clients' emotional processing and sense of self is through the use of *reflections*. These responses actively try to mirror what clients have said and distill the essence of their words. They try to capture the emotional meanings in clients' stories and facilitate exploration. When communicated in a tentative, inquiring manner, reflections engage clients' cognitive processing, often acting paradoxically to activate clients' self-reflection and reevaluation of their feelings and reactions. These types of reflections work to locate clients' experiences subjectively, leaving open the possibility of other ways of feeling and thinking about events; reflections may also act to deconstruct how clients view the world, unpacking hidden assumptions and implicit knowledge. The therapist's tentative stance communicates that clients are the experts of their own experience and provides an accepting, safe climate for them to explore it.

A number of different types of mirroring responses have been identified in EFT, including empathic understanding, empathic affirmations, empathic evocation, empathic exploration, empathic refocusing, empathic conjectures, and empathic doubling (Elliott et al., 2004: Greenberg & Elliott, 1997; J. Watson, 2002). Each of these reflections emphasizes distinct aspects and intentions of responding in a facilitative way to communicate understanding, acceptance, and prizing.

Empathic understanding responses are simple responses that convey simple understanding, acceptance, and concern about what the client has said. They may or may not focus on clients' affective experience:

> Client: I keep worrying that there is something wrong with me. I had another sleepless night because of this pain in my side.

> Therapist: Are you really worried that you may be ill?

Here the therapist indicates he is listening and that the client's concerns are legitimate and worthy of attention. This is a supportive response that implicitly asks the client to share more of her experience and to explore and reflect on her perceptions and bodily sensations.

Empathic affirmations are responses intended to validate the client's perspective. The therapist is congruently expressing his or her understanding and acceptance of the client's experience. The client is not asked to disclose more; rather, the therapist validates the client and communicates that what she or he is feeling makes sense. This reduces the client's anxiety and distress and increases the client's feelings of safety in the relationship, leaving her or him free to continue to explore her or his feelings:

> *Client:* I was so agitated after speaking to [my colleague]. She was so insistent that we do it her way! She wouldn't listen to me!
>
> *Therapist:* It sounds like she was quite emphatic and bullying. I can appreciate how upsetting that would be for you given your experiences with your brother.

Here the therapist reaffirms the client and communicates an understanding of the client's life history and how it comes into play in the present with the colleague at work.

Empathic evocations are responses that are used to bring clients' experiences and emotions alive in the session using rich, evocative, concrete, and connotative language. The intent here is not only to convey empathy, understanding, and acceptance of clients' experience in a congruent fashion but to heighten it to facilitate clients' access to their emotional experience so that they can differentiate and symbolize it in words:

> *Client:* I feel so responsible to ensure that everything goes right. I keep checking things and going over what needs to be done.
>
> *Therapist:* So, it so difficult to relax and trust that the others will take care of things. It's like you are keeping watch, on guard and monitoring everything all the time.

Here the therapist uses the metaphor of being on guard to bring the scene more alive and to heighten the sense of tension. The intent is to evoke the client's feelings more intensely so that they can be processed and the impact of events explored to find new ways of acting.

Empathic exploration responses focus on exploration and have a probing, tentative quality to examine the hidden depths and live edges of clients' experiences. These responses convey understanding and acceptance of the client's experience. However, the intent is to facilitate more exploration. These responses are not used when clients are distressed or feeling intense emotional pain. Those times call for validation and support. But when clients are calmer, more exploratory stances can be encouraged to better understand their experience and how they have formulated it:

> *Client:* [My boss] was so angry, shouting at me to get out of the way. I was confused at her reaction. It niggled me all day.

> *Therapist:* So it was confusing to you that she got so angry. You just could not let it go; it stayed with you?

Here the therapist reflects that the client feels confused by her boss's response, as well as by her own. The therapist maintains the focus on the client's reaction to encourage her to explore it further. The intent is to have the client explore and become aware of her perceptions and feelings so she can understand why she reacted as she did and understand the triggers for her reactions.

Empathic conjectures are attempts by the therapist to articulate that which is implicit in clients' narratives, especially with respect to how clients are feeling or experiencing certain events. Although the therapist conveys prizing, understanding, and acceptance of the clients experience, he or she is showing enhanced empathic attunement by going beyond what clients are saying and tentatively proffering a label or conjecture about what clients are feeling:

> *Client:* It was hard after my parents split up and my dad left. My mom blamed me for everything. She expected me to look after her, as well as myself.

> *Therapist:* So it was really hard for you after they split up. I imagine that you might have felt quite lonely and sad?

Here the therapist maintains a focus on the client's experience. The client is aware that it was hard for her mother, but the therapist supports her and focuses her response so the client will stay in touch with her experience by sharing a conjecture to further explore her feelings and experience. This is done in a very tentative and cautious way so that the client does not feel intruded on, but, instead encouraged to take a moment to look inside, see how the emotion felt, and put it into words. The therapist is modeling the metatask of EFT, that is, for clients to turn attention inward to become aware of their inner experience and put it into words so that they can reflect on and express it.

Empathic refocusing responses, while staying within clients' frames of reference, reveal an alternative perspective. In these responses the therapist demonstrates understanding of clients' behavior. However, the therapist stands just outside clients' frame of reference, providing a slightly different view. In the following example, the therapist highlights the client's tendency to assume all the responsibility and not allow herself to relax. This is an attempt to have her see herself from a different perspective, to elicit self-compassion, and to open up the possibility that there may be other ways of behaving or feeling about events. As before, this type of reflection is offered tentatively. It is important that the client not feel criticized or misunderstood:

> *Client:* I worry that [my son] will fail. I am constantly at him to do his homework and trying to help him develop a schedule to help him to study.

> *Therapist:* It sounds as if you are fretting and [are] worried about him. It seems as if you feel that the responsibility is all yours to get him through his course. It is hard for you to let go and trust him?

These types of responses are especially helpful when the therapist detects that clients are not attentive to their feelings and needs and do not seem to be taking care of themselves. At times in the session when this becomes apparent, the therapist might say, "I see you are concerned about everyone else but I wonder who is taking care of Monica?" In this way the therapist is bringing the client's attention to her own needs and to the fact that she might be forgotten and is suggesting that there is another frame of reference. Of course, this should be shared gently, with the therapist recognizing that it may take some time before the client can shift her frames of reference to allow for her experience and needs and to feel deserving enough to express them and have them met.

Empathic doubling responses are attempts to voice clients' thoughts and feelings as they focus on and try to articulate the impact of events. These responses are attempts by the therapist to put clients' experiences into words and to help them find the phrases to represent feelings and emotions that may have been silenced or never articulated. These responses go beyond conjectures as they attempt to give life and form to clients' experience, often in the client's voice. They are particularly useful in empty-chair exercises:

> *Client* *(in an empty-chair dialogue with her mother):* You made me responsible for everything. You never listened to me or cared about how I was feeling.
>
> *Therapist:* What was that like for you? It sounds as if you felt burdened and invisible?
>
> *Client:* Yes, I felt I had no impact, [that] there was nothing I could do.
>
> *Therapist:* "I felt so invisible; you didn't see me. You didn't care what I needed or want to know how I felt." Can you say that to her?

Here we see the therapist put into words what the client, as a child, might have felt and was unable to express. These responses convey a full empathic understanding of what it felt like to be the client in a specific situation. They build on the therapist's understanding of the client's life history as well as her sense of what the client might have needed from others. Again, the client has to show agreement or confirmation that this response does fit and reflect what she was feeling. The therapist must be sure to check with clients that his or her suggestions fit and be quick to discard them if they do not.

RESEARCH ON THE EFFECTS
OF A POSITIVE THERAPEUTIC RELATIONSHIP

A healing therapeutic relationship provides the fertile soil to promote change. Accumulated research evidence points to a strong relationship between the presence of the therapeutic conditions and positive outcomes in psychotherapy (Elliott, Bohart, Watson, & Greenberg, 2011; Elliott, Greenberg, Watson, Timulak, & Freire, 2013; Farber & Doolin, 2011; Horvath, Del Re, Flückiger, & Symonds, 2011; Kolden, Klein, Wang, & Austin, 2011). Recently, the second Task Force on the Effectiveness of the Therapeutic Relationship designated therapist empathy as "demonstrably effective," positive regard as "probably effective," and congruence or genuineness as "promising" (Norcross & Wampold, 2011). However, the therapeutic conditions cannot be seen in isolation from each other but rather as an interpersonal style, an attitude or way of being that conveys understanding and acceptance of clients by one who is experienced as sincere and trustworthy (Angus, Watson, Elliott, Schneider, & Timulak, 2015; Elliott et al., 2011). In EFT, this way of being with clients conveys a therapeutic presence (Geller & Greenberg, 2002; Geller, Greenberg, & Watson, 2010) that provides an essential background condition for implementing the more active interventions that promote changes in behavior and ways of being and is itself an active ingredient of change.

The presence of a therapist who is accepting and empathically attuned enables clients with GAD to become aware of their organismic experience and emotions, and to differentiate and to symbolize them in awareness. A sense that their therapist is present, attuned, accepting, warm, empathic, and genuine is important for clients to process their inner emotional experience and share their life stories to identify the specific events and stimuli that trigger their anxiety. To work effectively in therapy, clients with GAD need to develop a sense of safety and feel accepted so that they can be free to explore, allow, and express their emotional experience and learn new ways of being with the self and others.

DEVELOPING COLLABORATION AND A WORKING ALLIANCE

Agreement on the goals of therapy, as well as the methods used to achieve them, is central to building a positive working alliance and essential to positive outcomes in psychotherapy (Horvath et al., 2011; Norcross & Wampold, 2011). To obtain agreement successfully, the therapist needs to understand the client's objectives and be able to demonstrate that his or her way of working is relevant to the client's goals. Both participants need to agree that they are working toward the same goals and feel that they have the tools for developing a positive alliance. J. Watson and Greenberg (1994) argued that a positive therapeutic alliance enacts the relationship conditions of empathy, acceptance, and prizing. J. Watson and Geller (2005) obtained partial support for this hypothesis with their finding that the working alliance mediated the impact the therapist's empathy has on outcome.

In treatments with successful outcomes, it is clear that the therapist tailors his or her interventions to fit with the client's goals and intentions. Close collaboration between client and therapist, in which the former feels accepted and valued, builds feelings of trust and confidence in the relationship that are manifest in a positive, warm bond (Ackerman & Hilsenroth, 2003; Bachelor, 1988). A good therapeutic relationship is necessary if therapist and client are to work together effectively to solve the client's problems. To address clients' pain in GAD, the EFT therapist focuses on establishing collaborative relationships so that they can begin to work together to meet the client's objectives to overcome intense worry and fearfulness.

This coalescence of objectives and shared tasks is generally best accomplished when the participants feel good about each other and clients feel supported and positive about the therapist's intentions and regard for them, providing a sense of safety in the relationship. One of the first ways that the therapist does this is by working with clients on their worry dialogues, which are discussed in detail in Chapter 6 of this volume. Another way is for the therapist to reflect the clients' concerns and feelings and suggest ways of working that might be helpful. However, at all times the therapist follows the client's lead, trusting that the latter will know when she or he is ready and able to tackle specific issues.

The therapist's empathy and acceptance is important in forming and maintaining the therapeutic alliance and in negotiating agreement on the tasks and goals of therapy. The EFT therapist continually monitors his or her interactions with clients and watches how interventions are received. He or she is attentive to when clients may be acting deferential and not fully disclosing their feelings and reactions (Rennie, 1994). He or she listens and makes sure that clients have the space to open up and share their experience. When the therapist becomes aware that clients are having difficulty (e.g., shutting down or interrupting by becoming intellectual, changing the subject, being overly positive, falling silent), the therapist modifies his or her responses and attends to the client's behavior in the moment. The therapist reflects to clients what he or she sees happening in the process and asks clients how they are feeling or what they are doing to try to open up the conversation for further exploration of their experience in the session.

By being sensitive to the impact of his or her interventions on clients and to the overall quality of the alliance, the EFT therapist is alert for ruptures as well as moment-by-moment shifts in the relationship during a session and over the course of therapy. The EFT therapist tries to remain sensitively attuned to the client and updates his or her assumptions and working hypotheses to maintain alliances and determine the client's readiness to engage in specific tasks and ways of working. This sensitivity to clients' experience moment-by-moment in the session is integral to working successfully and effectively with clients as they explore their affective experience in EFT.

BUILDING TRUST AND SAFETY

Clients with GAD can have difficulty trusting the therapist as well as themselves. Their worries preoccupy them, and they may feel ashamed at not being able to manage their feelings. These clients often either assume too much responsibility for their own and others' well-being or see themselves as inadequate, weak, and unable to cope. In EFT, it can be important to work with clients to address their intense feelings of shame about their feelings of helplessness and powerlessness, as well as their sense of being weak and damaged. Clients who fear the loss of social support and who feel ashamed of their experiences are more likely to form poor alliances with the therapist (Kwan, Watson, & Stermac, 2000). Clients with intense anxiety are often ashamed of their feelings, as they feel overwhelmed and out of control. They try to harness their feelings and shut them down, interrupting their experience. These clients need to address their feelings of shame about their sense of vulnerability and fragility so they can begin to acknowledge and accept their feelings. The therapist can reflect on how clients are relating to their emotional experience—observing how they are shutting them down or interrupting them. Once clients agree that this is something that they would like to address, the therapist can suggest two-chair tasks to further the exploration and build alternative ways of reacting to the self. In addition, as clients internalize the therapist's acceptance and respect for their feelings, they become more accepting and compassionate toward themselves.

Clients with GAD are especially concerned with feeling helpless and out of control. They constantly worry about being ambushed or taken by surprise. They worry in an attempt to control the outcomes of events that directly or indirectly impact them and to protect themselves from abandonment, rejection, loss, and shame. Thus, it can be scary for them to think of confronting and experiencing painful feelings in session. However, in the context of an accepting, prizing, and empathic relationship, these clients slowly come to feel more comfortable sharing their experiences, as well as less concerned about being shamed or found wanting by their therapist and others. As the relationship develops, and a positive alliance is built, clients with GAD come to see that their feelings are an important source of information.

There are a number of phases in working with clients experiencing GAD. At first, clients with GAD are usually focused on their symptoms. The therapist needs to be sensitive to the toll that anxiety takes on clients. The sheer physical intensity of anxiety can be debilitating and all-consuming. Although the EFT therapist acknowledges, reflects, and empathizes with the client's physical symptoms, he or she also works with clients to share their stories and begin to attend to the emotional impact of events. Clients with GAD may be unaware of the sources of their distress, so the therapist needs to work with them to unpack memories to develop their life stories. Once they begin to develop a narrative of events and get a sense of what they have lived through, clients can begin to apprehend the impact of events and become more aware of their emotions. It is at this point that they start to pay more attention to their feelings.

Clients need to engage in the task of narrative construction so that they can look at the events in their lives and see how they have been treated and have learned to cope (Angus & Greenberg, 2011; J. Watson, Goldman, & Greenberg, 2007). To engage in this type of exploration, clients need to feel safe. Safety in the therapeutic relationship promotes exploration and enables clients to examine and look at aspects of their experience that might have been denied or were outside of awareness and of which they may be ashamed. When clients feel heard, understood, and supported, they are better able to begin to disclose their experience so that they can have the opportunity to become aware of it, label it, and examine and reflect on it to know and understand it better. As the therapist reflects clients' narratives, clients come to see things more clearly and to name what happened to them in their interactions with others (J. Watson & Rennie, 1994).

It can take time for clients to refocus on their feelings and the events in their lives that have contributed to their fear and vulnerability. The EFT therapist gently and patiently introduces clients to the importance of attending to their emotions to heal and resolve their anxiety. Clients need to agree that their feelings are important and valid. The EFT therapist facilitates the shift to feelings by reflecting their clients' experience, directing clients to what is happening in their bodies, asking how they are feeling, and reflecting clients' perceptions. Another way that the therapist turns clients' attention inward is by focusing clients on their anxiety splits (see Chapter 6, this volume). Once clients begin to see their role in making themselves anxious, the EFT therapist works with them to form new treatment goals to strengthen their sense of self (see Chapter 5) and change the ways in which clients relate to their emotional experience (see Chapter 7). As clients work on these aspects of their functioning, they start to identify and work on their attachment wounds and relational injuries (see Chapter 8, this volume). Each phase of the treatment requires the therapist to be patient and attentive to where the client is focused in the moment, while keeping a sense of the general direction in which the client is moving.

DEVELOPING THERAPIST RESPONSIVENESS

Being responsive and empathically attuned to clients' affect is an essential part of EFT. To be maximally responsive requires the therapist to grasp not only the surface meanings of clients' stories but their implicit and underlying meanings as well (Barrett-Lennard, 1997; J. Watson, 2002, 2007). To facilitate empathy, responsiveness, and understanding of their clients, EFT therapists engage in a number of activities, including actively imagining clients' stories, sensing into clients' experience, actively thinking about clients' experience, attending to their own bodily reactions, and drawing on his or her own personal experiences (Greenberg & Rushanski-Rosenberg, 2002; J. Watson & Greenberg, 2009).

Being empathic is a decision that the therapist makes as he or she listens carefully to what clients are saying in order to distill the essence of clients' experiences. The EFT therapist is intent and absorbed as he or she reflects on clients' subjective worldviews. He or she attends to clients' core feelings, grappling with the meaning in their words, taking them in and trying to "taste" the experience to get at their feelings. There is a sense that as the therapist walks closely beside the client, he or she is seeing things as the client does. While listening to clients, the EFT therapist actively searches to find the words or expressions that fit what the clients are experiencing. He or she tries to infer what the clients might be feeling or thinking as he or she listens for the "live edge" (Greenberg & Elliott, 1997; Rice, 1974; Rogers & Truax, 1967). However, what is inferred is offered as a conjecture in a tentative manner. The therapist often feels elated when his or her conjectures fit a client's experience, rather like finding the right key for a lock.

For example, when Monica, whom we met in the Introduction to this volume, initially spoke about her childhood, she spoke about being stupid and deserving of her mother's criticism. She observed that she was not as smart as her brother. When she said this, her therapist reflected, "It seemed as if you were not as smart as your brother; that somehow because you were stupid you deserved her criticism." Monica agreed and started crying, to which her therapist responded, "It just felt so awful to always be shouted at, to be made to feel stupid. It did not feel fair somehow." Here the therapist conjectured what it might have felt like as a child. She has gone slightly beyond what her client has reported or said to try to capture her client's experience by tentatively suggesting that it was unfair. In this way, she is trying to support the client to give voice to her experience. Monica responded by saying, "Yes it was so unfair, he was always her favorite; she didn't care for me." She began to cry more fully, allowing herself to experience the sadness that she felt as a child and that she was experiencing in the session as she spoke about it.

To get to the core of clients' experiences, the EFT therapist actively imagines the events in clients' stories. The therapist is able to heighten his or her understanding of clients' states by actively visualizing the details of the stories being told. The therapist plays movies in his or her head of the client's narratives and attends to the images that come up while listening to the client. Research studies show that mirror neurons fire when human beings observe and imagine others performing different actions (Ferrari, Gallese, Rizzolatti, & Fogassi, 2003; Gallese, 2005; Rizzolatti, 2005). However, deliberate acts of imagination produce stronger responses in the mirror neuron circuit than observation alone (Decety & Jackson, 2004). Therefore, by actively developing mental images of different situations, therapists can develop a better understanding of what is happening for clients than they would if they were just passively listening to their narratives (J. Watson & Greenberg, 2009).

Another way that the therapist builds a progressive understanding of the client's subjective experiences is by drawing on his or her own experiences. When trying to be empathic, the EFT therapist draws on his or her own store of general knowledge to better understand and appreciate clients' experiences. Clients' stories can evoke personal memories of similar feelings or experiences. These memories in turn can evoke images that the therapist can draw on to distill the essence of the client's experiences, which can then be shared as conjectures. Monica's therapist was able to recall times in her own childhood when she had been criticized by her mother after something had gone wrong and her little sister had not been chastised. This helped her get inside the situation that Monica was describing and conjecture what she might have felt at the time.

Therapists' empathy can be augmented further if they attend to their own bodily reactions as they try to imagine and gauge what clients are feeling (Greenberg & Rushanski-Rosenberg, 2002; J. Watson, 2007; J. Watson & Greenberg, 2009). Studies from neuroscience show that the physical correlates of empathy are automatic and out of the therapist's conscious control. However, the body is an important source of information to understand how different experiences impact others. Wilson (2001) suggested that, as a result of the activation of motor mirror neurons, we are able to use the implicit knowledge of our own bodies to track other people's actions. Hence, the therapist's bodily sensations and feelings can be useful guides that he or she can draw on to enhance his or her capacity to resonate and know where and when to focus his or her responses.

By becoming more aware of their own bodily reactions and translating them into words, therapists can reflect and capture clients' subjective experiences. For example, if a therapist's gut tightens when a client describes an intense or frightening situation, she or he can use that physical response to conjecture about the client's possible sense of anxiety and tension in the situation. Similarly, if a therapist experiences an ache in his or her chest when listening to a story of loss, this could be shared with the client as a tentative conjecture of the sad feelings stirred up by the situation. For example, the therapist might say, "I feel an ache in my chest when you tell me about that. How does it make you feel to share it with me?" The therapist is voicing an empathic response and focusing clients on their feelings in the session. It is important to note that, although resonating in this way, the therapist remains aware that the experience is not his or her own, so he or she is not debilitated or overwhelmed by it.

In addition to mirroring clients' feelings, the therapist may be aware of having complementary feelings of compassion and nurturance when clients are in pain. At these times, the therapist may experience feelings of tenderness or concern for clients. The therapist may be touched by clients' stories and feel a desire to protect them. These feelings can alert them to the need to be especially empathic and carefully attuned to clients' experiences. It is very important to be accepting of clients' experiences and feelings and show a willingness to explore them—especially difficult and painful feelings. The therapist's willingness and courage to explore the painful dark places in clients' lives gives clients the courage and support they need to fully process their experiences.

The EFT therapist consciously attends to clients' body posture, voice, and facial expressions for clues to their inner experiences. These observations can be further enhanced if the therapist enacts them to try to reflect physically what the client is experiencing. Thus, a therapist may reflect a client's body language by saying, for example, "I see that you are tightening your fist/ slumping in your chair. What is happening right now? How are you feeling?" The therapist might ask clients to exaggerate these postures to get a better sense of how they make them feel. Alternatively, the therapist might clench his or her fist or slump down to get a sense of the client's experience and share this with the client in a tentative fashion. These enactments can heighten awareness of the client's subjective experience. Enactments help to simulate similar sensations and feelings in the observer as are being experienced in the observed (Wilson & Knoblich, 2005). This mirroring process helps therapist and client to find the words to express and label the client's inner, subjective states more clearly (Elliott et al., 2004; Kennedy-Moore & Watson, 1999).

The EFT therapist recognizes that the manner in which clients tell their stories is an important marker of their emotional processing in a session (Elliott et al., 2004; J. Watson & Bohart, 2001). They listen to whether clients are giving rehearsed descriptions of scenes and whether they are rambling in the session or are focused on their physical symptoms. At these times the EFT therapist works to encourage clients to get more in touch with their emotional processing. One way they do this is by asking clients to give more detailed, specific, and vivid accounts of situations. For example, a therapist might say, "Can you play me a movie of that?" or "Can you describe concretely what happened?" Then, as the client describes the events, the therapist can reflect them to build a shared visual sense of what occurred. These descriptions provide the therapist with a context and an inside view of the client's world that enable the therapist to conjecture about the client's feelings states. Detailed, vivid, and clear stories facilitate the therapist's empathic process and his or her understanding of the clients' worldviews (Elliott et al., 2004; Rice & Saperia, 1984; J. Watson, 2002, 2015; J. Watson & Greenberg, 1996; J. Watson & Rennie, 1994).

The expression of empathy requires individuals to decenter (Jackson, Brunet, Meltzoff, & Decety, 2006; Rogers, 1957). Merging with another can result in emotional contagion such that people may experience and express distress at another's distress but not fully comprehend it. Thus, to fully comprehend another's experience, it is important to remain differentiated. To empathize effectively, the EFT therapist needs to modulate his or her distress and avoid emotional contagion when they work with clients who are experiencing a lot of pain (J. Watson, 2007). The capacity to empathize is a cognitively complex process that requires the therapist to be highly adaptable and cognitively fluid as she or he takes on the perspective of the other to build working hypotheses and update and revise them continually.

To be truly empathic, the therapist demonstrates cognitive and emotional aspects of empathy. Cognitive capacities include perspective taking, abstract reasoning, and cognitive flexibility. In his or her attempt to fully understand the other, the empathic therapist takes on the viewpoint of the other by imagining his or her cognitive and/or emotional state on the basis of visual, auditory, or situational cues. The therapist engages in abstract reasoning to make interpretations about other people's perspectives, motivations, or intentions, all the while remaining cognitively flexible to spontaneously and easily generate ideas about clients' cognitive and emotional states. The therapist is also able to shift attention back and forth to compare and contrast information about his or her own emotional and cognitive state with those of clients. Reactive flexibility requires that the therapist sort through his or her various hypotheses and rapidly update their working models of clients' emotional and cognitive states.

In addition, the empathic therapist demonstrates the emotional components of empathy, including recognizing clients' emotions, being emotionally responsive, and correctly identifying his or her own emotional and cognitive states as well as those of clients. The EFT practitioner focuses on being responsive moment-by-moment as he or she tracks clients' inner, subjective, and affective experience. To facilitate responsive attunement to clients' affect moment-by-moment in the session, the EFT therapist listens for poignancy and clients' expressions of emotional pain, as well as for intense emotional reactions. The therapist is focused on fostering clients' emotional processing in the session as clients attend to and become aware of their emotional experience and begin to label and differentiate it in words (Elliott et al., 2004; Greenberg, Rice, & Elliott, 1993; Klein, Mathieu-Coughlan, & Kiesler, 1986). The EFT therapist works to help clients process their affective experience to acquire an understanding of why they act as they do, to learn new ways of processing and regulating their emotions, and develop new ways of interacting with others (Elliott et al., 2004; J. Watson, 2002, 2015).

RUPTURES IN THE RELATIONSHIP

Sometimes clients may reject their therapist's concern, being unable to take it in as they are caught in the neglectful and rejecting worldview of another. These clients need time to receive and believe in their therapist's empathy and acceptance. At first they may challenge their therapist's sincerity and have difficulty believing that someone cares for them or sees them as intrinsically valuable and deserving. These clients may feel that they do not deserve support and understanding. However, with time and patience as their therapist continues to accept, validate, and empathize with their experience, these clients will soften and begin to internalize their therapist's attitudes to develop more self-compassion and self-acceptance along with greater self-protection and nurturing.

Some clients may complain that the treatment is not working, is taking too long, or that they are not achieving their goals. When clients complain or seem stuck, this can be a clue that they are unwilling or not ready to assume responsibility for their own well-being. At these times, the EFT therapist gently reflects the client's sense of being frustrated or overwhelmed. The therapist can return to following clients and reflecting their feelings and life narratives. Slowly, as they grow stronger and more trusting of their perceptions and feelings, clients develop the capacity to be more agentic. Their strength and confidence are fostered in an empathic, accepting, prizing, and congruent therapeutic relationship. At times, when clients are stuck and are unable to be compassionate toward themselves or are unable to protect themselves, the therapist can try to focus them on their experience to see whether there are other aspects of their experience that they might be ignoring or overlooking. Perhaps there are elements of their life histories that need further elaboration to foster a better understanding of their pain and what they need.

Alternatively, clients may be reluctant to face their pain, instead wishing that it would go away. At these times, the therapist might gently suggest that the client needs to process the pain for it to be alleviated, and the therapist is willing to enable this at the client's pace.

Another option is for the therapist to frame the client's reluctance as a conflict split using two-chair dialogues to see if they can work out how they might resolve their pain and commitment to therapy. When clients withdraw or express reluctance to engage in a certain task, their therapist can ask them what they are trying to do or accomplish in the session or ask them to focus on their body to become more aware of their organismic experience. It is important to encourage clients to become aware of how they are processing their emotional experience to lay the framework for other tasks like two-chair (see Chapters 6 and 7, this volume) and empty-chair dialogues (see Chapter 8) that will be introduced later in therapy (Elliott et al., 2004; Greenberg & Watson, 2006; McMullen & Watson, 2011). When clients are slow to internalize their therapist's attitudes and develop new ways of relating to themselves and their experience, the therapist may feel stuck. At these times, she or he might check in with clients to inquire how they are processing their experience and explore whether they are finding the treatment useful; this tactic may open up the conversation to determine if something is hindering the process and, together, develop ways of dealing with it.

It is important to consider that when clients with GAD complain about therapy or their therapist, this might be indicative of a transformation and the emergence of a new state of self-organization. Clients with GAD often avoid confrontation and do not easily express anger and frustration to others. The expression of irritation, frustration, and disappointment to their therapist may mark the emergence of a stronger sense of self and a willingness to take risks. The therapist needs to be able to hear the client's complaints and respond in an accepting, nondefensive, empathic, and congruent manner so that clients can continue to learn how to express their feelings and needs in relationship with others. Addressing discontent and dissatisfaction with the therapist enables clients to cultivate and develop new ways of being with the self and other. In the next chapter, we look at how the therapeutic relationship contributes to changes in clients before moving on to explore some of the more specific chair dialogues.

5

STRENGTHENING THE VULNERABLE SELF

One of the most important goals in emotion-focused therapy (EFT) is the development of a stronger, more resilient sense of self and more positive self-organizations. As we discussed in Chapter 1 of this volume, EFT formulations see a vulnerable sense of self and negative self-organization as being at the core of generalized anxiety disorder (GAD). When individuals, at an early age, are required to take on too much responsibility for their own and others' safety and well-being, and lack adequate skills and capacities to do this effectively, a vulnerable sense of self develops that feels weak, alone, helpless, or overburdened. These individuals are unable to regulate and process their affective experience in positive ways, and their identity formation is compromised. Therefore, they do not develop feelings of self-worth, self-esteem, self-compassion, self-acceptance, or self-protection. Rather, the negative self-organizations that develop in clients with GAD involve a basic sense of insecurity and painful feelings of fear and anxiety. There is a sense of being intensely vulnerable and alone.

http://dx.doi.org/10.1037/0000018-006
Emotion-Focused Therapy for Generalized Anxiety, by J. C. Watson and L. S. Greenberg

Clients' painful feelings and sense of vulnerability are further compounded by negative beliefs and evaluations of themselves as well as negative ways of relating to their feelings and subjective experience. When their negative and vulnerable self-organization is activated, individuals feel distressed; their trust in the self and others is compromised, and a state of emotional vulnerability takes hold, along with the belief that they cannot cope. Bereft of adequate support and protection, individuals feel weak and inadequate, developing rigid expectations of themselves as they try to cope and ensure their safety and survival (Rogers, 1961), constantly worrying as they try to anticipate threats to their well-being.

As described in Chapter 1 of this volume, clients' capacity to regulate their affect and develop positive self-organizations is rooted in early childhood interactions and continues to develop in interactions with others across the lifespan (Benjamin, 1993; Blatt, Zuroff, Hawley, & Auerbach, 2010; Rogers, 1959; Siegel, 2012; Sullivan, 1953; J. Watson et al., 2007). People's sense of self develops in social interactions, particularly in their attachment relationships, but also with peers and society at large (Rogers, 1959; Schore, 1994, 2003; Siegel, 2012; Sullivan, 1953; Vygotsky, 1978). Mammals develop confidence in their capacity to navigate the world through their interactions and relationships with caregivers (Rogers, 1959; Schore, 1994, 2003; Siegel, 2012; Sullivan, 1953). They test the limits of their abilities and learn when to turn to others for assistance and support and acquire ways to survive in their habitats and environments. The capacity to feel safe and confident in order to explore and develop skills for survival can be compromised in environments that are hostile and neglectful, providing insufficient protection and support, so that people do not internalize self-compassion, self-protection, and ways to self-soothe. Research shows that clients with GAD are insecurely attached. These individuals have more negative views of the self, more negative self-concepts, experience more self-doubt, and have lower confidence in their ability to cope with stress than more securely attached individuals (Griffin & Bartholomew, 1994; Hazan & Shaver, 1987; Marganska, Gallagher, & Miranda, 2013).

Thus, one of the most important tasks in EFT is for clients to develop the capacity to regulate their affective experience in more positive ways and to develop greater trust and confidence in themselves and their perceptions. They need to acquire a sense of mastery and competence, and more positive ways of relating to themselves and others that enhance their well-being and access more positive self-states. Clients with GAD need to become more self-accepting, self-compassionate, and self-protective, as well as more confident in their capacity to cope with the challenges of living. One of the primary ways in which the EFT therapist works with clients with GAD to develop trust in their subjective experience and perceptions, regulate their emotions in more positive ways, and help them feel strong enough to negotiate with others to meet their needs and stand up and protect themselves is by providing a positive and healing therapeutic relationship.

FOSTERING MORE POSITIVE SELF-ORGANIZATIONS

A healing therapeutic relationship provides the soil from which a stronger sense of self can develop. As we discussed in Chapter 4 of this volume, the EFT therapist emphasizes the importance of positive therapeutic relationships, characterized by presence, empathic attunement, acceptance, sincerity, congruence, and valuing of the other, to strengthen clients' sense of self. Each of these attitudes is important in providing an antidote to the sense of vulnerability and the fear that are at the heart of GAD.

In EFT, the therapeutic relationship is seen as serving a number of important functions that contribute to clients' developing a stronger sense of self and more positive self-organizations. These include clients developing more coherent life stories to help clients make sense of their experience and identify sources of pain, processing their emotions and affective experience to enhance their sense of mastery and the belief that they can cope, internalizing their therapist's attitudes to create more positive ways of regulating their affective experience, and rebalancing their sense of responsibility and agency to take better care of themselves.

Just as people's sense of self develops in social interactions, so too can it be changed in a supportive, caring relationship with a therapist. Positive therapeutic relationships support clients when they feel vulnerable, enabling them to become more self-confident and helping them build a more confident and resilient sense of self so that they are able to balance the needs of the self and others in more satisfying ways and feel more self-assured and trusting in their relationships (Barrett-Lennard, 1997; J. Watson, 2002). Clients internalize their therapist's positive attitudes. They become more accepting of themselves and their subjective experience, learn to value their experience, including emotions and perceptions, come to trust themselves, and develop more supportive and protective ways of caring for themselves.

In EFT, clients are encouraged to become aware of their experience, including their emotions and perceptions, to accept and validate them, and to use them as guides for future actions to try to meet their needs (Barrett-Lennard, 1997; Benjamin, 1974; Blatt et al., 2010; Rogers, 1951; Schore, 2003). Acceptance and understanding by another is an important antidote to feelings of vulnerability and fear. Research shows that clients who feel accepted by their therapist are more tolerant and self-accepting. The therapist's acceptance and empathy increases clients' self-esteem (McMullen &

Watson, 2015) and facilitates their knowledge and awareness of their feelings, providing them with the opportunity to symbolize and reflect on their emotional experience to modulate and regulate it better (Malin & Pos, 2015; Mlotek, 2013; Prosser & Watson, 2007; J. Watson, Steckley, & McMullen, 2014). The capacity to modulate the experience and expression of emotion cultivates feelings of mastery and competence as clients manage internal states of arousal and distress more optimally and in ways that they experience as self-enhancing.

SYMBOLIZING EXPERIENCE

Developing More Coherent Narratives

Strengthening the self is a slow process that begins with clients sharing their life stories and developing narratives to make sense of their experience. In neglectful and harmful environments that contribute to painful feelings of intense fear, sadness, shame, and distress, individuals may not have the opportunity to make sense of their experience. As a result, events are poorly encoded, and specific stimuli related to threat may not be adequately symbolized or represented in awareness. Consequently, reactions triggered by different situations are experienced as coming "out of the blue." Clients with GAD often report a sense of being ambushed when their anxiety is activated or becomes heightened, leaving them feeling out of control and unable to cope.

Before clients can begin to process their emotions and organismic experience effectively, they need to organize their experience and episodic memories to fully apprehend and understand what has happened to them. Hence, an important goal for clinicians working with clients with GAD is to encourage them to make sense of their experience, to name it and describe it in order for them to become more aware of the links between their reactions and different stimuli as they reconstruct and develop narratives about their lives (Angus & Greenberg, 2011; Rice, 1974; J. Watson, Goldman, & Greenberg, 2007; J. Watson & Rennie, 1994). Narratives and stories about the events in clients' lives provide the contexts and reference points of the terrain that will be explored in therapy. It is the episodic memories embedded in clients' narratives that will need to be activated to facilitate the emotional processing that leads to change.

Telling stories is important—they help to make sense of an experience. Stories provide an account of events that contribute to the integration and formation of who people are (Angus & Greenberg, 2011). Stories reveal implicit meanings and experiences (Siegel, 2012). It has been observed that as children begin to develop self-regulating capacities during development, they begin to tell stories to order and make sense of their experience. Siegel (2012) suggested that story telling contributes to the interhemispheric processing of events that facilitates self-regulation and the development of alternative self-states, leading to a more coherent sense of self. The capacity to tell stories and provide accounts of experience develops in relationship with significant others, who help children recall, organize, and derive meaning from their experiences (Schore, 2003; Siegel, 2012).

Clients, too, need to tell their stories and process events along with their reactions and organismic/bodily felt experience. In the process of developing narratives, they access not only known autobiographical memories but implicit experiences as well. These are the experiences that were not in awareness or adequately symbolized but that can provide important information to guide healing. As we discussed in Chapter 1, and observed in the case example of Monica, clients with GAD may not have had the opportunity to develop coherent life histories that have been validated by others. Instead, their stories are often told from the viewpoint of others or may be incoherent, as the events in their lives were so painful and intense that they were inadequately processed. It is essential for client and therapist to understand the roads the client has traveled. Making sense of experience and beginning to articulate the cause-and-effect relationships evident in their life histories are important processes for clients with GAD.

Identifying Triggers for Anxiety

To facilitate clients' rendering of their stories, the EFT therapist listens attentively and reflects clients' experience with acceptance and empathy as they share their memories and flesh out their life histories and experiences. As they put their experiences into words, clients attend to their subjective experience in a new way as they register and express implicit understandings and identify the triggers for their anxiety. Through this process, clients come to see and acknowledge aspects of their experience that previously were unseen or unacknowledged. They come to see how events unfolded and identify the important, or nodal, events in their lives that contributed to who they are and their ways of being in the world.

Once the events and experiences have been described and processed, clients and the therapist can begin to understand the triggers for clients' reactions. The felt impact of events comes into view and is apprehended more fully as well as how the events shaped clients' treatment of the self and views of the self and others. The narratives provide windows into their clients' lives, enabling them to visualize and imagine their experiences, thereby enhancing the empathic process as we discussed in Chapter 4. An increased empathic understanding of what clients have experienced assists the therapist in formulating empathic conjectures about clients' inner experience or exploring and evoking seminal moments and life events that may have contributed to their anxiety and ways of being.

The EFT therapist validates clients' experiences, which in turn enables clients to develop greater confidence in their perceptions and experiences of the world. In the process they begin to see and name what has happened to them, whether it was neglect, emotional abuse, or the narcissistic distress of significant others. This labeling and naming of others' behaviors, along with the clear description of events, fosters increased trust in the self. As clients come to trust their perceptions, as well as their feelings, and make sense of their reactions, they gain an increased understanding of what has happened to them and how they have adapted.

Deconstructing Worldviews

In the process of developing their narratives, clients have the opportunity to deconstruct their worldviews and look at events through different lenses. An important function of empathic reflections and understanding is that the therapist offers a mirror to clients so they can see and reflect on what they are saying and experiencing. These types of responses enable clients to deconstruct their views, construals, and assumptions about the world, themselves, and others. This has been termed the *hermeneutic function of empathic responding* (Keil, 1996; J. Watson, 2015; J. Watson, Goldman, & Vanaerschot, 1998), which frees them to develop new ways to cope with threatening and overwhelming experiences.

As the therapist reflects clients' narratives, clients have the opportunity to see how they are constructing their life stories and worldviews. This opens the possibility for clients to look at their experiences differently. They have the opportunity to evaluate whether their views are accurate and whether their subjective experience is commensurate with events. Much as translators work to understand an author's intentions in a text, an empathic and accepting therapist works with clients to facilitate the deconstruction of their worldviews and to discover the subjectivity of their perceptions (J. Watson, 2002, 2015).

Seeing the hypothetical nature of their perceptions, construals, and assumptions, clients gain an increased range of action and choice. For example, if a client sees that another's aloofness might be due to shyness as opposed to hostility, he or she has alternative ways of responding other than feeling snubbed or injured. Becoming more reflective and seeing their worlds more clearly enables clients to develop alternative ways of addressing challenges and threats. They become more trusting of their perceptions and feelings as well as their ability to cope in the present. Developing coherent life histories, they acquire more positive self-states, freeing themselves from those that were formed as a result of earlier experiences of neglect, abandonment, and abuse (Siegel, 2012; J. Watson et al., 2007).

CHANGING NEGATIVE TREATMENT
OF THE SELF AND PROCESSING AFFECT

Early attachment experiences play an important role in peoples' capacities to regulate their emotions and neurophysiological functioning (Benjamin, 2003; DeSteno, Gross, & Kubzansky, 2013; Feshbach, 1997; Siegel, 2012; van der Kolk, 1994, 1996, 2005). Research shows that anxiously attached individuals with GAD have difficulty regulating their emotions (Marganska et al., 2013; McMullen, Watson, & Watson, 2014; J. Watson, McMullen, & Watson, 2014). They have difficulty accepting their emotions and controlling impulsive behaviors, and they show a lack of effective affect regulating strategies in times of distress.

Thus, clients with GAD are scared of being overwhelmed by their emotions. They do not know how to process them effectively and imagine that they will be engulfed by their feelings. They fear they will drown and be unable to surface or carry on effectively. Clients who have denied their feelings and ignored their bodies may not immediately be convinced or see the need to take their feelings into account. They might wish that their therapist could write a prescription or provide another solution to their pervasive feelings of dread and anxiety. They have great difficulty turning their attention inward. First, they do not know how to do this, and then they do not know what they should be looking for or experiencing. They are very much in their head as they worry and anticipate what might go wrong and try to manage and organize everything around them. The first task, then, is to work with them to attend to their bodies and help them develop labels for different bodily sensations using empathic responding and focusing.

Learning to Value Emotional Experience

The therapist can facilitate this by explaining the importance of processing painful emotional experiences. For example, a therapist might say, "I know this is difficult and that it seems as if you might not survive, but the pain is there, pulling you under. The only way to find relief is to process it so that you can find other ways of dealing with it that will be more satisfying and less painful." Over time and with practice, clients can learn to attend to the information registered in their bodies. In this process, clients come to recognize their feelings and begin to label them and name them appropriately as they acknowledge the impact that negative events have had on them. As they experience their therapist's acceptance and valuing of their feelings, they too come to value, trust, and accept them.

Clients' fear of their feelings is reduced as they come to experience the natural ebb and flow of their feelings in relationship with their therapist—becoming aware of their bodily sensations, accepting them, allowing them to bubble up, naming them, and reflecting on them. The process follows a natural cycle that has an order such that clients come to see that even the most intense emotions can be experienced and expressed, that their feelings will run their course and subside.

Differentiating Feelings

To facilitate the differentiation and labeling of feelings after clients have shared their life histories, the EFT therapist gently encourages clients to become aware of the impact their experiences have had on them. Often clients' stories are colored by a dominant feeling of anger, sadness, or fear. These feelings are generally undifferentiated in terms of their triggers and other feelings. Using empathic responding, the EFT therapist assists clients as they begin to clearly identify the triggers for their feelings. If clients become more aware of their feelings in a differentiated manner, alternative ways of acting and behaving are revealed as different needs arise—every feeling has a need that can direct behavior. Another way that the EFT therapist uses to assist clients to become more aware of and label their feelings is to ask them to attend to their body and their organismic experience. Clients are encouraged to focus on their bodily felt experience to become aware of it, label it, and reflect on it so that they can meet their needs in more life-enhancing ways. This emotional processing cycle begins to lay the groundwork for the development of more optimal affect regulation strategies.

As clients differentiate their feelings, they feel better able to cope with them and begin to experience the relief that comes when feelings are expressed. They glimpse the value of understanding their feelings and what they are communicating, seeing that they are providing direction and information about how to respond and cope with events. With this realization, clients are better able to allow their emotional experience, letting it into awareness so that it can be worked on in the session and reprocessed. They no longer feel ambushed by their feelings or terrified and anxious about their capacity to cope. Instead of fearing disintegration, clients develop more effective ways of processing and regulating their feelings so that they do not feel ashamed and out of control. In the process they begin to develop a stronger, more resilient sense of self.

Internalizing Self-Soothing

In EFT, clients become more accepting of their feelings and perceptions, better able to tolerate their feelings, and learn to self-soothe to modulate the intensity of their feelings. The capacity to protect and soothe the self and regulate affective experience develops initially through the internalization of the soothing and regulatory functions of a protective other (Bowlby, 1988; Fosha, 2000; Siegel, 2012; Sroufe, 1996; Stern, 1985). Two important ways that the EFT therapist works to improve clients' affect regulation is through the internalization of a self-soothing capacity and by changing negative ways of treating the self or regulating emotions (J. Watson, 2012).

In EFT, self-soothing is developed interpersonally by means of the therapist's presence, empathic attunement, and responsiveness to clients' affect and through acceptance and validation of clients' subjective experience. Directly experiencing aroused affect, expressing it, and being soothed by relational or nonverbal means is a right hemisphere process (Schore, 2003) and builds individuals' capacities for self-soothing. It has been suggested that the therapeutic relationship facilitates the dyadic regulation of emotion through the provision of safety, security, and connection (Fosha, 2000; Porges, 2011a, 2011b; Siegel, 2012). This type of interaction breaks clients' sense of isolation, confirms self-experience, and promotes self-empathy. Moreover, extrapolating from Porges's (2011a) polyvagal theory, it is likely that in healing therapeutic relationships, clients learn to down-regulate their biological systems so as to engender calm and more relaxed states of being.

The development of more effective strategies to regulate affective experience and provide soothing is essential to coping with intense feelings of anxiety and fear and to combat a vulnerable sense of self. Effective modulation of emotional experience is facilitated through the expression and symbolization of feelings. The capacity to modulate affective experience contributes to feelings of competence and self-esteem. Naming or labeling feelings is an essential task in EFT, especially with the use of empathic reflections that convey understanding, acceptance, prizing, and genuineness. By responding empathically, the therapist actively works with clients to become aware of their bodily felt experience and emotions, and to find the labels for their feelings. This process helps to modulate clients' level of arousal and enables them to reflect on their feelings and emotions to understand the impact of events and to identify what they need to protect or nourish themselves moving forward.

For example, Monica, the client who was presented in the Introduction, was unable to articulate her feelings when she first came to therapy. She was primarily aware of her anxiety and sense of foreboding. As the therapist began to explore her childhood, Monica began to realize how sad, lonely, and rejected she had felt. She got in touch with her sense of helplessness and how unfair her mother's treatment of her had been. This process of differentiating her feelings happened over a period of time. As she began to name and differentiate her feelings, the processes by which she regulated them became more apparent, as did the childhood wounds and attachment injuries.

The therapist's prizing, acceptance, and empathic attunement to clients' affective experience provides the scaffolding for clients to regulate their affect and internalize ways of self-soothing. Feeling felt creates a resonance of minds that is pleasurable and essential to survival (Siegel, 2012). In EFT, the therapist works to be empathically attuned to clients' emotional experience, to mirror it so that clients have the opportunity to see it more clearly and acknowledge their experience in awareness. People experience a sense of relief and comfort when they feel understood and accepted by another, especially when they are experiencing intense, painful emotions (Fosha, 2000; Greenberg, Rice, & Elliott, 1993; Schore, 2003; Siegel, 2012; J. Watson, 2002). Similarly, positive therapeutic relationships can be seen to facilitate changes in clients' affect regulation as they internalize the therapeutic conditions of presence, prizing, empathy, and acceptance to regulate their emotions and affective experience and develop more positive self-talk and ways of soothing themselves.

Changing Negative Treatment of the Self

As discussed in Chapter 1 of this volume, clients with GAD have developed ways of regulating their intense feelings of vulnerability that are maladaptive over the long haul. Typically, these clients are not fully aware of their affective experience—they have shut down their distress and are unaware of what triggers it. By developing an external focus of attention, they attempt to control events and protect themselves to the exclusion of their subjective experience and feelings, using worry as one of the primary ways of modulating experience.

Securely attached individuals are more confident about managing their emotions; better able to focus on their goals; and better able to be aware of, label, and accept their emotions when things are difficult than clients who are insecurely attached with GAD (Marganska et al., 2013). As we discussed in Chapter 2, clients with GAD reject, ignore, dismiss, and undervalue their feelings. Therefore, their affect regulating capacities are diminished and underdeveloped, leaving them feeling continually challenged as they experience themselves as weak, vulnerable, and ineffective in mastering and coping with their environments.

An important focus in EFT with clients with GAD is to work with clients to see the negative ways in which they may be regulating their affect and relating to their experience. To do this, the therapist makes observations about how clients are treating their experience and themselves. For example, she or he may say, "I see you interrupting and silencing yourself; what is happening inside?" or "you seem impatient with her—what is that about?" This information is gleaned from clients' narratives and life histories as the therapist works with them to process and become aware of their emotions. Negative ways clients can treat themselves are also highlighted in two-chair or empty-chair dialogues (see Chapters 6–9, this volume).

To identify clients' negative behaviors, the therapist can use the structural analysis of social behavior (Benjamin, 1974), the circumplex model discussed in Chapter 4 to assess clients' and the therapist's interactions. The circumplex model (Benjamin, 1979, 1993) can be used to determine whether clients are relating positively or negatively to their experience. The therapist can assess whether clients are displaying behaviors and ways of being that indicate that they are relating positively to their experience by being accepting, attentive, validating, empathic, guiding, protective, caring, and nurturing of themselves or whether they are relating negatively and being forgetful, neglectful, abandoning, rejecting, threatening, exploitative, blaming, intrusive, and controlling of themselves and their experience. For example, when clients ignore their feelings, overburden themselves, or drink excessively, these may be signs that they are not attending to their feelings and are being neglectful of themselves.

In EFT, identifying how clients are relating to themselves and others can be useful to develop case formulations with respect to how clients are regulating and managing their emotions. Clients with GAD are typically not respectful of their feelings, they do not accept them; instead, they tend to neglect, silence, and block their organismic experience as they attend to the needs of others, either because others are unavailable or because they are too present. The therapist attends to clients' behaviors as they share their narratives as well as when they engage in chair dialogues, either as the self or the other, to determine whether the clients are relating negatively or positively to their emotions. As these behaviors emerge, the therapist can reflect them to the clients to make them aware and suggest ways of working with these processes to alleviate clients' anxiety.

As they attend to their feelings, clients are encouraged to become aware of how they are treating their organismic experience. Initially the therapist may suggest that they are stifling, silencing, neglecting, or ignoring their organismic experience. For example, a client may say, "My feelings are not important" or "Feelings don't count; they are silly," or he or she might not wish to acknowledge his or her pain, rejecting it as a sign of weakness. The therapist can respond with empathic refocusing and observe that clients are invalidating or rejecting their feelings and then check whether this fits with clients' experience or not. As clients become more aware of their behaviors and ways of relating to their experiences, they are better able to recognize and address the negative impact of their behaviors on themselves in therapy.

It may take time for clients to see their own behaviors as negative. However, the EFT therapist is patient, trusting that clients will develop the capacity to recognize and categorize these different behaviors and ways of being as they internalize their therapist's attitudes. Once clients perceive how they are relating to their experience and see how these behaviors are contributing to their pain, they usually resolve to change them and learn to be more self-compassionate and self-protective. The EFT therapist uses two-chair dialogues to work with clients' negative ways of treating experience. These can be seen not only in the content of clients' self-talk but also in their demeanor and manner of expression, as is elaborated in Chapter 7 of this volume.

Changing these internalized negative behaviors is not simple or easy. The therapist cannot merely prescribe or tell clients what they need to do. Clients with GAD have spent years developing ways of coping to protect themselves from pain to survive in neglectful and hostile environments. Those who have spent years dismissing their experience or denying it will not immediately turn their attention inward and value and appreciate their feelings. It requires patience on the part of the client and the therapist, as the client develops the strength to cope with the pain and trust that he or she will not disintegrate but rather process and transform it.

An individual's sense of self is weakened and their confidence is undermined when they internalize negative ways of treating their experience. As a result, their sense of what they need is impaired and their confidence in their perceptions and their ability to cope is undermined. They lose a sense of direction as well as their capacity to protect and nourish themselves. To change these negative ways of relating to experience, clients need to internalize their therapist's feelings of empathy, acceptance, and positive regard so that they can process their feelings of helplessness and terror and learn how to reassure and soothe themselves to modulate their feelings of distress (additional strategies for developing self-soothing are presented in Chapter 9). As clients grow stronger and become more self-accepting and compassionate, they come to see themselves as deserving of inclusion and acceptance. They are able to access their anger to protect themselves and stand up for what they need and deserve. The development of self-acceptance in the relationship with a therapist who is accepting and attentive to clients' experience is essential to attaining a stronger sense of self and enhancing emotion regulation capacities. The following case example illustrates these changes.

CASE EXAMPLE: OVERBURDENING THE SELF

Ginny, a 58-year-old woman, came to therapy for the treatment of GAD. Although she had been in therapy before, she had not been able to master her generalized anxiety. She was very effective at work but she still worried about losing her job and her partner of 15 years. Given her preoccupation with work and her partner, her focus of attention was constantly outside of herself—it was focused on others. Ginny was unable to reference her own feelings except so far as she was worried and knew she felt anxious much of the time.

She found it difficult to tolerate other people's negative emotions, wishing they were different and that they would see the world more positively, as she did. She had a great deal of difficulty accepting her own vulnerability and neediness. She could not admit that she wanted others to care for her, because she was invested in seeing herself as "the helper" and the one who took care of other people's needs. She was very competent in this role and took much pleasure and pride in it. As a result, she was not able to recognize when she needed succor and thus was not able to ask for care and support. She tended to deny her own feelings and needs, just as she was unable to respond to her partner's needs, telling her partner to "just cheer up" or "think more positively."

The therapist assumed an accepting, empathic stance to reflect Ginny's concerns and to try to focus Ginny on her feelings. It took a number of sessions for Ginny to become aware that her attention was constantly focused outside and that she had difficulty turning her attention inward to her own body and feelings. To facilitate her attention to her feelings, the therapist worked with Ginny to differentiate her experience using empathic exploration responses.

> *Therapist:* So, somehow you have difficulty when [your partner] complains?
>
> *Client:* Yes, I just wish she would make the best of it.
>
> *Therapist:* There is something about seeing her sad or unhappy?
>
> *Client:* Well, it just drags us down. She needs to control herself more.
>
> *Therapist:* You feel dragged down somehow—sad, hopeless—what?
>
> *Client:* I'm not sure. It seems things are more difficult if she is always complaining. It feels heavy.
>
> *Therapist:* When she complains, it feels like a burden for you—it is heavy?
>
> *Client:* I guess that is it. I feel I have to fix it or that I am letting her down, disappointing her.
>
> *Therapist:* Somehow you feel you are responsible for what goes wrong in her life? What is that about?

Here the therapist tried to focus Ginny on her partner's behavior to have her explore her perceptions and the triggers for her own behavior. The therapist used empathic exploratory reflections to keep Ginny focused and move the exploration forward.

Through tasks like focusing and empathic responding, Ginny slowly turned her attention inward. As she became more aware of how she attended to other people and responded to their feelings, she saw how she neglected herself and did not address her needs in her relationship. Her therapist noted that she had difficulty being vulnerable. Ginny admitted that she judged herself as needy and despicable for needing support or care. Ginny's negative treatment and ways of relating to herself became clearer during a worry dialogue (see Chapter 6, this volume). As she became more aware of her own feelings and needs, her therapist began to work on Ginny's negative treatment of the self and her relationships with others using two-chair and empty-chair dialogues.

Research shows that clients internalize the ways that their therapist treats them, which in turn facilitates changes in how they relate to their subjective experience (Benjamin, 1974; Ulvenes et al., 2014; J. Watson, Steckley, & McMullen, 2014). J. Watson, Steckley, and McMullen (2014) found that clients who experienced their therapist as empathic showed a decrease in negative self-treatment and an increase in their level of security in close interpersonal relationships. Moreover, these changes mediated the role of the therapist's empathy on outcome, accounting for moderate to large amounts of variance in clients' attachment styles, and negative self-treatment after controlling for the therapeutic alliance. Decreases in clients' negative self-treatment, including self-silencing, neglectful, critical and hostile behaviors, as well as insecure attachment in the later stage of therapy, mediated the impact of the therapist's empathy on outcome.

These findings provide preliminary support for the view that clients' perception and experience of the therapist's empathy contributes to changes in how they treat themselves and their experience, and that these changes facilitate improvement in clients' self-reported functioning, including dysfunctional attitudes, self-esteem, interpersonal difficulties, and depression at the end of therapy. Interestingly, the effect of the therapist's empathy on all outcome indices was stronger for clients who were more insecure in their attachment relationships. Empathy may be even more important for clients who are insecurely attached to help them engage effectively in psychotherapy than it is for those who are more securely attached at the beginning of therapy. The more insecure clients who perceived their therapist as empathic made significant changes and were less insecure, more self-accepting, and better able to regulate their emotions at the end of therapy than they were at its beginning (Prosser & Watson, 2007; J. Watson, Steckley, & McMullen, 2014).

Thus, the experience of the therapist's positive attitude toward clients is internalized and contributes to changes in interactions with the self and others. As the therapist listens attentively to clients and accepts and reflects their experience, they model positive ways of being and relating to the self and their subjective experience. Barrett-Lennard (1997) referred to this as developing self-empathy or self-compassion. Empathic, accepting, supportive, protective, and nurturing interactions with others build positive, protective, and nurturing ways of relating to the self. The internalization of positive ways of relating to oneself and one's experience results in the development of behaviors that are more self-affirming, self-accepting, self-protective, and self-soothing. As clients develop new, more positive ways of treating their experience, their self-concepts become transformed. They experience a sense of self-worth, come to view themselves as deserving of better treatment, are less judgmental of themselves and their experience, and feel more self-confident (Barrett-Lennard, 1997; Bozarth, 2001; Rogers, 1975; J. Watson, 2015).

The process of strengthening the self and internalizing positive attitudes and behaviors toward the self is a fundamental change process in EFT. In empathic and accepting relationships clients build self-compassion so that they can hear and attend to their pain. They are better able to process their pain, listen to what is needed, and respond so that it can be accepted and validated and new ways of coping devised. With the development of more positive ways of treating their affective experience, clients are able to make the changes necessary to resolve specific tasks like two-chair (see Chapters 6 and 7, this volume) and empty-chair dialogues (see Chapter 8). To resolve these tasks successfully, clients need to develop self-compassion and access anger to be more self-assertive. They have to feel deserving and entitled to their feelings and needs so they can counteract negative ways of treating their experience in two-chair work or give voice to silenced aspects of their experience in empty-chair work. However, to be more self-assertive, clients need to feel strong enough to stand alone and withstand challenges from others and the world at large.

It is in the relationship with their therapist that clients revise their views of the self and others (Barrett-Lennard, 1997; Benjamin, 1993; Blatt et al., 2010; J. Watson, Steckley, & McMullen, 2014). Before they are able to change the negative ways they relate to their experience and resolve relational injuries in two-chair or empty-chair dialogues, some clients may need to internalize more positive ways of relating to themselves. How to develop these more positive ways of relating to the self can be ascertained in chair dialogues, as we discuss in the following chapters. These more positive behaviors continue to develop over the course of psychotherapy as clients interact with their therapist and come to better understand their own needs, respect them, and learn to assert them and/or express them to others to receive the support and care they need and deserve (Benjamin, 1993; Schore, 2003; J. Watson et al., 2007).

REBALANCING RESPONSIBILITY IN A RELATIONSHIP AND REDEFINING THE SELF

Positive relationships facilitate the development of agency and self-identity. An important goal in EFT is for clients to become more self-directed and agentic. This is especially important for clients with GAD, whose development of agency may have been thwarted by caretakers who were neglectful or overly intrusive. Navigating connections is one of the complexities of being human and living in community (Benjamin, 1974; Greenberg, 2011; Schore, 2003; Siegel, 2012). Individuals are self-organizing organisms made up of internal processes and in continual interaction with their environment. They become more self-governing and self-regulating as they mature (Bohart & Tallman, 1999; Damasio, 1994, 1999; Rogers, 1959; Schore, 2003). However, if this process is interrupted, dysfunction and anxiety can result. To be fully functioning and strong, individuals need to be aware of and accurately represent their inner organismic experience, as well as that of others and integrate the information from both sources to find solutions for living that are optimal for individuals and the community (Schore, 2003; Siegel, 2012; J. Watson, 2011). At its core, optimal functioning implies differentiation of experience.

Two types of differentiation are facilitated by the therapist's empathic responding and acceptance of the clients' experiences: (a) the differentiation of clients' subjective experience and (b) the differentiation of the self and others. To become fully functioning and to form their own identity, individuals need to be able to discriminate and label their inner and outer experience and differentiate it from the experience of others. This latter process does not require individuals to be totally independent of others but rather it means that they can differentiate their experience from the experience of others and they can clearly represent their experience, along with the experience of others, in consciousness to be self-regulating and self-governing. Fully functioning individuals are responsible for their own well-being and are able to negotiate their needs respectfully and effectively with others (J. Watson, 2011).

As emotional beings in interaction with others and who have the capacity for empathy, individuals can subserve their feelings and needs to remain connected with others (Benjamin, 1993; Bowen, 1976; Rogers, 1959; Sullivan, 1953). In so doing, they forfeit meeting their needs for identity, mastery, and competence, leading to feelings of anxiety as these essential needs remain unmet. When individuals sacrifice their needs and feelings to remain connected, they may silence, reject, neglect, or otherwise misattribute them and take on the needs and feelings of others as their own (Greenberg, 2011; J. Watson, 2011).

Alternatively, when neglected and unprotected, individuals may become so self-reliant that they are unable to reach for support when they need it. By silencing their pain, they remain fragile and vulnerable, their process of differentiation is stalled, and healthy functioning is compromised. The process of differentiation is vital to healthy and adaptive functioning—it is essential not only to the well-being of individuals but also to that of couples, families, communities, and, ultimately, the survival of the species and planet. A secure bond with another who is accepting and empathic begins to support and allow for differentiation of the self and others in clients with GAD as they begin to know and understand their emotional experience and develop greater confidence and trust in themselves to protect and support themselves in interaction with others.

An important task for clients with GAD is to redress the imbalance between the self and others, to rebalance the scales. Clients who have assumed too much responsibility for regulating their environments and the needs of others need to assume less responsibility, and instead, hold others more accountable and expect them to assume greater care for their own well-being (Benjamin, 1993; Blatt et al., 2010). Often clients who assume a lot of responsibility have done so in an attempt to protect and care for themselves in relationships with others. However, this often results in these clients overburdening themselves, as they constantly worry about the needs and feelings of others while neglecting their own. Thus, it is important for clients with GAD to share the burden of responsibility more equally so that they can attend to their own needs and seek assistance and support from others when necessary. This is one of the important objectives in empty-chair dialogues that we discuss in Chapter 8 of this volume.

In contrast, there are those clients who have been overly controlled and managed by significant others and whose ability or capacity to cope has been undermined. These clients also have difficulty trusting themselves and their subjective experience. They tend to dismiss and undermine their own feelings, suppressing them in favor of those from anxious, overly protective others who interrupt clients' differentiation and their capacity to develop and individuate (Bowen, 1976, 1978; Schore, 2003). Both these types of self-organization represent an imbalance in relating and require the sacrifice of the self to attend to the needs of others. In the first scenario, the others are neglectful, helpless, or unavailable, and clients are required to do the caretaking; in the second scenario, clients' needs and self-regulation are compromised because others intrude and assume control and management of clients' feelings and actions. These two different types of relationships result in clients' silencing their needs in the service of others, contribute to impaired emotional processing, and foster the development of negative self-organizations and a lack of self-confidence. To become more self-protective, clients need to draw on assertive anger and require others to assume more responsibility for their own well-being and/or to give up control and become less intrusive. As they redress this imbalance, clients redefine their boundaries and improve the differentiation between the self and others. They come to feel strong enough to request more support and assume less responsibility for their own and others' well-being, and they come to expect others to assume more responsibility and greater initiative for their own well-being and survival. This rebalancing of agency and responsibility is illustrated in the case of Alex.

CASE EXAMPLE: THE IMPACT OF AN INTRUSIVE OTHER

Alex came to therapy when he was 35 years old. He was anxious much of the time. He worked as a successful accountant but worried continuously about his wife, children, and clients. He reported that as a child, his mother had been very overbearing. She would constantly remind him to be careful. She expressed concerns and fears when he would go to play with friends and monitored his schoolwork, sometimes doing his homework for him. As a result, Alex became quite fearful and cautious. He realized he was communicating this anxiety and fear to his family. Seeing how undermined he had been as a child, his therapist worked at being present, attentively listening, and empathically responding to Alex's fears and concerns.

At first, he was very protective of his mother. Alex saw her as having sacrificed herself for him and his brothers after she gave up her career to stay home. But with time, as Alex explored his childhood, he came to see how intrusive his mother had been. He saw how her fears and tendency to take over had undermined his confidence in himself. He realized how critical he was of himself. Having internalized his mother's fears, he saw himself as incompetent. As Alex internalized his therapist's attitudes of respect and prizing, he came to trust his experience more and accessed assertive anger toward his mother. This led to some empty-chair dialogues during which he was able to assert his competence and tell his mother how damaging her intrusive behavior had been. Alex set limits on their relationship and reduced the number of times she called him during the week. In addition, he learned how to self-soothe when he began to feel distressed, and he became more self-compassionate and less critical of his abilities. He stopped worrying as much about his work and relaxed more around his family and colleagues.

WORKING IN CLIENTS' PROXIMAL ZONES OF DEVELOPMENT

Clients come to therapy with different capacities, depending on the degree to which these have been subverted or thwarted. Earlier negative life experiences and more neglectful and harsh interactions are more likely to cause one or more of these capacities to be underdeveloped. This can be seen most clearly in clients with GAD who have comorbid disorders, including substance abuse, depression, and personality disorders. Thus, some clients may have poorly developed narratives and need to spend time to develop more coherent life histories before moving on to the tasks of emotional processing and changing their relationship with the self and others. Other clients may have more developed narratives and life histories, but less developed emotional processing and affect regulation capacities. The focus for them in therapy is to improve their emotional processing capacity and relationship with the self. Yet others who have coherent narratives and some capacity to regulate their emotions may be fearful of standing up to others and challenging their relationships. These clients need to build a stronger sense of self so that they can feel more confident and assertive.

The EFT therapist is constantly evaluating changes in clients' sense of self and their self-organizations. Initially they work with clients to understand what has happened to them and to reconstruct their life stories. Concurrently, the therapist is evaluating clients' emotional processing and sense of agency and responsibility, along with their self-organizations. Client and therapist weave in and out of working with these different processes across therapy as the client shares and develops her or his narratives and life histories, acquires improved emotional processing and affect regulation capacities, develops more positive self-concepts and ways of regulating experience, and rebalances her or his sense of responsibility and agency. Each of these processes becomes figural at different times in therapy as clients work to overcome their anxiety.

The therapist needs to be aware of these differences so that he or she can adjust and work at clients' proximal stage of development to facilitate healing and strengthen their vulnerable sense of self. Originally, Vygotsky (1978) used the term *proximal stage of development* with reference to the development of children's cognitive capacities (Zaretskii, 2009). However, he suggested that the concept was relevant to the development of personality in general. Here we are applying it to the development of individuals' self-regulation and self-organization, and more specifically, to their emotional processing and regulating capacities in psychotherapy.

Thus, at different times, clients may need to focus on developing their life histories to access autobiographical information and implicit experience to organize and make sense of the events in their lives. At other times, they may need to attend to their emotional processing, working with their therapist to represent their bodily experience and symbolize their feelings so they can better understand the impact of events and what they need to promote their well-being and enhance their social and emotional functioning. At still other times in therapy, they will be working on how they relate to their emotional experience, becoming more aware of negative ways of treating themselves in order to develop more positive ways of relating to their experience. Finally, in parallel, they may also be working on differentiating from and standing up to others, drawing on assertive anger to heal attachment injuries, and becoming more self-protective. All of these changes are facilitated as clients internalize their therapist's attitudes and develop greater self-assertion and self-compassion along with new ways of self-soothing.

CONCLUSION

The vulnerable self at the core of GAD should be the focus of treatment. It is important right from the start to pay attention to strengthening clients' fragile sense of self by providing acceptance, empathy, prizing, and congruence, usually in the form of reflections, process observations, questions, focusing exercises, and by following the client's lead (Elliott, Watson, Goldman, & Greenberg, 2004). Developing a stronger sense of self helps clients to engage in the tasks of therapy, including becoming aware of, tolerating, and exploring painful underlying feelings of fear, sadness, and shame and effectively differentiating themselves from significant others. The core insecurity of the vulnerable self is transformed as clients internalize their therapist's empathy, acceptance, attunement, responsiveness, prizing, and sincerity. Their awareness of their emotions increases, they improve their capacity to regulate and soothe painful emotional states, and they acquire more positive ways of treating themselves. In the process, clients also develop more coherent life stories and rebalance their sense of agency and self-identity, which contributes to their feeling stronger and better able to cope with life's challenges.

Changes in clients' self-organizations can be slow and may require the therapist to be patient as clients internalize their therapist's positive attitudes and behaviors. With continual empathic responding, prizing, and acceptance from the therapist, clients will grow strong enough to stand alone and feel more positive about themselves. They will develop a greater sense of mastery as they become more self-directed, self-compassionate, self-affirming, and assertive. In the next few chapters, we discuss how to work with two-chair dialogues for worry splits and negative ways of treating experience, as well as how to work with empty-chair dialogues to address attachment wounds, as clients access greater self-compassion and self-protective anger.

6

WORKING WITH WORRY:
ANXIETY SPLITS

In emotion-focused therapy (EFT), worry is viewed as a way of protecting against experiences that would activate painful underlying emotions (e.g., fear, sadness, shame). As discussed in Chapter 1 of this volume, these primary feelings often emanate from unresolved attachment and identity issues, which result in insecurity. They reflect past emotional, physical, and psychological traumas, including large-T trauma (e.g., severe sexual and physical abuse), the accumulation of small-t traumas (e.g., less severe interpersonal injuries), and/or experiences of neglect and humiliation that people are unable to soothe with more accepting and compassionate ways of relating to the self. Clients with generalized anxiety disorder (GAD) can show marked difficulty in accessing anger and being self-assertive, along with a lack of confidence in their ability and capacity to manage and protect themselves from the demands of their environments. Although EFT treatment for GAD needs to focus on all these difficulties, it often starts by working with clients' worry.

http://dx.doi.org/10.1037/0000018-007
Emotion-Focused Therapy for Generalized Anxiety, by J. C. Watson and L. S. Greenberg

THE WORRY DIALOGUE

Worry is approached using a two-chair dialogue. This intervention is used to address negative ways of relating to the self and was originally used to work with conflict splits (Greenberg, 1979; Greenberg, Rice, & Elliott, 1993; J. Watson, Goldman, & Greenberg, 2007). The worry dialogue is a variant of a self-critical dialogue, which is described in more detail elsewhere (Greenberg & Watson, 2006; Elliott, Watson, Goldman, & Greenberg, 2004). It differs from a self-critical dialogue, which is related to negative self-evaluative depressive processes. In anxiety splits, there is a voice that worries and catastrophizes instead of being critical and evaluative. In self-critical split work, the critic softens into compassion, whereas in anxiety the worrier self softens into sadness, fear, and pain as a result of neglect and abandonment. Early on in the development of EFT, before discrimination had been made between a "critic" and a "protector," Greenberg and Dompierre (1981) observed that the critical voice softened into compassion or fear. It was in situations when the critic was catastrophizing that a softening into fear occurred. The discrimination between these two types of dialogues was not made at the time but has become clearer in distinguishing between self-evaluation and worry.

Thus, in contrast to self-critical splits, the worry dialogue in clients with GAD is characterized by an apprehensive voice that catastrophizes and makes the self anxious. This voice creates anxiety by fearing the worst, reminding clients of past dangers, and imagining future ones. To heighten clients' awareness of this voice and the manner in which it creates worry, the therapist can suggest they engage in a worry dialogue. In EFT, worry is externalized and separated into a dialogue between two parts of the self. One part is characterized as the worrier self or anxiety producer, whose messages to be vigilant and avoid situations are meant to protect the self from imagined catastrophes and other negative outcomes, but actually create tension and anxiety. The other part is characterized as the self that feels the impact of the worry and constant vigilance.

Conceptualizing the worry process in this dual way leads to a view of worry as a protector or guardian of the self. The protector is constantly vigilant as it searches for threats to safety and security and tries to prevent future danger, protecting the individual from experiencing feelings of humiliation, rejection, intense self-criticism, loneliness, and neglect. It worries about how the person is behaving and will be perceived, seeing him or her as solely responsible for the outcome of events. This pressure of being solely responsible for the well-being and safety of the self and others has the effect of scaring and overburdening vulnerable clients. As a consequence, the self feels anxious and unable to relax, with the unintended effect of feelings of weakness, tiredness, and helplessness. Worry is seen as a symptom in EFT, with the attendant anxiety conceptualized as a secondary reactive emotional response, which obscures the more primary fundamental feelings of fear, sadness, vulnerability, shame, and inadequacy.

As worry often predominates and is experienced as debilitating by clients, it is important to address it early. It helps to establish collaboration between therapist and client, given that worry and the attendant anxiety are the presenting problems. Often the priority for anxious clients is to have help dealing with their worry, and they expect their therapist to focus on it early in treatment. Therefore, the focus on worry and its attendant anxiety is consistent with clients' phenomenology. It supports the development of a positive therapeutic alliance and helps clients to cope with their anxiety early on in the therapy.

Clients experience anxiety as something that happens to them outside of their conscious control. By working with the anxiety in a two-chair dialogue, a split process is clearly formulated, in which one self worries and catastrophizes and the self feels scared, stressed, and tired. This formulation helps clients see themselves as agents in the construction of their anxiety and as able to change what they are doing to transform their state of being anxious and overwhelmed. They move from seeing their anxiety as something that happens to them to something they contribute to and play a role in doing to themselves. The first step, then, is to suggest to clients that they articulate the messages that they are telling themselves—the warnings and demands that they ensure things work out just right. Once these are expressed, the self reacts and expresses the impact of the demands and the dialogue begins to unfold. The steps in this dialogue are shown in Figure 6.1.

The opportunity to suggest a two-chair dialogue arises when clients begin to talk about their worries, accompanied by some indication that they

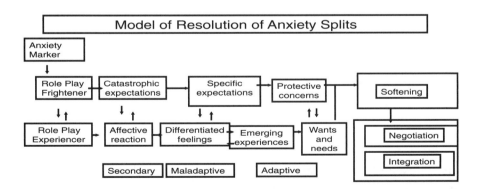

Figure 6.1. Model of the resolution of anxiety splits.

recognize that their worries are troublesome, possibly exaggerated, not fully warranted, or out of control. Worry is often expressed as a need to behave in a certain way to avoid anticipated catastrophes or negative outcomes. For example, one client's father had died of a heart attack when she was 9. As a result, she feared her husband would have a heart attack, and she would call him at work to check in with him regularly throughout the day. This concern for the physical well-being of those she loved extended to her daughter and her son. She would worry when they were out late, thinking thoughts such as, "Is my daughter safe? It's too late for her to be out alone; it's dangerous at night."

Markers for Worry Dialogues

Clients' statements that express worry are seen as markers for the therapist to suggest two-chair work (e.g., "I worry so much: I worry about my husband, my daughter, my son; I even worry about all the people in my building" or "I feel so anxious and afraid like I have no protective skin"). These statements are seen as *markers*, or opportunities, for the therapist to suggest to clients that they engage in a dialogue between the self that frightens them and the self that experiences the impact of the worries and concerns (Greenberg et al., 1993). If clients agree, they are asked to sit in one chair and express their worries and fears to their other self in the opposite chair. Once the worries have been expressed, the therapist asks clients to move to the opposite chair to experience the anxiety their worries and fears have produced. This dialogue is used to bring the whole process of how clients bring their anxiety to life in the session.

The following is an example of an anxiety marker that arose in a session with an anxious client:

> *Client:* I'm a bit tense today and [have been] for the last couple of days. It's like something is going to happen and I'm waiting for it; [I feel] like I am on guard.
>
> *Therapist:* I see, [you feel] tense and on guard?
>
> *Client:* Yeah.
>
> *Therapist:* So, you are somehow preparing to protect yourself?
>
> *Client:* Yes, so I'll know when it's going to happen and it won't be a shock.

In this example, the therapist suggested a two-chair task to have the client express her worries and clearly articulate what she said to herself to prepare for what might be in store. The therapist coached the client to enact the worrier self:

Therapist: I'm going to ask you to be that [self] that makes you anxious and tense so we can have a dialogue between the [self] that worries and the [self] that is anxious.

Client: Okay.

Therapist: You are worried—it sounds like you want to prepare yourself for something or to protect yourself against some danger.

Client: I'm thinking about the worry, just talking about it makes me tense.

Therapist: Will you come over [to the other chair]. This is the [self] that worries, and says things like "something bad could happen—be careful" or "don't forget to look at those files." Can you be this [self] and tell your other self "what if . . ." What does this [self] say?

In the first few dialogues, the goal is to enable clients to become aware of the messages that contribute to feelings of anxiety and tension. Increasing their awareness of the process begins to highlight that clients are agents in the process and that their anxiety is evoked by what they are saying to themselves to guard against negative outcomes.

Expressing Worries

In the two-chair dialogue, clients are asked to be as specific as possible in expressing their worries. This is designed to evoke the anxiety experience in the session and identify what clients are saying vividly and concretely. The worrying protective self is encouraged to voice concrete and specific fears and worries (e.g., failing to meet a deadline, a pet dying). The more specific and concrete the fears, the more likely that episodic, situational, or emotionally painful memories will be evoked. As the messages are expressed, the therapist attends not only to the content but also to the manner in which the worrying protective self expresses concerns. This can be speedy and frenetic or demanding and relentless. Alternatively, it might have a ruminative quality as the worries are repeated again and again. Sometimes it is the warning tones, or manner, accompanying the worrying and catastrophizing phrases of "what if" or "be careful" that contribute to clients' feelings of tension and anxiety. Often clients do not pay attention to the manner in which they speak to themselves, attending only to the content of their inner dialogues. They concentrate on what is said but not on the relationship between the parts. By paying special attention to the nonverbal elements of the dialogue, the therapist reflects not just the content but also the nonverbal elements, including vocal intonations, gestures, postures, and facial expressions, thereby drawing clients' attention to the affective tone of the worrying protective self as well as to the specific content of their worries.

Expressing the Impact of Worrying

After the worrying messages have been expressed, clients are asked to move to the other chair and express how they react to the protective self's admonitions and warnings. The therapist guides clients beyond a global cognitive reaction of "I feel anxious" to a differentiated sense of what actually comes alive in the body in the moment. This might evoke a feeling of being shaky or tense, with butterflies in the stomach or an urge to escape. As the feelings are articulated in language, the exploration deepens. The process of enactment with anxious clients during the initial period of therapy thus focuses first on activating the protective self's worrier voice to evoke helpless, exhausted, and anxious feelings. This secondary emotion points toward the more primary feelings of vulnerability, insecurity, and weakness.

Next, we provide an illustration of the two-chair task used for worry dialogues. The client is a 62-year-old woman who has suffered from anxiety most of her life. Her therapist suggested they work with the client's worry and asked her to describe a situation that causes her anxiety so as to access her fears:

Therapist: Let's try to get a sense of how your worry actually works.

Client: I imagine my brother lying on the floor. That just came up to my mind right away after calling [him on the phone] two or three times.

The client imagined that her brother had collapsed.

Client: And I said to myself he is just [right] there; he is trying to grab the phone.

Therapist: Okay, talk me through it first. When does the anxiety first hit you? Make it as if it was a movie.

The therapist asked the client to be very specific to try to get a sense of the exact moment the anxiety was triggered.

Client: I called [my brother] and again the machine came on and I [thought], "Oh something has happened. He's just lying on the floor trying to get someone to help him. He's in pain."

After the client described the situation, the therapist suggested they work with a two-chair dialogue to help her express her worry and see its impact:

Therapist: Let's try something, okay? You tell me if at any point this does not feel right to you. I want you to come over [to this other chair]? I will help you through this, okay? Imagine that you're [sitting in the opposite chair and I want you to] scare her. What do you do? What are those thoughts that you have? "[My] brother is on the floor; he could be dead"? "He could be lying there, helpless, suffering"? "He could be in pain and no one's there to help him"? Can you scare her, can you do that to her?

Client: You want me to talk to [myself like] I'm somebody else?

Here the client expressed confusion about the nature of the task. Her therapist explained that they are trying to give voice to two different parts of herself.

Therapist: It's like this part; this is part of you.

Client: Okay, so this is like an out-of-body experience?

Therapist: Well it's like, you know when you have [this voice] in your head [having these thoughts]? It's not a crazy voice, but it's thinking, "He could be lying on the floor in pain." You can imagine he's reaching [out] but he can't get to the phone and you can get an image of this and that is frightening. That's not an out-of-body experience, it's [more] like putting the worry in this chair—the voice that scares you. Does that make sense to you?

Client: Yes, okay. I'm me inside; it's my [voice].

In this example, the therapist explained the chair dialogue. Initially, the client compared it with an out of body experience. However, the therapist reassured her and she agreed to try to engage in the dialogue. The therapist continued to engage in some further psychoeducation to introduce and clarify the task, and the role of the worrier self, so the client could understand the purpose of the task:

Therapist: Exactly. It's part of you, but it's like this is the [self] that worries, that gets sick with worry; this is the worrier voice. Does that make sense to you?

Client: Yeah.

Therapist: Can you take a minute just to try to picture yourself when we are here and take a minute and go back to the time when you were thinking about your brother? Scare [yourself], tell [yourself] how [your brother is] going for the phone, how he is in pain he can't get to it. He could have fallen, he could have . . . what?

The therapist structured the dialogue and provided some possible thoughts in a sentence or two to get the dialogue going using empathic doubling responses.

This was done in a tentative searching way to encourage the client to come up with phrases that matched her experience. With this, the client began to engage in the dialogue:

Client: He could hurt himself.

Therapist: Tell [yourself in the opposite chair], tell her, scare her.

Client: Why are you not there with him?

Therapist: "Why are you not there with him." Say more to her about that.

Client: He might be dying on the floor and trying to reach the phone and suffering. Okay, it could be my [fault], I thought it could be my fault.

Therapist: Tell her: "It's your fault; if you were there [you could help him]." What would you tell her? What would happen if you had been there?

The therapist was trying to amplify the client's experience to evoke emotion. The client felt as if it would be her fault if her brother fell. This assumption of responsibility for the well-being of others or for preventing disasters is characteristic of many people with GAD. Shifting the load of responsibility to others for things that don't work out is an important change that ensues as clients become more compassionate and protective of themselves. The therapist encouraged the client to continue with the dialogue:

Client: If I had been there I could have called the doctor or called the emergency [number]. [I could have done] something for him.

Therapist: You could have helped him. You could have phoned, but you weren't there. Tell her "You weren't there."

The therapist tried to amplify the anxiety-producing voice to evoke experience in the self.

Client: You weren't there and you don't even have a passport to take a plane and go there.

Therapist: Yeah.

Client: So, it would have taken too long for you; you should have thought of that before.

Therapist: You should have thought of that before. You wouldn't be in this mess and he wouldn't be in pain on the floor if you had thought about this before. Can you tell her?

Client: Why don't you have a passport ready? You know your brother is on his own and you have problems but, on the other hand . . .

Therapist: On the other hand?

The therapist followed the client's shift:

Client: In my mind, I remember him saying [I] don't have to worry because [he has] his friends.

Therapist: Okay, come over [to this other chair]. This voice is saying to the other [worrier] voice "but, he told me not to worry." Tell her.

The therapist heard that the client was able to counter her sense of having to assume full responsibility for her brother's well-being. He suggested that the client move chairs to offer reassurance and to absolve the worrier self from responsibility.

Client: Don't worry because he told me he has his friends; somebody is going to go there at one point when he's not calling or they can't get in touch with him. Somebody is going to go there, even the person [who] looks after the building; he might go there.

Therapist: Yeah, so it's not [your] fault; he told [you] to not worry about it.

The therapist was supporting the client's emerging new voice of reassurance and self-soothing. The client became more self-protective and set limits on her responsibility. She recognized that others can play a role in looking out for her brother's well-being.

Client: I worry about him because I love him, but on the other hand how can I be [responsible for] a person that I [haven't seen] for so many years? His wife passed away, but I don't have control of that.

Therapist: How can you, it's destiny, "you can't blame me."

Client: No, you can't blame me and [in] the end I'm going to find out, somebody is going to call me, whatever happens. He might be in the hospital [and] if anything, I would just have to get a quick passport . . .

Therapist: So these are all the reasonable things right? But it's not really something [you] could have done.

Client: Yeah, but I should have been there. Why aren't you there?

Even though the client was able to recognize and express limits, the worrier voice that demanded and expected that she take care of others emerged once again. The therapist shifted back to the blaming, worry dialogue and continued to work with it in the chairs.

Therapist: I guess trying to help, why aren't you there? Can you come over [to the other chair] again?

Client:	It is guilt; I do feel guilty.
Therapist:	Tell her why she's wrong; tell her why she's bad, what should she be doing instead? "You should be there with your brother."
Client:	You should try to be there, but the problem as I see it right now is I have a problem. It's February and I have to deal with my taxes. I have a big mess in my taxes.
Therapist:	Come over [to this chair again].

Because opposition emerged, the therapist moved the client back to the self-chair. The client was defending herself and was focusing on the demands in her life.

Client:	I know he's more important than whatever. Unfortunately, it's a big mess that I have right now and I have to fix it.
Therapist:	Okay, so tell her.
Client:	Nobody else can do this. I have to do my taxes.
Therapist:	"I'm the only one who can do this." So you are saying, "What do you expect of me?" To [the worrier] voice you're saying, "What do you want me to do? I've got so much on my plate." It's like, what [are you] supposed to do? [You're] just buried.
Client:	Yeah, I'm buried.

The therapist offered an evocative reflection to amplify the client's experience. There was a sense of her being suffocated by her demands.

Client:	I'm buried and at this moment, I'm the only one that is always calling and no one helps me. I'm the responsible one.

As the client's experience of being burdened and alone began to emerge, the therapist focused her on her own organismic reaction.

Therapist:	You're on your own. What happens to you when you're on your own?
Client:	It feels like I have a lot of weight on my shoulders.
Therapist:	Tell her [in the other chair] about the weight, tell her what it feels like in your body, what's it like to carry this weight around.

The therapist asked the client to express and amplify her experience. This is important in clients with GAD, as they often silence their needs and feelings for others. Here the client expressed the full impact.

Client:	Well, it's depressing.
Therapist:	You feel depressed, alone?

The therapist conjectured about the client's feelings.

Client: Yes, I don't like being alone. My husband says I have to look for somebody to call, I'm always trying to find somebody to call and have a chat.

Therapist: Because [you're] so lonely and alone?

Client: Because my husband listens to me, but he's 64 years old and he has his [own] problems.

The client recognized that she can confide in her husband for support. However, she then went on to speak about not having the type of connection that she would like with him and that, although he is a good guy, he doesn't help her that much. As she spoke about this lack of connection, she observed that she was overtaken by anxiety at times.

Client: All of a sudden, I'm doing something and something comes to me. I don't know exactly what it is but it attacks my stomach, my mind and it's like I'm thinking: Look at the situation I'm in, my eyes are not good, and you know my husband needs a few things that have put us in trouble. I have to do my taxes; this is a big mess because I stopped working in September and then I had severance pay and I had to keep all those papers.

Once again the therapist encouraged the client to express her worries in a chair dialogue:

Therapist: Can you come over [to this chair]? All these things snow her in, lay them all on her. This is what you do right? This is your worry.

Client: And my husband has a problem with his hips; he has to retire.

Therapist: So all these things bury her; all these things come on like, "can you do it, can you just do it." Cover her up with all these things.

Client: How are you going to get an apartment? Are you going to get an apartment? Because you know the one that makes the most income is your husband, but he is the one that has bad credit, so how are we going to [get an apartment]. I'm thinking we're going to sleep in the park.

Therapist: So you're going to be homeless.

Client: Yeah, but I never thought [that] 4 years ago when I had my job, when my husband had his job, and everything went well. Everything was [fine] and then, I started thinking that there is a fine line [between] being homeless and [not being] homeless. It's a fine line.

Therapist: Tell her about this fine line; tell her how close she is. Scare her.

The client continued to worry and scare herself. Following her, the therapist tried to heighten her fears to make the client more aware of the process in which she engaged. However, the client was in the process of reorganizing and moved to reassuring herself about how she would cope with the prospect of becoming homeless.

Client: You know, I don't think you're going to be homeless because we do have a house that we are renting, but the rent is so high because of the bills that we have to pay. But for now, even if we have to travel, we are going to have it. But in the future if we don't find a place to live that is cheaper than the one that we already have we're going to have to leave and we are going to have to go back home, where the money that we make, is going to be worth more because we're going to be able to live with a thousand dollars.

At this point, an emotional reorganization took place and a possible solution emerged. The client sounded more confident, so her therapist shifted gears. Following the client's lead, the therapist asked her to change chairs so that she could reassure herself:

Therapist: Okay, so come back over [to the other chair]. This is you speaking; this is the [self] that is telling [you], "I'm doing what I can; I'm not going to be homeless."

Client: No, I don't think so.

Therapist: Tell her about that.

Client: Money is going to come in anyways from my husband's pensions, work pension and his old age and his government pension, which he split with me.

Therapist: Tell her.

Client: We are going to be okay.

Therapist: Tell her, tell her how you are going to be okay.

Client: We are going to be okay because if it's not one way, it's another; I'm sure that we will be able to get an apartment because not only is there my pension but between my old age and my pension from the bank, I'm going to have enough per month. Just because other things went wrong doesn't mean that we won't be able to get it.

Therapist: Tell her what it feels like when she snows you over with these worries; tell her what you need from her.

Here the therapist supports the client's awareness of the emerging new adaptive emotion of assertive anger:

Client: I'm annoyed—shut up.

Therapist: Tell her [to shut up].

Client: Don't tell me these things anymore because I know that we're going to be okay.

Therapist: [She's] not helping [you, she's] making it worse. Tell her about [how she's] making it worse.

Client: You are making it worse because your thoughts are coming back all the time and saying this and that and [I know] I am going to be able to afford it.

Therapist: So, it's like just shut up.

Client: Yeah, shut up [and] leave me alone.

Therapist: What do you feel now?

Client: I'm mad at you. I have money in the bank; I have enough money and my husband has enough money to help.

In these excerpts, we see that the process is nonlinear and often proceeds with one step forward as the client began to stand up to the critic, then one step backward as she engaged in catastrophizing, and then two steps forward as she finally was able to reassure herself, access assertive anger, and set limits and boundaries. However, she still needs to address the painful feelings underlying the worry.

Sometimes clients are reluctant to scare themselves or enact the worrying process in the session. In the following example, Maria, a 63-year-old woman who has suffered from anxiety for most of her life, was talking about her experience of anxiety during the week. She expressed reluctance to scare herself in the session. However, her therapist encouraged her to face her fear rather than trying to cope with it by distraction or avoidance. The segment began with Maria talking to the therapist about a friend's son who received treatment for cancer:

Client: [My friend] went through his chemo and everything. She says now he is okay, thank God, but I was thinking her son is the same age as my son and I [thought about] what I would do if that happened to me.

Therapist: So, you can't even imagine what would happen?

Client: No, and [my friend] is still working and everything.

The therapist heard a marker for a worry dialogue and suggested to Maria that they work with it in chairs.

Therapist: Can you come over [to this other chair]; let's try something? I want you to scare her. This is the voice inside of you that comes in—imagine it saying [your son] got sick and this [empty chair] over here [if the self] that feels your fear. Scare her, tell her what's going to happen. "He could get sick."

The therapist was trying to help activate the client's anxiety-producing voice:

Client: He could get sick.

Therapist: So scare her.

Client: And he would be alone because things happen. My son does not have anyone; I don't see that he has anybody.

Therapist: So your son is alone; he has no one. [You] don't see anyone coming along.

Client: Except for some friends. I don't see that he has anybody.

Therapist: So, he has no one and he may never have anybody, is that it?

Client: Yes!

Therapist: Tell her.

Client: Think of what can he do. Can he grab the phone and just call someone? I would like to be close to him.

Therapist: He could be so alone that no one would be there for him.

The therapist was trying to heighten the client's worry dialogue to get at her catastrophic self-talk so she could experience the full impact of it and how it made her feel.

Client: He would have to look for someone, a friend, or call a social worker or somebody, my daughter [maybe]. I told them, even though they don't talk too much to each other, you are brother and sister, so if anything happens to you, your sister is the first person that has to come.

In this excerpt, the client was continuing to speak about her concerns with her therapist and did not engage fully in the two-chair dialogue. So once again the therapist encouraged her to express her concerns to the other chair.

Therapist: So what do you think is going to happen to you? What do you say? Scare her with that. What is going to happen to him? Really bring it alive . . . I'm sure you have imagined it.

Client: Are you talking like if he gets cancer or something?

Therapist:	Is that what you imagine?
Client:	I do not imagine anything because it scares me. I just try to not to think about it. They are going to be happy all of their lives.
Therapist:	Yeah, but does that work?
Client:	No, it does not work but when I think about it I just try to think about something else.
Therapist:	Let's try to scare her, with the anxiety; this distracting doesn't work for you. So we have to try and chip away at it.

The therapist provided a rationale for the client. He observed that the avoidance did not help and that she still felt anxious. Although the client had engaged in two-chair dialogues previously, she was reluctant to deal with her anxiety about her son in this manner. The therapist took time to build an alliance and achieved agreement on the tasks and goals for therapy. He encouraged the client to engage in the dialogue to express and intensify the voice that catastrophizes. The client agreed and enacted how she frightens herself, then the therapist moved her to the other chair to access her experience of the worrier voice. To increase the client's access to her bodily experience, the therapist used reflections and focusing. It often takes more than one dialogue before clients can engage in each phase.

It is important to note that worry dialogues and other chair dialogues do not necessarily resolve in one session. Therapist and client may have to cycle back to address the client's catastrophic and negative self-talk as they work through the phases of resolution. In the following excerpt, taken from Maria's third worry dialogue, she spoke about the toll the worry took on her. Her therapist highlighted how exhausted she was by it.

Therapist:	It must take a lot of energy to constantly hear that voice. It must be tiring?
Client:	It is exhausting.
Therapist:	Like it will never end, you just feel so tired.
Client:	Yeah. It's just 24 hours a day.
Therapist:	Just experience it, inside, the way you feel as a result of that voice, "What if this might happen. This can happen. Do this. Don't do that." What happens inside? What does it feel like?
Client:	It's like a bee buzzing in my ear, always bothering me and I can't get away. And sometimes I feel like I'm just going to collapse or at least go on strike. Just stop!

The client began to be more aware of and express the physical toll the worry takes on her and her fear that she would collapse from sheer exhaustion. She spoke of how the exhaustion felt overwhelming and never ending. She said "stop," indicating a change in state as she tried to set a limit and assert herself. The therapist empathically tracked the client's experience working with her to differentiate it, as the client described her core fear of collapsing.

Client: It's trying to hold [everything] together so I can function.

Therapist: Yeah, I see. So it's like [you] feel like collapsing but [you] can't.

Client: Yeah.

Therapist: Because [you] have to cope, to manage everything.

Client: Yeah. And the constant [worrying].

Therapist: But it's just that extra pressure or something?

Client: Yeah. That's exactly it.

Therapist: And the feeling is like what you are saying, it's like pain. And something like exhaustion?

Client: Yeah. I just feel so shaky inside, like I don't have any ground to stand on, like a building that might collapse.

Therapist: So just so shaky, so insecure.

Client: Yeah, insecure . . . nobody, nothing to give me the support I need.

Therapist: [You feel] so alone and shaky.

Client: Just weak and tired.

Therapist: [You feel] just exhausted—tell her.

Client: I'm just exhausted.

Therapist: Tell her what you feel and what you need.

Expressing Needs

Once clients have experienced and expressed their core fear and symbolized it clearly, the therapist can promote transformation by asking for the need embedded in the emotion. This activates a resilient sense of agency in the personality, which begins to assert itself. Thus, an important step in EFT is to ask clients what they need after they have accessed core primary feelings. Here the client said she was utterly exhausted, so the therapist asked what she needed. The core primary emotion helped the therapist conjecture the client's need if it was difficult for the client to identify. The primary core feeling acted as a referent against which the conjecture or need can be checked for fit. The therapist conjectured what the client might need:

Client: [There is] tiredness and anger.

Therapist: Yeah, but anger almost like "give me break or something"? Or stop?

Client: Just leave me alone; let me be.

Therapist: Okay.

Client: Just be quiet.

Therapist: Okay. Be quiet.

Client: [I need you to] back off. I need some peace and quiet. [I need] a break.

Therapist: Yes? Tell her [to] back off.

Client: Back off give me a break. Be quiet.

Therapist: Yeah, be quiet. What do you feel as you say this?

The therapist asked the client to check inside. This is a very important step to determine whether what clients are saying is congruent with their experience. It lets clients and therapist access a new experience that is emerging in the moment, reflecting the process of changing emotion with emotion, as clients accesses anger and becomes more self-assertive.

Client: [I feel] kind of angry.

Therapist: Your anger is very important. Maybe put your feet on the ground, sit up, and take a breath. Tell her this again.

Client: Just be quiet. Stop buzzing in my head all the time. Leave me alone.

Therapist: [You] need [her] to stop.

The client expressed her needs clearly and assertively. The therapist asked her to move back to the chair with the [worrier] self to see how it would respond:

Therapist: Okay. Could you change [back to the other chair]? So now as a [worrier self], what's your response from inside?

Client: If I stop keeping on top of you, you'll get into trouble?

Therapist: Okay. So [you] can't stop. Yes? Tell her.

Client: I can't stop because if I stop who knows what would happen. I hold everything together for you and the family. What if your son doesn't take his medication? What if your daughter doesn't get a job?

Therapist: Okay.

Client: I make sure things are going okay. I make sure things go well enough.

Therapist: Okay, so [you are] keeping you on top of things.

Client: Be careful, anything can always happen so you have to be vigilant.

Therapist: Okay, but it's almost driven by fear that you could fall apart. Yes? If [you weren't] managing you, [what would happen]?

Client: I'd fall apart. Everything would fall apart.

Therapist: You and others would fall apart; the whole place [would fall apart]; the whole family would fall apart. Yes?

Client: Yes.

Therapist: Okay. So [you] can't give [yourself] a break. Yes? Tell her.

Client: I can't give you a break. I can't let you stop. I can't let you relax.

The client's worrying voice was clear. Some of her tension and need to be vigilant, could be experienced. As the therapist sense of these feelings were more heightened, he suggested the client change chairs.

Therapist: Can you change chairs? What happens on this side?

Client: Let me deal with my life. If you carry on like this I'm going to collapse.

Therapist: Okay.

Client: And I need for this to stop. Calm down!

Therapist: Tell her again. I need you to stop, calm down.

Client: I need you to calm down.

Therapist: What do you feel in your body now as you say this?

Client: Definitely, I need you to calm down. I'm mad at you for riding me like this all the time.

In this example, the therapist worked with the client to assert her needs. Once again the client accessed protective anger as she tried to stand up to the worry. This enabled her to reassert her need and ask that the worrier self trust her. We can see here that the worry was based on a set of affective–cognitive schemes, or a self-organization, that contained its own emotions and motivations. It was fundamentally afraid and attempted to protect the self. It is important to capture this feeling and motivation in the worrier chair. In this exchange, the client was able to access protective anger and requested the worrier self to back off. This type of resolution is more likely in clients whose GAD emanates from overprotective, intrusive others. In these cases, a boundary must be established so that clients can develop a sense of trust and competence in their own abilities and capacities. However, in other attachment injuries the expression of anger or the request to stop can be experienced as silencing and can create intense distress in the worrier chair.

Partial Resolution

At the end of the dialogue, the client stood up to her worrier self. This represented partial resolution of the worry dialogue; it is important to realize that this two-chair dialogue involved working on the symptom and that more work is needed, both for this change to take hold and to get at the underlying determinants of the anxious worrying, which comes from a core insecure sense of self and an inability to self-soothe. In the last turn in the worry chair, the client said: "Be careful, anything can always happen so you have to be vigilant [otherwise] I'd fall apart. Everything would fall apart." This points to the client's underlying feeling of basic insecurity and the deep sense of responsibility she assumes for the safety of others.

The worrier self is driven by an underlying fear for the safety and security of the self and others. It is this core pain that needs to be worked on as the next step in the therapy. It is important for the self that feels exhausted to stand up to the driving worrier self; however, it is also important to be able to soothe and reassure the worrier self. In the absence of soothing, the worrier self, especially in cases where clients have been neglected and abused, can dissolve into an early self-state that expresses sadness and pain that it is not being attended to and has never been adequately protected and nurtured. In this case, anger was experienced as rejection and dismissal of the worrier self's fears and concerns. When this happens, it is important to name the process of self-silencing and the dismissal of painful feelings, and to begin to work on clients' negative self-treatment to develop self-empathy, self-compassion, and self-soothing. These processes are discussed in Chapters 5, 7, and 9 of this volume.

In the next example, the client had some capacity for self-empathy and self-soothing and was able to consider alternative ways of being. Here the client was responding from the chair as the worrier self. She was able to see that it would be better not to worry, but she observed that she does not know how to stop herself. After the client asked the worrier self to stop, the therapist had her move to the other chair and respond as the worrier self:

> *Therapist:* Okay, could you come back here to the [other chair with the worrier self]? Your self [in the other chair] is saying, "I need

you to stop frightening me," right? This harms [you] and [your] life. [You] need [the worrier self] to stop this. What is your response from inside? Can you see the pain that comes with being frightened? What do you say to [your other self]?

Client: Yes. That's what I want.

Therapist: Okay, so [you] would be willing.

Client: I would be willing. It is just this fear that makes me behave as I do. But I can't relax really.

Therapist: Tell her [you] cannot let [her].

Client: I can't. I can't let you relax.

Therapist: Yes, tell her [you] won't let [her] relax.

Here the therapist heightened the client's agency. The client said she was unable, and the therapist suggested that the client did not want to. The client recognized her agency in her next response. We see her reorganize herself as she declined to express the therapist's statement and instead said the following:

Client: No, I'm not going to say that.

Therapist: Okay.

Client: I will try and give you a break.

Therapist: Yeah, instead of overwhelming [her].

Client: I will try to help you . . . me, if you took some risks doing some things in spite of me. But I'm always here to catch you. The safety net is always ready. I think that would help me, then I would become a bit more relaxed.

Therapist: Yes, because the other self is saying, "I'm a very responsible person even without you."

Client: Yeah.

Here the worrier self was able to acknowledge the pain that was caused by the worrying. The worrier self was willing to try to change and encouraged the other self to act in spite of the client's fears, knowing that she would be there to catch herself. The worrier self recognized, with the therapist's help, that the other self was responsible and would take care without continually being monitored by the worrier self. This worrier self was like an overprotective other that was restricting the client's agency and self-identity. We see the fear that drove the worrier self as well as its vulnerability and uncertainty, which needed support from the other self to relax. Building the capacity to be supportive of the worrier self and self-soothe is an important step in reducing anxiety.

Accessing Compassionate Self-Soothing

As discussed in Chapter 5, the capacity for self-soothing is an ongoing process throughout the therapy. Additional ways to facilitate and build the capacity to self-soothe are described in Chapter 9. In the following example, the client consolidated her position of greater confidence in the self-chair. She was able to soothe the worrier self by saying that she was to be trusted:

Client: Trust me, I'm going to find a way. I'm going to be able to handle it.

Therapist: [You're capable]. [You're] able. So this side [of yourself] is saying you know, "just trust me. I can handle this; I have some control now and I'm going to make it okay for us. I'll protect us."

Client: I will take it a day at a time, because I notice that worrying about the future has no meaning whatsoever.

Therapist: Yes, it doesn't help us at all.

Client: It doesn't help us at all.

Therapist: It actually makes it worse, and it makes you worse.

Client: Yes, like when you think in the future because you don't know what's going to happen, you tend to exaggerate to make it bigger.

Once the worrier self softened and was able to perceive its impact and be reassured by the other self, the client relaxed. The therapist invited the client back to the chair with the other self to check for the impact of receiving the compassionate softening. In this example, the worrier self was able to respond with compassion to the other self and acknowledged that the worrying was having a deleterious and negative effect on the client. However, at other times the worrier self needed to have its pain acknowledged and recognized. This is often linked with the self that has developed in circumstances of neglect and abuse with very little, if any, support. In addition, the self had tended to ignore pain and weakness in an attempt to remain strong and cope with life crises and painful events. In these cases, the therapist can assist the process by responding with compassion and validating the worrier self's pain, which is rooted in painful childhood experiences of neglect. With the recognition that the pain must be recognized and addressed, the stage is set to move to empty-chair work with significant attachment figures and to an exploration of how the core insecurity developed. This process is explored in Chapter 8.

WORKING AT THE GROWTH EDGE TO FACILITATE CHANGE

The overall focus when working to evoke adaptive emotion, as an antidote to helplessness or another maladaptive state, is to work at the client's growth edge. The therapist's responses need to be within the client's grasp or on the edges of his or her awareness. For example, if someone who is experiencing helplessness or exhaustion says in a shaky a manner that they can manage or shows a flicker of strength, the therapist can support this by reflecting it. Responding at clients' growth edges means being neither too far ahead nor too far behind clients but at the same level. The therapist's responses need to be sufficiently close to where clients are experientially, so as to provide stepping-stones for them to move out of their exhaustion or helplessness. If the therapist is two steps ahead, this can be impeding. Thus to encourage a client to assert that "I can cope" after she or he just said, "I feel so weak and shaky" would be too far ahead. However, a therapist saying to a client, "You're just feeling so fragile, so afraid" when the client has said, "I feel a little stronger" would be too far behind. The therapist needs to be alert to when a growth edge has begun to emerge or to when clients' experience has shifted and new and important ways of experiencing have emerged that suggest that a developmental shift to a more resilient level of organization is possible. The therapist, however, must also be aware that clients may be cautious about moving to a new level of organization out of fear of the unknown. In these cases, the therapist must provide sufficient support to their clients in their current state and be careful to communicate understanding of the fear of novelty and change, and at the same time, encourage the elaboration and expression of the more resilient growth edge.

FRAMING THE ATTACHMENT WOUND

In a subsequent session, when Maria and her therapist were working on another worry dialogue, the client began to focus her attachment wound: her feeling of sadness and lonely abandonment in childhood. This was triggered previously when the client began to think of how disconnected she was from her husband. However, it was not clearly articulated earlier. Now the client was able to name this pain and she and the therapist began to focus on it.

Therapist: So how are you doing?

Client: Okay. I remember what you told me to work on my feelings, being aware of them, and I tried. Still there are some times that I got busy or I did something else, but in the couple of times that I was able to get into this thing, I noticed something. It doesn't come on by itself. I call it. I noticed because, I was quietly sitting, I was just about to read the newspaper or something, and I thought about my son or my daughter or something, and I brought it on.

This indicated the client's new awareness of how the anxiety starts. She recognized her agency in the process.

Therapist: So, [you're] creating this worry in some way?

Client: I'm bringing it on with the problems that I have.

Therapist: So, somehow "I create this—I have the power over it?"

Client: [Power over] bringing it on, yeah. I was surprised because I thought this will come on its own, but no. Then I grab that and I said okay so I'm thinking about my son. So what is it what is the worst that can happen?

Therapist: So you were thinking about your son and then you were aware of [something]?

Client: [I was aware] of this feeling.

Therapist: We've established a very clear link between worrying about your kids and this place, so that's a little new. Go ahead.

Client: Yes, that's new. It is new! Because I always thought, this is just something that happens. But then I realize that [it's not, it's something that is] with me.

Therapist: Then what was the feeling like when it [happened]?

Client: It's like an empty thing, an empty pain. It's like a sadness.

Here the client accessed her core painful feelings of sadness and emptiness, the source of her fear.

Therapist: Yes, this emptiness.

Client: But I didn't run away from it.

The client approached and accepted her feelings. The therapist continued to explore them with her.

Therapist: That's great. What did that feel like?

Client: I always look for something: I make myself a cup of tea, I turn on the T.V., I talk to my husband, I read the newspaper, I talk to my neighbor, I do something.

The client previously tried to distract herself and ignore and suppress the painful feelings of sadness and fear instead of attending to them. This time, with the therapist's support and encouragement, she was able to confront those feelings and reflect on them to come up with some solutions. As a result, she felt more competent.

Therapist:	What was it like not to run from it?
Client:	I felt in control. So I started thinking okay, so to get rid of this, I have to think about it. I had to, like you said, grab the bull by the horns.
Therapist:	So what [did] this mean for you?
Client:	It was just like this thing is not just happening. It's not just coming. It's produced by me.
Therapist:	"[It's produced] by me."
Client:	And it's as I experience [in] my esophagus, my stomach, something.
Therapist:	This uneasiness is up to you, but it's almost like what can you do for yourself to make yourself feel better as opposed to just waiting for someone else to do something so you can feel better?
Client:	It seems like it's been a while that we've been talking and it's been a while that I've been thinking about these things and the other day I just thought, because you told me to confront this, I'm just going to try to see what is the problem I have in terms of that time. And I feel the hole; I can I can the sorrow and emptiness that I felt with my mother.

The client accepted and acknowledged a previously disallowed feeling. This is a marker for unfinished business work. It is an indicator of unprocessed feelings that require attention. Although the therapist would not necessarily shift to empty-chair work at this point in the session, it will be important to address in later sessions. Instead, the therapist conjectured what the sadness was about and began to frame the unfinished business task. The therapist focused the client on her sadness to try to help her understand it better.

Therapist:	Can you speak from that place?
Client:	The sadness is because of the situation.
Therapist:	Yes, it's sad.
Client:	I was so alone and afraid with my mother, [who was] always sick in bed, and [I was] alone in the house.

Here the client accessed her primary maladaptive emotion scheme. She recalled the fear associated with her mother being ill and her being alone as a child trying to cope. Clients with GAD often develop a sense of vulnerability and helplessness in response to not being able to cope or a fear of consequences that would be threatening and overwhelming.

DEVELOPING A MORE RESILIENT SELF-ORGANIZATION

The first sign of resolution of all types of anxiety splits, whether or not they involve worry and helplessness, is the emergence of new experiencing during the deepening phase of the work (Elliott et al., 2004; Greenberg, 1984; Greenberg & Watson, 2006). At this point, it is very important that the therapist empathically affirm clients' emerging new experience. This is the beginning of the emergence of a more resilient self-organization. When clients have worked through their helplessness or weakness to reach a more core adaptive emotion, they generally feel sadness, pain, and sometimes anger. With every primary emotion is an associated need (Greenberg, 2002, 2011). Needs are associated with action tendencies and direct clients toward meeting needs and attaining goals that are highly relevant to their well-being. Although it is essential to recognize and affirm clients' underlying feelings, the therapist must listen for associated needs and direct clients to express these in an assertive manner to the worrier self and the self that catastrophizes. Adaptive needs are at the core of the resilient self's tendency to survive and thrive. At times, the therapist can encourage clients to express a statement of need, aiming to heighten clients' experience and encourage a shift in their self-organizations thereby helping to empower them. This heightening or assertion of a need strengthens the self and promotes change.

The accessing of underlying needs—for example, for support, comfort, recognition, respect—while in part affirming and relieving, often requires a working through of the pain of not having had these needs met in the past. Resolving these old attachment wounds often requires clients to grieve for what was lost and not received in the past before they can begin to look for ways of meeting their needs in the future. Accessing needs in the present, however, opens pathways in the brain to new emotional states and to alternative ways of attaining those states of being (Davidson, 2000a, 2000b). Thus, accessing needs based in core primary feelings is a crucial step in mobilizing resilience and support for the self.

SOFTENING INTO THE FEAR AND SADNESS

Anxiety splits can partially resolve with a statement by the worrying self about its underlying fear, sadness, or anger. This is a plea to the self to acknowledge the underlying pain of being damaged, wounded, and hurt, or of having been intruded on. If these painful emotions are recognized and the worrier self is validated, then clients can move to a state of greater resilience and become more aware and acknowledge the impact of their worrying. The worrier self no longer expresses its needs as worry and catastrophizing to frighten the self, but instead, it expresses them in a congruent statement of an underlying fear and vulnerability that often stems from past trauma and/or childhood attachment wounds. In contrast, worry dialogues that are the result of intrusive others, who have undermined the client's capacity to cope, can often resolve with the expression of assertive anger as clients define a boundary between the self and others, and sets limits on others' behavior.

DIFFICULTIES WORKING WITH THE WORRY DIALOGUE

The worry dialogue brings anxiety alive in the session, and some clients may panic or become overwhelmed by it. At these times, the therapist needs to be prepared to help clients distance or soothe themselves if the anxiety becomes too intense. To do this, the therapist can encourage clients to regulate their breathing and label their physical sensations as they attend to their awareness of the room and look at the therapist. Working with the anxiety process does not have to be done using a two-chair task, if clients find this difficult or challenging. It can be done without enactment using questions and reflections of feelings. In this case, the therapist keeps track of the different parts of the self and works with them one at a time in sequence. The use of enactment using two-chairs, however, enlivens the experience and helps to accentuate and clarify the process with the added advantage of making the nonverbal aspects of the inner dialogue more accessible and visible.

Transforming Blame and Defensiveness

In EFT, the therapist encourage clients with GAD to evoke their worry and sense of helplessness in the session so that they can work through it to generate new responses as an antidote to the feelings of helplessness and worry. An essential element of working in an emotion-focused way is that the therapist does not encourage clients to dispute their anxiety. It is not productive for clients to engage in a blame/defend game. Thus, it is important to avoid letting clients get stuck in a dialogue about the truth or the rationality of the catastrophic worry. Rather, the goal is to see the dialogue as one related to revealing how feelings are produced and to evoking feelings to make them amenable to change.

Rather than responding to the worried, catastrophic content, clients are encouraged to become aware of the emotional impact of the worrier self. The therapist might ask, "What does it feel like to be told that you are responsible to make sure it is safe or that disaster is around the corner if you are not on guard. What happens inside as you hear those words?" Clients are encouraged to speak from the bodily felt experience of anxiety or helplessness, to experience the impact of the worrier self rather than to agree or disagree with the validity of the catastrophic thoughts.

The therapist can help clients access their bodily felt sense by empathically observing nonverbal and paralinguistic indicators of clients' current state of anxiety. The therapist might say, "I see that you're shaking/slumping in your chair/your voice has become thin. Are you feeling scared? What's the shaking/slumping/thin voice saying?" Another possibility to help evoke clients' feelings, as discussed in Chapter 4, is for the therapist to offer empathic conjectures that "feel into" clients' experiential states of helplessness. Often clients may be only dimly aware of these. For example, a therapist might say, "I guess this awful feeling of helplessness comes up?" Or the therapist might capture the feeling of anxiety with a reflective question by asking, "What is it like to have to be on guard all the time?"

Working With the Collapsed Self in the Worry Dialogue

When a client's voice in the chair with the experiencing self collapses, seems to fall into helplessness, and is unable to offer an alternative state to the worrier self, this can be difficult for client and therapist. Accepting and staying with the anxious helpless sense of self is often the most difficult part of this work. First, clients' tendency is to avoid or escape the awful feeling. Next, the therapist may have a similar tendency to try to "help" or change clients and find quick solutions. However, rather than trying to modify a client's behavior, the therapist is encouraged to try to accept his or her feelings. The therapist needs to promote staying with the present experience of anxious helplessness and following the process. The therapist's goal is to provide a safe, accepting environment, validate the client's experience, and turn the client's attention inward to the experience of vulnerability and helplessness. This helps clients to differentiate their vulnerability and helplessness. These then develop into more core primary feelings of fear, sadness, and basic insecurity.

Helping people face their vulnerability and helplessness is often key in dealing with anxiety, so clients can accept the pain they have been avoiding. To differentiate and elaborate overwhelming helplessness and get some perspective on it, the therapist might focus on the bodily-sensorimotor aspects of the feeling or empathically reflect the meaning of the helplessness and inquire into what it is about. They can also ask clients to identify what the worst part is. The therapist may teach clients the purpose of "staying with helplessness."

He or she can explain that feelings of vulnerability and helplessness lead to anxiety. He or she can point out that the vulnerability and helplessness often are reactions to more primary feelings, such as basic fear of abandonment, sadness, and anger, that have been obscured or blocked and that are important to discover, express, and resolve. These obscured and unresolved feelings need to be expressed in order to identify primary needs and develop an antidote to the anxiety and a changed view of the self and their problems. Once clients' negative ways of coping have been identified, the therapist can suggest working with them in two-chair dialogues again. The goal is to access the denied and ignored emotional responses that underlie the sense of worry and anxiety.

Another way of dealing with collapse or defeat in the chair dialogue, when resilience does not emerge and clients seem stuck, is to try to heighten the worry. The therapist can encourage the worrier self to intensify its catastrophizing and scaring behavior and actions so that the response can be evoked in the experiencing self. The therapist also can use vocal tone to amplify the worrying messages in an attempt to evoke feelings in clients. This is an attempt to heighten the impact of the worrier self to try to make clients more aware of what they are doing and to access their organismic responses. When the worrier self is very distressed, it can be useful to help clients become more aware of the catastrophic feelings of fear as it worries about negative outcomes.

If the dialogues are to resolve, clients must have the capacity to empathize with and recognize their pain. Empathic conjectures, evocative language that highlights the most poignant aspects of clients' experience and focuses on the person's bodily felt sense, can help to access the underlying core pain. Empathic affirmation of core feelings (i.e., sadness, anger, fear, shame) and an internal focus on feelings and needs invariably lead to the emergence of more proactive, healthy aspects of the self. As clients learn to better process and regulate their affective states and internalize their therapist's acceptance and empathy, they begin to develop self-empathy and self-acceptance and be guided by their primary emotions to promote survival and well-being. This is a painful process through which clients struggle with hope and courage to find their own healthy, nurturing voice.

After a client has expressed her painful emotions of sadness, fear, and shame and is able to be empathic and compassionate toward herself, then therapist and client can shift the focus to the client's underlying vulnerability and attachment injuries to deal with the sources of her pain. These are the markers for empty-chair work. However, if the worrier self is unable to respond with empathy and compassion to the chair with the experiencing self, stating that it has been neglected, ignored, and dismissed, then this is a marker for more relational work to strengthen the self and build self-compassion and self-acceptance (see Chapters 4 and 5), as well as more focused work on negative self-treatment (see Chapter 7). The therapeutic work continues along these two parallel tracks: working to resolve the repeated and chronic attachment injuries that are the source of the pain, as well as the negative ways that people have learned to regulate and process their emotions.

Regardless of which marker appears first, the marker for empty-chair work or the marker for two-chair work, the path to resolution of GAD needs to move to a focus on clients' underlying painful emotions of sadness, fear, anger, and basic insecurity and the circumstances in which these developed to access the adaptive sadness of grief, protective and empowering anger, and self-compassion to transform the maladaptive emotions and their action tendencies. The resolution of worry dialogues points to unfinished business and negative treatment of the self, which are discussed in the following chapters.

7

CHANGING NEGATIVE TREATMENT OF THE SELF: TWO-CHAIR DIALOGUES

An important process underlying generalized anxiety disorder (GAD) is that of changing clients' negative ways of relating to themselves and their experience, which have developed as a means to cope with and adapt to threatening and painful life experiences. To survive and cope in negative environments, people may learn to deny, avoid, or suppress their feelings and perceptions if they seem too threatening and overwhelming or are dismissed and rejected by others. This learning may occur, for example, if caretakers or others distort or deny the reality of children's experiences. Alternatively, it may develop as a way of coping with rejection, neglect, and insufficient interpersonal or physical support.

To address the negative ways that clients relate to themselves, the emotion-focused therapy (EFT) therapist suggests two-chair dialogues (Elliott, Watson, Goldman, & Greenberg, 2004; Greenberg, Rice, & Elliott, 1993). These dialogues are between different aspects of the self. They have been used to resolve conflict splits, self-criticism, and other negative ways of relating to

http://dx.doi.org/10.1037/0000018-008
Emotion-Focused Therapy for Generalized Anxiety, by J. C. Watson and L. S. Greenberg

clients' experience (J. Watson, 2011; J. Watson, Goldman, & Greenberg, 2007). The objective with two-chair dialogues is to highlight the negative self-statements and behaviors so that clients are more aware of them. Once these negative behaviors are more visible, the therapist can support clients as they experience the impact of these behaviors. It is through experiencing the impact fully and acknowledging the pain caused by these negative ways of relating to the self that clients are able to identify their needs for support and compassion, express these needs, and develop more positive ways of relating to their experience. In terms of GAD, this means that clients need to stop silencing, denying, or ignoring their experience and learn to attend to it so they can soothe and protect themselves.

Without adequate ways of self-soothing, people may suppress and ignore pain in an attempt to overcome and survive at any cost. In the previous chapter, we showed how working through clients' worry dialogues leads to the painful emotions and situations that underlie their anxiety, as well as the negative ways of relating to the self that have developed to cope with the pain, which contribute to the maintenance of their anxiety. In this chapter, we describe how to work with the negative ways of treating experience, such as self-interruption, oppressive control, self-criticism, and self-blame.

In threatening situations (e.g., intense conflict between parents; witnessing or receiving abuse, rejection, or neglect; absence of parental warmth and concern), it can be difficult to process experience adequately. Anxiety inhibits adequate processing of information as well as emotional processing (Staal, 2004). When people feel afraid and at risk, emotions can be interrupted and shut down, they can be distorted in such a way that people feel they are to blame, or actions and events may not be accurately named and acknowledged. These experiences can lead to a variety of ways of relating to the self, such as self-blame, self-silencing, and self-neglect in the form of a disavowal of what is occurring and a suppression of the attendant emotional experience and feelings.

Some of the negative ways that people may relate to themselves are illustrated in the following case example. Jennifer was the youngest child of older parents. Her father was resentful that she had been born, as he had wished to pursue an alternative lifestyle. Her mother was beaten down and wistful, filled with regret for lost dreams of life on a grander scale. Her mother felt stifled and overpowered in her marriage and sought comfort from her daughters to boost her sense of self and achievement. When Jennifer was born, her two older siblings were 10 and 12 years old, entering adolescence and moving away from the family circle. Jennifer described her father as angry and sadistic, given to ridiculing the children, especially Jennifer. He seemed to delight in making his children feel powerless as he threatened to strike them and growled orders demanding obedience. Jennifer's siblings, taking a cue from their father, would often gang up and bully her. They would tease Jennifer, making her feel very small and weak. As the youngest, Jennifer grew up with a strong sense of being unwanted and a burden to her parents. She felt rejected and viewed herself as disposable. She would have nightmares of being suffocated or drowned. She worried that if she ever needed intensive care or became disabled, her father would dispose of her as he did the animals he hunted.

When Jennifer came to therapy she was in a constant state of underlying anxiety and fear. She worried about her health as well as her ability to earn money. Although successful at her career, she did not feel satisfied and saw her life as blighted. The therapist began to work with her anxiety, starting with a worry dialogue. As Jennifer worked through the worry dialogue, the pain of being rejected and her strategy of shutting out feelings of pain and vulnerability became clear. She rejected her vulnerability and sadness as signs of weakness. Initially, it was difficult for Jennifer to accept that she played a role in how she treated herself. She attributed her pain and unhappiness to her parents and siblings and blamed them for her "blighted" existence.

At first, the therapist focused on developing a better understanding of Jennifer's childhood experiences and representing them in awareness more fully and completely. Another important focus during this phase of therapy was for the therapist to provide empathy and acceptance so that Jennifer could begin to build more positive ways of treating her experience.

During this phase, Jennifer began to work in empty-chair dialogues to address the pain of how she had been treated by her siblings and parents. This work of dealing with her deep sadness and shame as a result of their abuse and apparent lack of care and support took time, as she began to see things more clearly and acknowledge the impact of their behavior. However, Jennifer realized that she was unable to assert herself in the empty-chair dialogues or even acknowledge to herself and her therapist that she deserved better. It became clear to her that she was self-rejecting and that she numbed herself to keep from feeling the pain fully. She blamed herself for her parents' treatment, and saw herself as unlovable. Observing her difficulties in asserting herself with her parents, Jennifer realized that she needed to address her relationship with herself and the negative ways in which she thought about herself and treated her own experience.

TWO-CHAIR DIALOGUES FOR NEGATIVE
TREATMENT OF THE SELF

Before Jennifer could resolve the pain with her parents and siblings, she decided to work on her relationship with herself. She saw this as key to feeling better about herself, which was one of her goals in coming to therapy. Jennifer began to engage in two-chair dialogues and two-chair enactments to become more aware of how she negated her feelings and was blaming and contemptuous of herself, interrupted her feelings, and silenced herself. In two-chair dialogues, the negative ways people treat themselves and their experience are identified, differentiated, and expressed, including rejecting, denigrating, or neglecting behaviors and messages. In two-chair enactments, people engage in actions to interrupt their own feeling, such as constricting, suppressing, or blanking out.

Markers of Negative Treatment of the Self

As she engaged in the chair work, it became clear to the therapist and Jennifer that any sensation of pain that she experienced was a sign of weakness that was scorned and repudiated. She also tightened up and numbed herself. Consequently, when feelings of sadness and vulnerability were evoked in chair work or when she described her childhood memories, she would immediately interrupt the experience by becoming very intellectual and blanking out. Jennifer actively rejected herself and her experience. Initially, she could not tolerate experiencing or seeing herself as weak and powerless. At these times she would shut down any feelings and revert to a more intellectual engagement with her experience and her therapist. It was easier for Jennifer to access anger, frustration, and complaint than sadness and vulnerability. It was clear that her negative ways of treating herself, including silencing, blaming, and interrupting her experience, were deeply rooted and that she needed to develop more positive ways of treating herself and attending to her pain. Her therapist continued to work with empathic, accepting reflections to promote Jennifer's internalization of more positive ways of treating her experience.

To protect herself in her family, Jennifer had actively tried to hide any feelings of pain. She felt that expressing emotion or showing pain when she was bullied and threatened would give the perpetrator satisfaction. She also learned early on that any sign of weakness or emotion was reviled and ridiculed. So she tried to be strong and in control at all times. Clearly, Jennifer had internalized her family's values toward her. She negated and neglected her own pain, refusing to acknowledge or even admit any hurt. When painful feelings were evoked in the session, she would become numb and distracted and move to an intellectual stance of analyzing, describing, and blaming her parents. She felt strong when expressing anger, so she was able to move to that position quickly and away from any feelings that left her feeling weak, powerless, and small.

Clients with GAD are not aware that they are interrupting, silencing, dismissing, or denying their emotions and experience. Therefore, the first step for the therapist is to explore how they are treating themselves. This increases their awareness of how they are relating to their experience and provides them with an opportunity to see the negative impact or implications of engaging with their emotional experience in these ways. Awareness of how they block themselves and what they are preventing themselves from doing and feeling begins to build as they experience that they are unable to assert themselves with others from their past who caused them harm and distress, or unable to achieve certain objectives in their career, or relate satisfactorily to others in the present.

These ways of behaving become evident in two-chair work as well as through comments clients make about their experience. For example, emotions may be denied or dismissed in two-chair work, or clients may dismiss their feelings and refuse to engage with them in the session. At these times, the therapist is able to observe and comment on how clients interrupt the flow of their experience. At other times, clients may collapse in empty-chair work when talking to an imagined other, or they may drift away, change the subject, revert to blaming themselves, or complain about others. These are markers to the therapist to shift focus in the session and suggest to clients that they engage in two-chair work to address their negative ways of relating to their experience (e.g., when they disparage and interrupt it).

Expressing and Enacting Negative Treatment of the Self

With the client's agreement, the therapist can suggest that they work together on the blocks and interruptions to their experience to explore how clients are treating themselves and their emotions. At first, Jennifer did not see how she was treating her own experience. She felt that it was her parents and family who were to blame and wished she could transform her childhood. Slowly, as she and her therapist worked together to process her feelings, she began to see how she was interrupting her experience and saw that this was something that she was doing to herself when she felt distress to avoid painful feelings of helplessness, fear, and sadness at being rejected and bullied. She became more aware that she drifted away when she began to feel sad. Jennifer stifled her own growth tendency by curtailing and restricting her feelings as she tried to adapt to her negative home environment. She would worry about her behavior and her safety. Her "wounded child" would demand that she take care to protect herself from harm. The therapist began to work with Jennifer on how she shut down her emotions and made herself feel bad about exploring alternative career options. She negated her experience by telling herself she was going to be homeless and a pauper and that she should stop dreaming about more rewarding work. This is illustrated in the following excerpt.

> *Client:* Stop dreaming; that's useless. Nobody cares about your ideas. Shape up; get serious. You need to earn money and take care of me.

| Therapist: | So, this side is dismissing you and telling you to shape up? Come over here to the [other] chair. [Now], tell her what it feels like when she says, "Stop dreaming and shape up!" |
| Client: | She's right. Dreams won't get me anywhere. I have to keep doing what I'm doing. |

Working With the Collapsed Self

Here there is an impasse: The dialogue has been stifled and only one perspective dominates. This is referred to as a *collapsed self*. It is an indication that the therapist needs to work on separating the two sides more so that the client can become more aware of how she relates to herself and can begin to experience herself as an agent who does this to herself. This will enable her to acknowledge and experience the impact of the negative treatment of herself and provide her with the information to identify her needs.

When clients are unable to be aware of and express their emotions in the face of negative self-treatment, it may be an indication that the therapist needs to spend more time attending to the relational tasks, providing empathy, acceptance, understanding, and positive regard for the clients' experiences and working with them to elaborate and symbolize the experiences in awareness. This work supports clients as they acquire the skills to process their emotions and build a stronger sense of self as well as more positive ways of relating to their feelings and experiences. As was discussed in Chapter 4, the provision of a supportive, empathically attuned, accepting, and sincere other facilitates the internalization of new and more positive behaviors and ways of treating the self and the emotional experience. Receiving acceptance, validation, attentive listening, and empathic attunement from their therapist, clients develop the capacity to listen to and acknowledge their feelings and begin to symbolize them in awareness and use them as a guide to their needs and behaviors.

Expressing Feelings and Needs

As clients are better able to tolerate and attend to their own feelings and needs, and as they feel stronger and better able to confront their pain, it is possible to return to two-chair dialogues and enactments so that clients can express the impact of being treated badly or having their experiences distorted, shunned, or neglected and request that they be treated better.

In the case of Jennifer, she was able to say that it felt suffocating to silence herself and not express her feelings. However, the part of her that was scared of expressing her feelings was unable to listen. She had developed a rule to keep herself safe that required that she not feel or express her feelings to others. Her mother had dismissed her as a nuisance when Jennifer expressed feelings of need and distress. Given her own burdens and disappointments, she needed Jennifer to be happy and content and not demand too much. Jennifer stifled her needs and tried to do as her mother wished so as to receive care and protection from her siblings.

Client:	You need to continue working. How else will we survive? Stop dreaming!
Therapist:	Come back over [to this other chair]. What do you say to her when she says that you *must* continue working and that she does not want to hear about you taking time for you?
Client:	It feels hard, like she won't listen to me. It reminds me of my mother; it was always on her terms.
Therapist:	Can you tell her what is hard about it?
Client:	I am tired; I can't keep doing this. I am so unhappy. I hate it! It's suffocating, joyless.
Therapist:	Yes. Tell her how unhappy you are.
Client:	I hate you pushing and controlling me.
Therapist:	Okay, come back over [the first chair]. How does this self respond? Jennifer says she hates it, that you are pushing her. It makes her very unhappy. It takes the joy away.
Client:	I don't care. You need to look after me. Nobody ever cares for me. I am hurting too and you don't care. Nobody has cared about me. You must look after me!

Expressing Core Pain

The worrier self, or anxious critic, is unable to respond empathically to the self that is tired and unhappy. Instead, lacking positive ways of treating the self as well as self-compassion and empathy, the worrier self dissolves into an early developmental self-state of painful vulnerability and neglect. The client's vulnerability could be seen in both chairs. The worrier self accused the other self of not attending and taking care of her. When asked to stop worrying, the worrier self refused, feeling like she was once again being neglected and instead demanded attention. The client in the experiencing chair felt so beaten down and exhausted that she was not able to respond to this anxious critic. Instead, she responded by saying that she is unable to care for her worrier self, as there was no one to care for her either. She also expressed some disgust at the whining, needy worrier. This is a marker for a second underlying split that indicates negative self-treatment, with the client unable to accept or respond to any sign of weakness. Instead, she was self-rejecting, demanding that she be strong and stoical and not give in to or express pain. This is a sign that the therapist needs to continue to work with the client to build self-empathy and self-compassion so that the client can learn to soothe the pain and find alternative ways of responding to it.

> *Therapist:* So, this [self] is in pain too? It does not feel like there was anybody there looking after her?
>
> *Client:* Nobody cared about me; why should I care about her? She is supposed to look after me!

An anxious, worrier self developed at a very young stage in this client. It is the part of the self that developed to adapt to being scorned and neglected as a young child. The pain was so intense that she could not take account of the experiencing self's request to stop pushing her to make money instead of trying to find a more satisfying career.

> *Therapist:* What do you need from her? Tell her.
>
> *Client:* You have to take care of me!
>
> *Therapist:* Okay, come back over [the chair with the worrier self]. What happens when you hear that [self] say she is in pain and needs you to look after her?
>
> *Client:* I am in pain too. I cannot take care of her. I am needy too. Someone else needs to look after us.
>
> *Therapist:* You look disgusted as you say that.
>
> *Client:* Well, she is weak and repulsive. You have to be strong. My father despised weakness. He would ridicule people at work for being weak and spineless. It is totally unacceptable.

Building Self-Compassion and Self-Care

Jennifer did not have the inner resources or capacity to attend to her pain. She preferred to turn away and repudiate it. She and the therapist began to do more relational work and continue with the two-chair dialogues around her negative self-treatment. It took a few more sessions before she was able to be more compassionate toward herself and allow herself to feel her sadness and express her pain. The beginning of a shift can be seen in the following excerpt:

> *Client:* There is so much pain over here and there was nobody to soothe me or care for me.
>
> *Therapist:* So it just feels so painful over here?
>
> *Client:* Yes. I need someone to take care of me. I did not receive any love.

Therapist:	Okay, come over [to the experiencing chair]. What happens over here when she says she is in such pain and that nobody took care of her?
Client:	I know, I can see her pain, but I don't have the resources. I don't know how to take care of her. Nobody showed me how. Somebody else needs to look after us. I need support as well.
Therapist:	So both sides just feel needy—they both need support?
Client:	Yes, anyway I don't want to see her weak and needy.

At this point, the therapist acknowledged how hard it is for either side to admit and address the pain of the other. She suggested that the two sides represent early emotion schemes and ways of being in the world that would take time to soften and develop. Once again, they moved back to more relational tasks as the therapist worked with Jennifer to strengthen her sense of self and foster her capacity to attend to and process her feelings. Over time, Jennifer became more open to her feelings of neglect and pain in the chair with her worrier self. Although she was still reluctant to support that self and was overwhelmed at the thought of caring for her and listening to her pain, this shifted with time. To facilitate this process, the therapist encouraged Jennifer to express and share the pain that the worrier self feels:

Therapist:	Can you tell Jennifer about your pain? What was it like for you as a child feeling that no one cared for you?
Client:	It was so scary. I felt like garbage, totally disposable. No one cared if I lived or died and they took such pleasure in taunting me.
Therapist:	What was it like when they taunted you?
Client:	I didn't let them see. I was not going to give them the pleasure of seeing me hurt. I shut down completely. I had to be strong. I couldn't be weak.
Therapist:	So, you shut down, you hid your pain?
Client:	Yes. That was the only way to survive. That was how I got them to leave me alone. If they felt they won, they would have continued, but if I hid my pain, they would go away. That was better than their taunting. They ridiculed me when they saw me cry.
Therapist:	So you learned really early on that if they saw your pain, it would be worse. Better to hide it and pretend you did not feel anything.
Client:	Yes. I could not feel vulnerable.

The therapist suggested that this behavior, which was so useful in helping her survive in her family, is getting in the way of Jennifer's leading a more satisfying, happier life now. With time, Jennifer came to acknowledge and recognize that she needed to change how she related to herself. She recalled that when she had come to therapy she had said that she wanted to be rid of the fear and to feel relaxed and good about herself. The therapist continued to work with the client on her feelings of neglect and sense of powerlessness at home. She became quite grief stricken and sad giving up her wish to be cared for by her parents and siblings. For a time, she continued to blame herself, saying it was her fault that they did not love and cherish her. With time, Jennifer came to acknowledge that she had not deserved their negative treatment, but, rather, as a small child she had deserved to be loved and to have parents who cared for her and were attentive to her needs for protection and support. These changes required that she come to value herself and feel supported and safe as she shared her pain. As Jennifer began to shift to feeling more deserving and able to hear and attend to her pain in the two-chair dialogues, she was able to engage in empty-chair exercises with her parents and siblings. In these dialogues, she could hold them accountable for their behavior and set higher expectations for herself in her work and her relationships with others.

As Jennifer became less self-silencing, emotions like sadness and rage began to bubble up. She found herself expressing her feelings more. This was scary and unfamiliar. She wanted to learn how to express her feelings in ways that did not seem so out of control. Therapist and client continued to work on this, engaging in two-chair dialogues and two-chair enactments around Jennifer's fears of expressing herself to others and the various behaviors she used to shut herself down. As she began to address her feelings more and speak out, her fears about her health diminished. She felt less anxious and became more committed to doing things that she valued and enjoyed. Jennifer changed her job and began to travel more.

NAVIGATING CHALLENGES IN TWO-CHAIR WORK

It can take time to work through the different phases of these forms of two-chair work, which include (a) building awareness of the negative ways of treating emotional experience and experiencing oneself as an agent, (b) accessing core pain and attending to and experiencing the emotional impact and representing it in words, (c) expressing needs based on the feelings and felt impact, and finally (d) responding in a caring and supportive way that allows for transformation. Clients often stall at each stage. When this happens, it provides the therapist with an indication of the work that clients still need to do to process their emotional experience and develop positive ways of relating to themselves and their emotions. Each of these stages is described next.

Building Awareness of Negative Treatment of the Self

An important task in EFT is to facilitate clients' awareness and felt sense of their emotional experience. This can be done in a variety of ways, including the therapist reflecting and mirroring clients' experiences in an empathic, accepting, prizing manner as clients describe the events in their lives and construct their narratives; teaching clients to focus on their inner experience and symbolize it in words; and engaging in chair work to enable clients to attend to the impact of self-interruptions (two-chair enactments), work with self-critical statements and other negative ways of treating the self (two-chair dialogues), or express the impact of the others' behavior and attitudes (empty-chair work). Attending to their inner experience and representing it in words is the first step in clients' learning to process their experiences in new ways.

The EFT therapist and his or her clients work together to become aware of clients' negative treatment, including their self-talk, attitudes toward their experience, and other behaviors. One of the first tasks in two-chair work is to have clients become more aware of these negative behaviors and express them to access the felt impact. In two-chair work, difficulties with processing emotions can become clearer when clients are trying to access and represent the impact of negative ways of treating their experience, whether it be self-criticism, self-neglect, or self-silencing. When asked to do this, clients may go blank and say they do not know what they are feeling; they may say that they are not feeling anything; they may change the subject or express confusion; or they may agree with their self-criticism as be deserving of criticism and blame. These responses indicate a collapsed self, sometimes referred to as an impasse in the dialogue. These are markers that clients are blocked and that their experience is interrupted or shut down.

If clients are unable to attend to or represent their experience at this stage and are showing signs of self-interruption, the therapist can suggest they work on how they shut down their experience. Alternatively, client and therapist can temporarily forego two-chair work and return to more relational work on the basis of the client's narratives. Once clients have learned to attend, accept, and value their experience, they are better able to engage in two-chair dialogues and can express the impact their negative ways of treating their emotions have on them. This then leads to the next stage of treatment: accessing the core painful emotions and expressing the associated needs that flow from a recognition of the impact of their own or others' behavior in a situation, as well as their own felt sense of that situation.

Accessing Core Pain and Expressing Feelings and Needs

Clients need to access their interrupted painful experience at some degree of arousal. If it is simply processed at a more cognitive level, it will not give access to the unmet need it represents. If it is at too high a level of arousal, it will be disorganizing. Once clients experience their core pain, they are in a better position to express what they need. However, for some clients the link between feelings and needs has never been formed and they may feel lost and unable to articulate their needs. However, the more clients experience painful feelings at moderate levels of arousal, the clearer the unmet adaptive needs become.

When clients are baffled about what they need, their therapist can conjecture about it and make suggestions on the basis of his or her own experience of human needs and his or her experience with clients and others. For example, when clients say they feel exhausted from their struggles with their negative voice, the therapist might ask if they need a break. At these times, clients are encouraged to check inside to see if the therapist's suggestions fit and, if they do, to express it in two-chair work. However, if the suggestions do not fit, clients are encouraged to continue searching for what might fit better to ensure their well-being. A constant thread throughout the therapy is for clients to attend to, accept, symbolize, and express their emotions by checking inside to determine what they need. This can be framed simply by asking clients what they feel and what they need.

The EFT therapist thus encourages clients to engage in minifocusing exercises to attend to their feelings and their felt needs at points in the session when they seem blocked. Learning to attend to feelings, and needs that flow from them, can be a long learning process for those clients for whom this capacity has been extinguished in unresponsive and punishing environments. In chair work, expressing needs means stating them to another aspect of the self or other with the attendant worry and concern for how they will be received. Hence, clients need to feel strong enough to tolerate rejection and experience the attendant pain if others are nonresponsive, whether that be from the self or others. Expressing feelings and needs to another can be loaded for clients who have experienced others as uncaring and unsupportive of their feelings and needs. It requires courage to say them out loud. The strength and confidence to attend to and express feelings and needs develops in supportive relationships with the therapist and through the ongoing sharing of their experience with another who is accepting, empathic, prizing, and congruent. Once clients are able to express their needs in two-chair work, they are asked to respond to the expression of these needs from the opposite chair.

Facilitating the Expression of Care and Compassion

After a client has expressed his needs, the therapist asks him to respond from the opposite chair in a two-chair task. At this stage the therapist is able to get a read on whether the client has internalized the therapist's attitudes and has developed more positive ways of responding to his experiences. If positive ways of treating the self have been absorbed and internalized, clients are able to respond compassionately to their own pain and understand and accept the needs of their other self. The therapist also needs to empathize with and validate a client's painful feelings. This usually begins a negotiation in the client, as each side of the self recognizes what is necessary for a more satisfactory balance between the self and the demands of the environment.

However, if positive ways of treating experience have not been internalized then the response is likely to lack empathy and reflect rejection, disowning, or disavowal of a client's needs and feelings. This can be conceptualized as a self who is too wounded to take account of the client's feelings and needs. For example, when Jennifer first expressed her need for support and wished to express her feelings, her anxious self responded by dismissing Jennifer and saying that the anxious self's pain was greater. This is a marker or cue to the therapist that the client still needs to internalize more positive caring behaviors. The client needs to develop self-empathy, self-acceptance, and self-compassion to acknowledge and attend to her pain so that she can meet her needs more effectively. Dismissing emotion is a marker of negative self-treatment and self-silencing that needs to be addressed so clients can attend to and access their core pain to resolve their feelings of anxiety.

At times when clients continue to be self-silencing, oppressive, and controlling of their experience, the therapist returns to empathic listening, following, and acceptance of their experience. The objective is to continue working together with clients to process their pain, including attending, tolerating, labeling, and expressing it to an empathically attuned, accepting, warm, and sincere other. Then, slowly, clients internalize these behaviors so that they are better able to be empathic, supportive, accepting, and nurturing of themselves (J. Watson, Steckley, & McMullen, 2014). When clients feel stronger, they are able to engage in the different stages of the two-chair dialogue (e.g., representing the impact of negative behaviors, expressing needs and responding in a caring and supportive way).

The experiential therapist facilitates these processes by adopting a more relational stance as he or she works with clients to process their emotional experience, label it in words, validate and accept it, and demonstrate respect and acceptance for clients as they share their experience. In turn, as clients attend to their experience and process it with an empathic, accepting other, they come to internalize these attitudes toward themselves and their experience and learn to listen to their feelings and needs and how to support and nurture themselves. This often reflects a major turning point in therapy, especially for those clients who have been stuck and unable to respond with care and kindness to their needs for support, protection, and nurture.

TRANSFORMATION: DEVELOPING SELF-SOOTHING

To transform feelings of anxiety in clients with GAD, they need to find ways of soothing themselves to replace the protective worry. Some clients, those who have internalized self-compassion and are more self-protective, are able to generate a soothing phrase or mantra in the two-chair dialogue that speaks directly to their anxiety. But this is different for each client, as each has different ways of evaluating the self or trying to protect the self that trigger worry and anxiety. Jennifer, for example, needed to know that she was acceptable and deserved to belong. When she told herself in a two-chair dialogue, "You are acceptable and deserve to be loved and feel safe," she visibly relaxed, the tension flowed out of her body as her shoulders sank, and her breathing became more regular. It is important to note that it is the client who first articulates the words that directly address the trigger for her anxiety and who experiences them as key to soothing and diminishing anxiety.

In another case example, Miriam, who worried continuously about not coping at work and about having her partner leave her, had a slightly different mantra that helped her to relax. Miriam had a constant undercurrent of worry and fear. Her mother was highly anxious and had been unable to adequately care for Miriam after the birth of her second child. This had left Miriam feeling alone and struggling to survive at 18 months of age. Miriam learned early to be self-reliant and that if something was to happen, she needed to make it so. In addition, her mother was critical and expected Miriam to be helpful and self-sacrificing. As the therapist began working on her worry and unfinished business with her mother, the negative ways that Miriam treated herself became clear. Her default position was to assume that she had done something wrong and accept blame. She assumed responsibility for situations and other people's behavior. When she came to therapy, she was exhausted and feeling overburdened.

Miriam and her therapist began to work with her feelings of anxiety. She realized that she did not attend to herself for fear of being selfish. She and her therapist continued to do relational work and two-chair work to address the accusation that she was selfish. By saying she was selfish, she denied and ignored her own feelings for the sake of others. Miriam's therapist worked to have her see herself as more deserving of attention and care, and as a result she began to listen to and express her feelings and needs more. However, she still would find herself waking at night worrying. As the therapist began to explore with her the different situations that triggered her anxiety, it became clear that Miriam was very judgmental of herself. She would blame and criticize herself for poor outcomes and worry that she had done something wrong.

Her therapist suggested that she engage in two-chair work to try to transform the blame. Miriam recalled how her mother always blamed her and held her responsible for things that went wrong at home or with her baby brother. She realized that the phrases "It's your fault" and "You are responsible for what happens" were the triggers for her anxiety and worry. As Miriam became aware of how she felt when she said those phrases, and of how burdened and scared it made her feel worrying that things could go wrong, her therapist encouraged her to attend to the fear and speak to it in a two-chair dialogue. This encouraged Miriam to access more compassion for the scared, vulnerable side that felt she was always to blame.

Miriam was able to find the words that visibly eased her fear and to adopt a more supportive way of relating to her experience, saying, "You are not to blame" and "You are not responsible." Hearing these words, Miriam's body relaxed, she sighed in relief, and she felt an enormous burden slide from her shoulders. She began to cry thinking about how heavy and difficult it had been to assume that she must take care of and look after everybody. Miriam felt relieved to think that she could make mistakes and be human. Of course, she still felt concerned about letting people down, but she was much more accepting of herself and did not hold herself to such exacting standards. She accepted that she might make mistakes, that she did not have to be responsible for everything but could leave things for others to pick up.

It can be important for clients to identify the situations that trigger their anxiety and how they respond. For example, another client, Sandra, who saw herself as very loved and cared for by her family, was diagnosed with GAD. She constantly worried and was anxious about her relationship, the maintenance of her house, and her work. As the therapist worked with her worry dialogues, Sandra realized that she was constantly telling herself to get it right so people would like her. She told herself to be serious and careful so that she would not make any mistakes at work. She worried about her position at work even though she consistently received positive feedback. The therapist suggested a two-chair dialogue to address this worry. Sandra was able to tell her worrier self that she was tense and needed to relax. However, the worrier self responded by saying it was scared and could not stop worrying in case it was forgotten:

> Client: Please stop telling me to be careful. It makes me so tense and I feel so exhausted being vigilant and trying to ensure I don't make a mistake.

Therapist:	So this side is just so tired and exhausted. What do you need?
Client:	I need her to stop worrying. Stop telling me that "things will go wrong." I need her to calm down.
Therapist:	So you need her to ease off, to stop worrying you. Come over [to this other chair]. So how do you respond to her? She says, "I need some respite. I need you to calm down, I am so tired and exhausted."
Client:	I can't stop. I am so scared of being forgotten. No one will see me. I feel invisible. If I don't do things right, no one will notice me and I will be left alone.

As she shared this, she thought about what it must have been like in her house when she was very young. She recalled that when she was 2 years old her mother was hospitalized for depression following complications during a pregnancy that caused her to miscarry. Her father was away a lot as a result of his work. Sandra realized that her mother was distracted, depressed and grieving her miscarriage, and not able to be attentive and present. Sandra realized that she had to continually work to be noticed. As she came to this realization, she began to relax. She felt this realization fit her experience and explained what was going on for her. Her therapist suggested that she try to tell herself that "she was memorable and would not be forgotten." That struck the right note, and Sandra visibly relaxed and sighed. She remarked that she had thought it was because she had felt abandoned when her mother was hospitalized when she was a child, but that it never fit her inner felt sense properly. However, feeling forgotten was closer to her experience so that the mantra she would be remembered and seen was more appropriate. Returning to the other chair, the client proceeded:

Client:	You are memorable. I won't forget you and you do not have to work to get it right to be noticed and seen. You are visible.
Therapist:	So, you are reassuring her that she is important, that you do see her and will not forget her. Come over [to the other chair]. What is it like to hear her say that?
Client:	That's it, that's what I needed to hear. That feels so good.

After this, Sandra's anxiety lifted. She felt more joyful and less fearful. At times when she felt anxious in social situations or at work, she would recall that she was visible and that she did not have to bid for attention.

In contrast to clients like Jennifer and Miriam, there are those clients who are not subject to negative treatment or neglect but are overly protected. The message that these clients internalize is that they are unable to take care of themselves. This can leave them feeling vulnerable and at risk when confronting challenging circumstances. They can feel unsupported or overwhelmed. For example, Malcolm's mother was very protective of him. She and his grandmother were constantly attending to him and fretting that he was frail and subject to illness.

Malcolm's anxiety started when he was a young adult and first married, after he became ill on a plane while flying to the Caribbean for his honeymoon. He felt extremely nauseous, with gastric complications. As he struggled with the nausea, his wife was sleeping and unaware of his plight. He did not want to wake her and recalled feeling very alone and scared that he would throw up and shame himself and her on the plane. He saw his wife as very young, and dependent on him to be strong. She seemed child-like and helpless whenever he looked to her for support. She became scared when he was sick so that he felt he could not lean on her. This made Malcolm feel very alone and helpless. Subsequently, Malcolm was diagnosed with GAD as he experienced anxiety more regularly, worrying about his family's health and safety. He worried about his children and his wife's ability to care for them. He worried that he would antagonize people at work and jeopardize his family's well-being.

An important focus in therapy was to work with Malcolm to develop greater confidence in himself and his ability to cope. He realized that he became more anxious when he told himself that he could not cope in a two-chair dialogue. After processing the emotional impact of his early experience, he came to see how vulnerable and undermined he felt by his mother and grandmother with their constant fretting and worry about him. Their concern made him feel inept and helpless. He engaged in empty-chair work to express his feelings and to reassure them that he was capable. He told them to stop worrying and to trust him and have more confidence in him. After this exercise, he was able to reassure himself in a two-chair dialogue and respond to the side of him that was scared and afraid that he could not cope, saying, "I am strong and capable." As he said this, Malcolm realized that his anxiety began to dissolve. The therapist suggested that he attend to these feelings of relief and hold on to the phrase that "he was strong and capable" to counteract his anxiety. Although these words eased his anxiety, it was not enough to have the words available, he needed to be able to heed and believe them. This happened gradually as he learned to trust his emotional experience more, identified his needs, and found ways to meet them. Over the course of the therapy, he came to see himself as capable, strong, and a good provider for his family. He was also able to express his feelings to his wife, and she was able to respond to him with support and concern. Malcolm's mantra became "You are strong and capable—everything will be fine."

Clients move back and forth between two-chair work (resolving negative ways of treating their experience and acquiring more positive ways of treating themselves) and empty-chair work (giving voice to feelings and needs in interpersonal situations and differentiating them from others). Alternatively, they may focus on narrative retelling to help symbolize and organize traumatic experiences. These processes happen in parallel as clients come to symbolize their experiences and share them with their therapist. As they engage in these processes, clients reconstruct events to make sense of their feelings and perceptions. In the process they may reevaluate their perceptions and come to see events and others' behavior differently. These changes in perception may be at odds with previous accounts or even the accounts that others have of the same events. Learning to trust themselves and their experience is essential for clients to build self-confidence and become more resilient and self-assured about their capacity to cope with life challenges. This is enhanced as they begin to reprocess their emotional experiences by attending to their emotions, labelling them, and expressing them to others. Their emotions provide them with information to identify their needs so that they can use them as a guide to what they need and learn to meet them in ways that are more satisfying and fulfilling.

Another important part of the change process is clients' processing their painful experience with others, who failed or neglected to protect them, using empty-chair work, as well as learning how to self-soothe. Empty-chair work is an important task to address clients' core painful feelings and transform them with assertive anger, grief, and self-compassion. Learning to self-soothe is an integral part of this process. For some clients, this task may need to be an explicit lesson in how to care for the self and treat the self with compassion and kindness. Self-soothing is an important outcome of working with clients with GAD. It is an underlying process that develops as clients learn to process their emotions and label them and as they learn to find mantras that serve as the antidotes to their anxiety triggers. For some clients, soothing mantras are acquired during two-chair dialogues. However, for others, more explicit coaching to develop and acquire self-soothing behaviors can be helpful. These interventions are described in more detail in Chapter 9. Often clients can benefit from engaging in specific tasks to enhance their capacities to be more compassionate toward themselves and soothe their core painful feelings and insecure sense of self.

8

TRANSFORMING PAIN: WORKING WITH EMPTY-CHAIR DIALOGUES IN GENERALIZED ANXIETY DISORDER

As clients engage in two-chair worry dialogues and reconstruct their life narratives, they often identify relational injuries and interactions with others that may have contributed to painful feelings and an extreme sense of vulnerability. When painful feelings and relational injuries underlying worry and anxiety are brought to awareness, the therapist can suggest that clients begin to address them using empty-chair dialogues (Elliott, Watson, Goldman, & Greenberg, 2004; Greenberg & Paivio, 1997; Greenberg, Rice, & Elliott, 1993; J. Watson, 2006). The goal is for clients to access and express underlying core, maladaptive, painful feelings of fear, sadness, and shame that were experienced in relationships with others and transformed them. The objective of working with empty-chair dialogues is to help clients to process their core painful feelings and unmet needs.

http://dx.doi.org/10.1037/0000018-009
Emotion-Focused Therapy for Generalized Anxiety, by J. C. Watson and L. S. Greenberg
Copyright © 2017 by the American Psychological Association. All rights reserved.

To facilitate access to their feelings in empty-chair dialogues, clients are encouraged to access episodic memories, symbolize the impact of others' behaviors, and give voice to the feelings experienced in interaction with others. As clients become more aware of how they have been treated and express their painful feelings and process them with the therapist, they come to see the full impact of others' behaviors and recognize what they needed to receive from them. By expressing their feelings and asserting their needs as they dialogue with others, clients become more self-assertive and assume greater responsibility for their own well-being. They hold others more accountable for not providing them with protection and care, and they commit to protecting and caring for themselves moving forward. This results in greater differentiation of the self and others, as well as an increased sense of empowerment and mastery in their interactions with others.

The goal of empty-chair dialogues with others is to enable clients to give voice to their feelings and needs and develop new ways of being in relationships with others. As clients become more aware of their feelings and begin to experience them in the session, they may begin to recall specific episodic memories and times when they felt afraid and anxious or experienced painful feelings of sadness and shame in interaction with others. The therapist asks clients to imagine and describe the other who injured them to help clients access their feelings. Thus, imagining the other evokes feelings in the session that clients can then put into words. Often the feelings are not known or have not been expressed previously. However, in interaction with an empathically attuned therapist, clients' painful feelings can be voiced and heard. The therapist's empathy, acceptance, and warmth help clients become more conscious of others' behaviors and styles of relating, as well as the impact of the injuries on them. As clients become more aware of their emotions and feelings in interaction with the other, they can begin to express their feelings and share their distress and sense of responsibility, as well as apprehend what they need from the other and begin to see the other more clearly.

Empty-chair work is a powerful way to address wounds from the past resulting from emotional abandonment, rejection, abuse, criticism, overburdening, and overprotection. The therapist encourages clients to express painful feelings that were silenced or ignored to take care of the other or as a way of coping. In this process, clients begin to take better care of themselves and become more accepting of their limits, while expecting more from others. They begin to hold others accountable for their actions and relinquish some of the responsibility for outcomes. In this process, clients let go of ways of interacting with themselves and others that may have contributed to the development of an anxious self.

INITIATING EMPTY-CHAIR DIALOGUES TO RESOLVE ATTACHMENT INJURIES

There are a number of phases in the processing of painful emotions in generalized anxiety disorder (GAD) using empty-chair dialogues, including accessing, acknowledging, and attending to clients' pain and their relational injuries sustained in relationships with others; imagining the other by calling up an episodic memory; dialoguing with the other; and asserting and protecting themselves to claim more space as they feel more deserving of care and acceptance in relationships with others and expect that their needs and emotions be acknowledged and met. Before engaging in empty-chair dialogues, clients need to agree to work with their painful experiences in this way. Once they have agreed, the therapist can set up the task.

Markers for Attachment Injuries

Clients' complaints, descriptions, and memories of hurtful interactions and relational injuries indicate that empty-chair work might be useful to address these painful experiences. These types of client statements serve as markers or guides that clients may need to process distressing, negative interactions and events. Painful feelings associated with neglect, rejection, criticism, and harm point to the need for empty-chair dialogues. As we have discussed in earlier chapters, emotion-focused therapy (EFT) proposes that GAD develops when people feels that their emotional, psychological, and/ or physical survival is threatened in some way. There is a sense that the self is overwhelmed and unable to cope with intense painful feelings of fear, sadness, shame, and the resulting undifferentiated distress of not having these feelings attended to by caretakers. Hurt and unprotected, people learn to be vigilant and guard against harm or threat.

As we discussed in Chapter 1 of this volume, GAD often follows from experiences of being emotionally and physically abused, rejected, abandoned, or neglected, or it may be a result of other negative experiences that leave people feeling physically and emotionally vulnerable. These are the small invisible traumas that accumulate in attachment relationships with negative, cold, rejecting, hostile, demanding, and overburdening caretakers, or in relationships that are overly intrusive. A sense of inflated responsibility can develop in situations where people feel physically, emotionally, and psychologically at risk, or when they see caretakers in pain and unable to adequately care for or protect them. To compensate, people assume responsibility for their own well-being, as well as the well-being of others, to cope with their painful feelings and sense of threat. Alternatively, when others have been overly protective, clients may silence and sacrifice their needs for the sake of others, leading to enmeshment and stalled identity formation.

In clients with GAD, painful, threatening experiences are not fully symbolized in conscious awareness. Rather, the manner in which others have responded to clients' distress has led to the development of maladaptive emotion schemes and ways of processing emotion and dealing with subjective experiences, ways that are problematic and contribute to the development of worry and overresponsibility to ensure the client's safety and survival. To effectively address the worry and the difficulties with emotional processing and expression, core, painful, maladaptive emotional experiences need to be symbolized and transformed. As we have discussed in earlier chapters, the EFT therapist first works with clients to access their pain and construct narratives that adequately take account of clients' life histories (Angus & Greenberg, 2011; J. Watson, Goldman, & Greenberg, 2007). As clients work on their worry dialogues, the core pain experienced in interaction with others is highlighted so that clear markers of unfinished business emerge.

Evoking Feelings and Episodic Memories

The first step in facilitating clients' processing of their painful feelings is to help them identify the distressing, threatening experiences underlying their fear. Often the circumstances and the relationships that have contributed to the wounds that manifest as GAD have resulted in clients' being unable to fully symbolize their experience. By assuming emotional and psychological care of others, clients' own experience remains unsymbolized, unacknowledged, and unsupported. Moreover, their sense of competence and mastery may be undermined by intrusive, overly protective others such that they doubt their ability to cope. Their own feelings and needs may have been silenced or suppressed as clients developed ways of coping to try to maintain relationships with others and survive under difficult and constraining circumstances. The empty-chair task enables clients to give voice to previously implicit and unexpressed aspects of their experience. They are encouraged to attend to and access their experience so they can symbolize and express what they were feeling and experiencing in interaction with difficult and harmful others.

Once clients have accessed the feelings of fear or distress embedded in their worry, the therapist can begin to probe for the underlying pain. To help clients identify their pain, the therapist might ask the following questions: "What is the fear about?" "Can you recall the first time you became aware of or experienced these feelings?" or "What is so distressing to you right now?" These questions direct clients' attention inward and often bring up memories of times when they felt vulnerable and insecure. For example, Roger, who was being treated for GAD, recalled how hard it was for him as a child when his mother would become enraged and walk out of the house. At these times, he would feel that he had somehow failed her. He believed that he was to blame for her rage—that there was something terribly wrong with him. This sense of being inadequate and "wrong" remained with him into adulthood. As a result, he worried about his work and his relationships. He often felt guilty and formed relationships with people who were needy and required a lot of care. When they expressed disappointment or disapproval, he would begin to feel very anxious and that he was somehow guilty and unworthy of their love. After engaging in a worry dialogue, Roger became aware of how overwhelmed and inadequate he felt.

Often the triggers for clients' reactions are outside of conscious awareness. Thus, they respond automatically without realizing what they are doing. It is only as clients begin to present and describe different situations, events, and people in their lives, as well as the behaviors of others, that they have the opportunity to name the triggers and clearly see the behaviors of others that have caused them distress. During this process, clients come to see their experiences through a different lens, and recognize its negative impact on them. In the case of Roger, the effects of negative events made him feel afraid and responsible for the well-being of his mother and himself. The weight of the responsibility to ensure the well-being of the self and other, which people with GAD often assume, is debilitating. Even though the outcomes are often beyond clients' actual control, they constantly worry as they try to avert negative consequences for themselves and others. They remain vigilant and alert, to ensure that they maintain the attachment, love, support, and availability of others who were unable to assume responsibility for themselves and protect and care for the client.

Imagining the Other

To facilitate access of clients' painful emotions, the EFT therapist encourages them to visualize an imagined other in an empty-chair and attend to the painful feelings that come up as they imagine the interaction. Clients may imagine the other as he or she is currently or was in the past. Clients are asked to provide a physical description of the other, giving a sense of the other's presence to try to bring the person alive in the session. After this, it is important for the therapist to ask clients how the other is looking at them or what the expression is on the other's face. It is the other's facial expression that usually evokes an emotional response in clients. After being asked, a client might say, "She looks sad and helpless" or "He's frowning and angry." Once the other's expression is named, the therapist asks how it makes them feel as he or she encourages clients to engage in a dialogue with the other. Often clients' image of the other's expression characterizes and encapsulates the relationship, making it an important source of affective experience.

DIALOGUING WITH THE OTHER

Expressing Feelings

After the memory of the other has been evoked, the therapist focuses on supporting clients to access their feelings and put them into words. As clients symbolize their feelings, the therapist uses affirming and validating reflections to hold their pain as it is expressed. The therapist may also use empathic conjectures to help clients put their feelings into words; at other times he or she may use empathic doubling responses to try to represent how clients were feeling at the time of the emotional injury. These responses are offered tentatively and checked with clients. As clients try to give voice to their feelings and engage in dialogue with the other, the therapist can invite fuller expression by using his or her voice to evoke and meet the client's emotions. The therapist varies the vocal expressiveness as well as the tempo at which he or she speaks as he or she conveys concern, anger, or sadness. The primary objective is to work to support clients and invite their feelings into the room so that they can be clearly expressed and shared with the other. The therapist need to support clients as they give voice to their painful feelings of sadness, shame, and fear. To do this, he or she reflects clients' feelings as they are symbolized and put into words. Once clients have expressed how they feel, they are asked to state what they need from the other or what they wish they had received. It is important to work with clients to fully express their feelings and needs with the other, who injured them or caused them pain. Next, they are invited to respond as the other from the empty chair.

These dialogues can be short and intense, or they can be slow and drawn out. Full resolution of the empty-chair dialogue is usually marked by clients' accessing compassion and empathy for the self, the other, or both, by accessing protective anger and holding the other accountable for hurtful, neglectful, and threatening behaviors. Resolution often does not occur the first time clients engage in the empty-chair dialogue. Usually there are a number of dialogues across the course of therapy before full resolution occurs. When empty-chair dialogues are fully resolved, clients can claim space such that they fully own and inhabit their feelings, express their feelings to others, own their perceptions of the self and others, trust the information from their senses, express their needs, and feel deserving of care and attention.

Supporting Full Expression

Clients' bodies and nonverbal behavior are good guides as to whether they have resolved or fully expressed their feelings. The EFT therapist asks clients to check in with their bodies, particularly their core emotions, to determine whether all their feelings have been expressed. Often clients will express some feelings but hold back others, continuing to carry tension, fear, anger, or sadness in their gut or chest. If this is the case, the therapist continues to work with clients to fully express their feelings either in the current session or in later sessions as they return to resolve the relational injuries sustained. Once clients have fully expressed their feelings, they will express a sense of lightness, usually sighing and releasing their breath and sitting up and back in their chairs, looking more comfortable and relaxed. Their faces usually lighten and their eyes brighten. When the therapist notes this, it is good to ask clients to check in with their bodies to see how they are feeling and to share it so they and the therapist can be sure that the process has resolved and a significant shift in how they feel toward the other has occurred.

Feelings come alive in the session as clients access their episodic memories and these in turn evoke more feelings (Angus & Greenberg, 2011; J. Watson, 1996; J. Watson & Rennie, 1994). The process of symbolizing their inner and outer experience continues the process of narrative reconstruction as clients begin to recall events that left them feeling vulnerable, rejected, abandoned, and uncared for by others. As they engage in this process, clients may come to see others in a new light. This can involve recognizing that others were unavailable, egocentric, or hostile and unable to provide the necessary care, attention, and protection. Sometimes this may be unintentional, the consequence of a difficult life circumstance (e.g., a parent who is seriously ill or dies). Alternatively, it may be recognized that the other did not have the capacities, will, or skills to provide the care that was necessary. At other times, it may be because the other's needs were regarded as more paramount. This is illustrated in the following case example of Rachel.

Rachel, who came to therapy for the treatment of GAD, experienced intense anger and disappointment at her mother as she began to process the events of her childhood. Rachel was constantly anxious and worried about her work and her interactions with others. She and her mother moved in with her grandparents after Rachel's father died. She recalled that when she was small, she had seen her mother physically attacked by her grandparents. Both her grandparents would lash out at her mother when they were displeased, sometimes pulling her mother's hair or dragging her mother from the table. Her grandparents also would shout and threaten to hit Rachel if her mother did not behave. The client recalled being very scared in these situations and consequently was very concerned about annoying people or making them angry. As a result, she tended to silence her own feelings and wishes and focus on trying to ensure others were not displeased. She constantly worried about whether she was doing the right thing and tried to anticipate the needs of others. This was exhausting and made it difficult for her to relax. Rachel worried about her behavior as she tried to put others' needs first. She worried about her grades and how she performed at school. She was studying to be a health care professional, and she worried that her teachers and grandparents would be disapproving and angry with her if she did not excel in her studies.

Initially, Rachel presented with concerns about her best friend, who had declined to attend Rachel's birthday party. Rachel was very hurt and confused by this. She worried that she had done something to provoke her friend. She raked over recent times spent together to see what might have contributed to her friend's refusal. After engaging in the worry dialogue, Rachel recalled how terrified she had been at the dinner table. She would recall watching her mother and grandparents, hoping that they would be able to eat without anyone becoming angry. As she began to share the pain of growing up with her grandparents and to express her feelings of fear and sadness, she also expressed anger and disappointment with her mother for not being able to manage alone and for subjecting them both to her grandparents' abuse.

For example, after Rachel accessed her disappointment and anger, her therapist asked her whether she would like to do an empty-chair task with her mother so that Rachel could express her pain and her need for greater protection.

> Therapist: Would you be willing to do a task with your mom? It might help you to express your feelings to see if you can get some relief?
>
> Client: I am not sure she could handle me talking about [my grand-parents], I don't think I have ever spoken to her about them.
>
> Therapist: So, it is hard to speak to her about these feelings? Perhaps this might be an opportunity for you to express your feelings and not have to worry about her or how she will react. Would you be willing to try?

The therapist tried to provide a rationale for engaging in the empty-chair dialogue. Sometimes clients think they must speak to the other in person. However, here the therapist explained that by doing it in the session, they would not have to worry about the client's mother or her reaction and could focus exclusively on the client. The exercise can seem strange and awkward at first. Although she seemed hesitant, Rachel agreed:

> Client: Okay.
>
> Therapist: Okay, I am going to bring up [another] chair and I am going to ask you to imagine your mother in that chair opposite you. Can you describe her to me? What do you see? Can you help me get a sense of her?
>
> Client: She's small, fragile looking, a little like me, with brown curly hair.

<blockquote>
<dl>
<dt>Therapist:</dt>
<dd>So, she's [small]; what's the expression on her face as she looks at you?</dd>
</dl>
</blockquote>

This is a very important question because this is the stimulus that often evokes the most affect in clients. It is not usually pertinent whether the other has blonde hair or blue eyes, but the expression on the face communicates a lot of emotional information to clients as well as the therapist. The way clients imagine the other looking at them provides the first clue about the quality of the relationship with the other. It is the stimulus that often evokes clients' emotions during the session so that they can be labeled and expressed to the imagined other in the empty-chair task. Here Rachel described the look on her mother's face:

<blockquote>
<dl>
<dt>Client:</dt>
<dd>She looks distant. She's not really looking at me, she's just staring into space.</dd>
<dt>Therapist:</dt>
<dd>So, she is not looking at you but is staring off in the distance. How does that make you feel?</dd>
<dt>Client:</dt>
<dd>[It makes me feel] sad. I feel she's forgotten me. Like she can't see me or something.</dd>
</dl>
</blockquote>

Once clients access their feelings, the therapist encourages them to express themselves to the other whom they have imagined in the empty chair. In this excerpt, Rachel engaged in a dialogue with the imagined other, her mother, as she recalled her mother as staring off in the distance:

<blockquote>
<dl>
<dt>Therapist:</dt>
<dd>Can you say [how you feel] to her: "Mom, when I see you looking off in the distance, it's as if you have forgotten me. It makes me feel sad, alone?"</dd>
<dt>Client:</dt>
<dd>Yes. When you stare into the distance I feel forgotten. It makes me feel so lonely and sad. It's as if I'm not here.</dd>
<dt>Therapist:</dt>
<dd>It's lonely—you feel invisible somehow? What's that like for you?</dd>
<dt>Client:</dt>
<dd>It makes me anxious [and] a little scared. I feel I have to do something; like [I have to] take care of her.</dd>
<dt>Therapist:</dt>
<dd>You feel scared, as if you must do something? Can you tell her that? "I feel scared and responsible like I should take care of you."</dd>
<dt>Client:</dt>
<dd>Yes, it reminds me of when I was little. You would look so sad and stare out the window. I used to feel so alone, sad, [and] frightened. I felt I didn't exist for you.</dd>
<dt>Therapist:</dt>
<dd>So, you felt like you didn't exist and that made you sad and lonely. What did you need from her?</dd>
</dl>
</blockquote>

Client:	I needed you to attend to me. I needed you to see me. I was so scared when we were living with grandpa. I kept expecting [him] to beat me and it was so hard seeing them punish you. Why didn't you stand up to them? If only you had left, then it might have been different.
Therapist:	Okay, can you come over [to the other chair and speak as your mother]? What happens over here as you hear Rachel say, "I was so frightened living with grandpa—I wish you had left, I needed you to take care of me"?
Client:	I know it was hard, but where could I go? I couldn't look after us alone. I couldn't find work, and I didn't know what to do after your dad died.
Therapist:	What's she saying—she had no choice?
Client:	Yes. I didn't have a choice; it was the best I could do.
Therapist:	You did the best you could and what do you say to Rachel's pain?
Client:	I'm sorry, but I thought if I just kept quiet and tried to disappear, they would stop being angry with me, stop beating me.
Therapist:	Okay, come [back over to the first chair and speak as Rachel again]. What happens when you hear your mother say [she is] sorry but it was the best that [she] could do?
Client:	I know you did your best, it was just so hard watching them attack you. I used to be so scared. I would try to disappear and make myself invisible too.
Therapist:	You were terrified. What do you wish she could have done?
Client:	I wish you had been able to protect me. I wish we had been able to escape.
Therapist:	Tell her what it has been like for you.
Client:	Watching them beat up on you and be angry and attack you and seeing you take it and not do anything has made it hard for me to be angry or protect myself. I shut down to avoid my feelings. It has made it difficult for me to connect with others. I am always afraid people will leave me or punish me and get angry.
Therapist:	It has made you so scared and made it difficult to form relationships. What do you wish?
Client:	I wish you could have protected me.

The therapist encouraged Rachel to express her feelings and she expressed her wish that her mother had been stronger and able to protect them both. This is an important step forward because this is the first time Rachel has asked for assistance from her mother. Up to now, she had considered it her responsibility to care for them both. She constantly worried about their safety and well-being. At this point in the dialogue, she began to acknowledge that she was a child who needed protection from witnessing her mother's abuse at the hands of her grandparents. The therapist recognized that this was a marker and suggested some empty-chair work with the grandparents.

During her empty-chair dialogues with her grandparents, Rachel was able to fully express her pain at their treatment. She was able to tell them how scared she had been and how awful it was to see them attack her mother. She told them that she wished they had handled their anger differently and learned to deal with it better. She expressed her need for them to be more self-controlled and told them that their behavior was unacceptable. As she expressed her feelings, she became angry and more self-assertive, and with her therapist's support, she was able to set limits. She asserted that she no longer wanted to worry about others' feelings or be scared that she was annoying them. Rather, she said that she expected people to restrain themselves and to express their anger appropriately.

Through the process of expressing their feelings and identifying their needs, clients access protective anger to become more self-assertive and self-protective in interaction with others. Engaging in empty-chair tasks, clients come to distinguish their own feelings and needs from those of others. This is particularly important in clients with GAD, where clients have been subjected to role reversal and have had to take care of themselves as well as caretakers, sometimes from a very young age. Clients who successfully resolve negative interaction cycles with others are better able to see clearly what others have done and how they have responded. For example, some clients may realize that they silence themselves when others are distressed. Alternatively, other clients may realize that they interpret vocal intensity as a sign that someone is angry and will lash out.

Another case example is that of Abbie, a client who constantly worried about whether she had done something wrong. As she began to explore her feelings in therapy, she realized she silenced herself when she saw another in pain, and would attend to their needs at the expense of her own. It was only after she had identified the trigger, seeing others looking wounded or sad, that she was able to begin expressing her feelings and reduce the sense of responsibility she felt if another person was disappointed, distressed, or hurt. Abbie recalled that from a young age she had been told that she must look after her siblings and ensure that they come to no harm, as her mother was ill and unable to care for her children. Her mother was very depressed and felt overwhelmed by the responsibility of caring for her children. Abbie, aware of her mother's distress, fretted that she would die or be hospitalized, leaving her alone to care for her siblings. To help her mother and alleviate some of her distress, Abbie took on her mother's role in the family to try to ensure that she and her brothers would not be abandoned. As a result of this role reversal, Abbie worried and assumed responsibility for the well-being of herself and her siblings, taking care of their meals, transporting them around, helping them with homework, and catering to her mother's needs.

Assessing the Other's Response

After clients have expressed their feelings and needs to an imaginary other, they are asked to enact the other to get a sense of how she or he might respond. This aspect of the task provides very important diagnostic information to the therapist about the quality of clients' interactions with the other, as well as their internalized attitudes toward the self. Ideally, clients are able to imagine the other as compassionate and able to acknowledge and respond to their pain. At these times, the imagined other expresses sorrow for what has happened and wishes that the events had transpired differently so that clients did not have to suffer. If clients are able to imagine a compassionate other that empathizes with their pain, this is a good prognostic sign and it is likely that the task will resolve quickly. If clients are able to respond positively as the other, this suggests that the other has been benevolent and served a positive caretaking function that the client has been able to internalize. Alternatively, clients, independently over time, may have internalized a positive, caring attitude toward the self from the therapist or other positive interactions with others. At times, he or she must be attentive and balance clients' positive feelings and concerns for the other even as the therapist encourages clients to be more assertive and express their needs. In this case, clients may need to express their recognition of the other's pain or difficulties as well as acknowledge that they required protection and care as a child.

However, if the other has been egocentric and oblivious to the client's needs so that he or she is unable to respond to the client's pain, then it is likely that the client will need support from the therapist to internalize more positive and caring attitudes and behaviors. If the other remains negative in the face of the client's expressed pain, then the therapist can step in and name what the other is doing (e.g., ignoring the client's pain, making excuses that focus attention on the other's pain, being critical, dismissing the client and minimizing his or her pain). By naming what the other is doing or portraying in the empty-chair dialogue, the therapist helps make the other's behavior visible. Once it is clear, the therapist can refocus on the client to inquire how he or she feels when the other responds in a negative way. At this point, when the other responds negatively, the therapist disengages the client from the dialogue with the other, and steps in to process the pain with the client. The therapist assumes the role of the concerned and empathic other. The goal is to help clients to become more accepting and receptive of their emotional experience; to validate their perceptions; and to help them become more compassionate, kind, and nurturing toward themselves.

If the other's response is negative, the client may need to grieve the absence of adequate nurture, support, and empathy from them. For example, a client who has recognized that her wish could never be met referred to it as the "baby wish"—the desire to be cared for and nurtured in a way that would have enabled her to grow up strong and confident in herself and trusting and sure about the support of others. It is this wish that needs to be relinquished. Once clients have grieved the lack of support with an empathically attuned and accepting therapist, they often feel stronger and more deserving. They may then reenter a dialogue with the other and hold him or her accountable for the neglect and failure to adequately protect, nurture, and support the client.

In the previous case example of Rachel, it was witnessing her mother's physical abuse that led to the development of GAD. However, sometimes the neglect and painful experiences are not visible, as is often the case with emotional neglect or overprotection. In these cases, it can be helpful for the therapist to reflect on how the other responds to the client's expression of painful emotions and needs. The client may not have represented the other's behavior or ways of acting and responding in conscious awareness. Instead, the interactions may be outside of awareness and governed by well-worn patterns. This is shown in another case example. Jane, who was in her mid-40s when she came to therapy, had been anxious most of her adult life. She was diagnosed with GAD as she constantly worried about her physical health and safety. Her mother died of cancer when Jane was in her late 20s. Although she played the piano, Jane had been unable to realize her dream of becoming a musician because she lived in fear that if she were to be successful, she would be punished.

Jane was the youngest of four children and had grown up with three brothers. She had seen her father beat her brothers when they misbehaved or did not follow his orders. In turn, they had bullied Jane and were seldom held accountable for their behavior by either parent, though her mother would sometimes intervene. Jane was closer to her mother than anyone else in her family. However, her mother was unable to protect her, as she was often ill. Her mother leaned on Jane, and urged her to be successful to make her mother feel better about her life so that she could brag about her daughter to her relatives. As a consequence, Jane never felt good enough. She developed excessively high standards for herself that she could not live up to and felt pressured to be successful. In the meantime, she was unable to realize her own dreams and ambitions. As an adult, she was dissatisfied with her work as a music teacher and unable to establish a satisfactory intimate relationship with a partner.

Jane felt unwanted by her father, who she felt resented her. He did not protect her from her brothers, nor did he show love or care for her. He was harsh and authoritarian and did not display much kindness to any of his children. Jane felt rejected and unloved by him. It took her some time to share her life story and access memories from her childhood. In time, she began to share her memories and symbolize her experience. She had been in therapy previously, and though she had spoken about her experiences as a child, she was unable to connect to her feelings. Although she was able to express anger at her parents and siblings, she was unable to admit to feelings of fear, shame, and vulnerability. After a few months in therapy this changed as she began to access her more vulnerable feelings, which she had suppressed, as they had been used against her. Jane recalled that as a child she had learned not to cry and reveal her vulnerable feelings for fear of being punished, ridiculed, and/or shamed by her brothers.

Initially, Jane was focused on her constant worry about her health and physical well-being. During the worry dialogues, she realized that her concern for her safety had started in childhood as a result of her brothers' bullying and her sense that her father did not care about what happened to her as well as her mother's unavailability as a result of her illness and high expectations. Her therapist suggested some empty-chair work to help her symbolize and express more fully how she had been treated and to try to give voice to her suppressed feelings. The therapist asked if she would like to work with her dad and Jane agreed. After setting up the chairs, the therapist asked Jane if she could conjure up a memory of her father:

> *Therapist:* Can you imagine your dad in the chair across from you?
>
> *Client:* Yes.
>
> *Therapist:* Describe him to me so I can get a sense of him.
>
> *Client:* He was tall with dark wavy hair, some gray at the sides.
>
> *Therapist:* Tall and dark. And what is the expression on his face as he looks at you?
>
> *Client:* He looks impatient, stern. I was always scared that he was cross with me.
>
> *Therapist:* What happens in you when you see him there looking impatient [and] cross?

The therapist asked the client to attend to her bodily reaction in response to her image of her father. This focused Jane's attention inward so that she could become more aware of her reactions and feelings and label them. Once she was in touch with her own reactions, she was encouraged to express them to the imagined other.

> *Client:* I get a knot in my stomach. I just feel sick. I want to disappear [and] fade into the background so he does not see me.

> *Therapist:* So, he's scary. You feel you have to disappear?

> *Client:* Yes. I know he doesn't want me around. I was a nuisance to him. I got in the way of his plans. He did not want a girl. I felt he despised me.

> *Therapist:* He made you feel unwanted? Can you say this to him—"I felt you despised me? I felt you didn't want me."

The therapist helped the client put her feelings into direct speech. Clients may need some encouragement with this, especially if the other has been abusive or harsh. With the therapist's encouragement, Jane was able to confront her father and express her feelings.

> *Client:* I felt so rejected by you. I never felt you wanted me. I was always scared, waiting for you to lash out at me. When you hit the boys, I wanted to disappear into the shadows. I was terrified of you.

> *Therapist:* So, you were so terrified of him? Can you tell him how scared you were?

> *Client:* I was terrified. I used to hide and wait until everything had calmed down and the shouting stopped.

> *Therapist:* What did you need from him?

> *Client:* Nothing. I tried never to need anything from him. He resented me so much.

> *Therapist:* So, it [was] hard to tell him what you needed—you tried to be self-sufficient?

> *Client:* Yes. It seemed the only way to survive.

> *Therapist:* What was it like to have him resent you so? What did the little girl feel like?

The therapist tried to heighten the client's access to her vulnerable feelings and needs. She emphasized what it was like for the little girl. This helped to make the episodic memory more vivid and evoke the client's feelings to make it easier for her to label and express them and symbolize the attendant need.

> *Client:* I felt so rejected, so unwanted. I wish he'd loved me. I wish he'd made me feel special and cared for.

Therapist:	Of course you did. You needed to feel special, to feel accepted and loved. Can you tell him that?
Client:	I felt you resented me so much. I just wish you had loved me.
Therapist:	It is just so painful; you wish he had loved you. What are the tears saying?

The therapist empathically reflected the client's pain. The use of empathic doubling responses, as well as empathic validation and evocation (see Chapter 4, this volume), is essential throughout this task.

One of the objectives in doing empty-chair work is to provide an opportunity for clients to give full expression to their feelings. The task enables clients to symbolize and give voice to parts of their experience that were not processed and expressed previously. This context not only enables clients to symbolize their experiences in awareness but also provides the opportunity for them to be soothed and supported by an accepting, empathic, and prizing other. Receiving acceptance and support from their therapist provides clients with a new and different experience of being vulnerable with another person. It allows clients the opportunity to rely on and be supported by someone else when in distress. With time clients can begin to internalize some of these more positive ways of treating their experience, so that they can be more accepting and valuing of their feelings, treating them with the respect and care that they deserve.

Naming the Other's Behaviors

In the next excerpt, the therapist continued to work with Jane to process her pain by asking her to name her father's behaviors and how she was treated by him.

Client:	I don't know it's so painful. He didn't protect me from my brothers.
Therapist:	So, is this something you would like to say? "You didn't protect me. You let them bully me."
Client:	Yes. I needed protection but it was almost like you [encouraged] them. You didn't care. Except once when they were making too much noise and you were working, then you got angry with all of us.
Therapist:	What did you need?
Client:	I needed a father who would protect me and love me, not [one that would] shout and make me feel unwanted and unloved.

Therapist:	So you needed his love and protection. Come over [to the opposite chair]. How does he respond when you say that?
Client:	He gets angry. What are you saying, of course I cared for you. You had a home; I fed you. That was more than I had. I had to leave home at 15 and fend for myself on the streets. You're too soft (with a dismissive hand gesture).
Therapist:	So what is he doing? What is this hand gesture saying? It sounds as if he is dismissing you, ridiculing you? Is that right?

The therapist tried to have the client symbolize and name what the other was doing, how the other was treating her. Asking clients to do this in empty-chair dialogues helps to make clear what the other does and how they behave toward the client. Naming the client's as well as the other's behaviors can be very revealing and clarifying of the relationship that clients have with others as well as with themselves. To do this, the therapist attends to clients' non-verbal behaviors. The therapist can ask his or herself what clients are doing or what expression is on clients' faces. The answers can be gleaned from clients' nonverbal behaviors, facial expressions, and tone of voice. Instead of focusing on the content of what clients are saying, the therapist focuses on the overall tone or message. The therapist can ask him- or herself what attitude is being conveyed (e.g., Is the client pleading? Is the other being compassionate? Is the client or other being dismissive and invalidating the client's experience?). The objective is to distill the essence of the behavior and put it into words so that clients become more aware of it.

As was described in Chapter 5, the structural analysis of social behavior interpersonal circumplex (Benjamin, 1974) can be used as a guide to how clients are treating themselves as well as how they experience others' treatment of them. By standing back and attending to the quality and type of interaction, the therapist can see the behavior of clients' imagined others, name it to make it more visible and, bring it into conscious awareness. When the behavior of the other becomes visible, clients are better able to see this behavior in themselves and the other, better able to apprehend its impact, and process their feelings and needs in the face of the other's negative treatment. Clients form links between their feelings and the other's behaviors, and these are acknowledged and validated by an empathically attuned therapist. As discussed in Chapter 5, this type of therapeutic interaction can be very healing for clients.

Some clients may find it hard to name the behavior of their imagined others; they may be afraid to see it clearly and starkly. These clients may need time to develop a stronger sense of self so that they can see the other's negative behaviors more clearly and cope with its implications for them and their relationships. To see the other's behavior as negative may be experienced as a betrayal if clients are enmeshed with and see the world through the eyes of their imagined other. Alternatively, to fully appreciate how negative the other has been may leave clients feeling very alone and vulnerable in the world. Thus, clients have to feel strong enough to stand alone and protect themselves. However, once they are able to do so, the conscious naming of the other's behavior enables it to be seen clearly and in a fresh, new way. This is useful because it helps clients to recognize that they are treating themselves and their experiences in a similar way and can heighten their awareness of the behavior of others in their lives, past and present. The increased clarity allows them to distinguish positive and negative interactions with others so as to form and maintain more positive relationships.

After the therapist named Jane's father's behavior as ridicule, Jane responded positively:

Client: Yes, that is what he did!

Therapist: What does he say when he sees you crying?

Client: Stop sniveling and whining. I'll give you something to whine about.

Therapist: He is not able to see your pain? He gets defensive and threatening. Come back over [to the original chair and speak as yourself]. What is it like for you when he dismisses and threatens you?

Client: I kind of give up. I feel hopeless and a little angry. He's not going to change.

Therapist: So, part of you gives up, feels defeated. What is the anger about?

Client: It's not right that he treats me like that, but what's the point?

Here Jane gave up. She felt some anger but became deflated as she experienced her father's scorn. She was not able to stand up to him or hold him accountable. In fact, she internalized her father's rejection of her so that she too was scornful of her vulnerability and unable to be compassionate or caring about her pain.

As discussed in Chapter 7, it is these inner splits of intense self-rejection in the face of feeling vulnerable that need to be addressed in GAD. Jane needed to develop a more self-accepting and caring attitude toward herself before she could stand up to her father and begin to see herself as deserving of love and protection. In Chapter 9, we describe the process of internalizing self-acceptance and self-compassion so that clients can soothe and take care of themselves when they feel vulnerable and in pain.

In later dialogues with her father, Jane acknowledged how hard it was for her to listen to or attend to her pain because to express pain and vulnerability was to be weak and risk rejection. With time, she was able to experience her pain and sadness and express these feelings to her therapist. She recognized how much she wanted attention and slowly began to internalize ways of treating herself that were more positive. She learned to attend to her feelings and to put them into words. At first she thought she would drown in the pain and be overwhelmed by it, but slowly she began to feel stronger, realizing that the pain waxed and waned and that she was able to bear it and find ways of comforting herself. Some clients may experience intense grief when they realize their imagined other can never meet their needs for love and protection. These clients need time to grieve to transform their pain and move on to try to meet their needs in the future.

TRANSFORMATION

Accessing and Expressing Self-Compassion and Self-Protective Anger

Relinquishing the "baby wish" for love and acceptance can take time, as clients internalize their therapist's attitudes of acceptance, empathy, and positive regard and in turn develop empathy for themselves as well as the capacity for self-soothing and self-compassion (Barrett-Lennard, 1997; J. Watson, Steckley, & McMullen, 2014). As they relinquish the wish to be protected, cared for, and loved by the other, clients come to accept that they will need to care of and soothe themselves and be more compassionate toward their feelings and needs. This state of differentiation, which clearly sees the other and the implications for the self along with the capacity to take care of the self and meet its needs, can feel lonely and scary to many clients, even as it paradoxically empowers them to ensure that they act in ways that are more self-protective and self-nurturing.

As we consider the role of clients' developing empathy for the self and the other, it can be useful to differentiate among different components of empathy, including perspective taking, abstract reasoning, and cognitive flexibility (Rankin et al., 2006). The task of enacting the other requires cognitive flexibility and the capacity to take the perspective of the other and engage in abstract reasoning about their motives, feelings, and intentions, which provides a more distant analytical view of the other. If clients can take the perspective of the other, the other's motivations become clearer. In cases where there have been positive interactions with another, perspective taking is useful so that clients can come to understand the other better. However, if the other has been very negative and malevolent and clients have spent much time and effort immersed in the other's worldview, then it is more important that self-empathy be developed so that clients can take better care of themselves in the relationship and assert boundaries with others (Greenberg & Paivio, 1997; Paivio & Pascual-Leone, 2010; J. Watson, 2006).

In cases in which the interaction has been mostly negative it may not be possible for clients to assume the role of the other in the empty-chair dialogue (Greenberg & Paivio, 1997; J. Watson, 2006). If they do, they may reenact the other's negative behavior toward them. The absence of compassion or positive caring from the other in the empty-chair dialogue is an indication that additional relational work with the therapist, rooted in the therapeutic attitudes of empathy, acceptance, prizing, and positive regard for clients and their experiences, is necessary to build and strengthen more positive ways of treating the self, including feelings and perceptions. In addition, clients may need some coaching and support to develop self-soothing (see Chapter 9, this volume). Once these attitudes have been internalized, clients are more easily able to empathize with their wounded, hurt self and provide the necessary compassion, acceptance, and soothing to relieve their pain. As clients let go of their pain, they often report feeling a sense of release, of opening up and being able to breathe more easily. The experience of tension and the painful feelings of sadness, fear, and shame that they have been holding in their bodies dissolve and give way to a sense of relief.

As was discussed in Chapter 3, clients experience negative circumstances and traumas at different developmental stages. The earlier in the developmental cycle that clients experience difficult interactions with the other or their environment, the more rigid the client's personality configuration and the more impaired their capacity for making sense of experiencing, processing and regulating their emotions and for developing a confident strong sense of self. These clients are less likely to internalize self-compassion and self-acceptance and develop optimal ways of processing emotion. The earlier clients experience negative interactions and environments or the more severe these are, the more likely they will reject themselves and silence their emotional experience in favor of trying to attend to and placate the other, or they may avoid their experience altogether. Either way, clients neglect their own experience and themselves as they try to cope with and adapt to negative environments.

Inhibited processing of emotion is evident in people who have insecure attachment styles. Often these clients may not have represented the other's behavior as egocentric or narcissistic. Rather, a lot of effort may have been invested in trying to see the world from the other's perspective, such that the client's own experiences have been overlooked, denied, and inadequately symbolized in awareness. This is how clients have tried to maintain security as children and ensure their basic needs for safety, love, and protection were met. However, this comes at a huge cost to the differentiation of the self (Bowen, 1976, 1978; Erikson, 1959; Sullivan, 1953; J. Watson, 2011), such that the tasks of becoming agentic and self-governing to develop an identity and learn to effectively process, regulate, and express emotions are interrupted and impeded. Instead, these clients tend to dismiss their perceptions and their feelings, fail to label them and symbolize them in awareness, driven rather by the needs of the other as they try to maintain safety and protect themselves from harm.

In the case example of Jane, these changes provided a glimpse into the development of a more differentiated and empathic stance toward the self. She and her therapist engaged in empty-chair dialogues with her brothers, giving her the opportunity to tell them how their behavior had affected her. She expressed the pain she experienced as a result of their bullying as well as her anger and disappointment that they had not protected her. At first, as Jane imagined her brothers, they were defensive, but then she was able to imagine them apologizing for their treatment of her. As she represented them, they explained that they saw her as being favored because Dad did not beat her. This made them resentful. Jane acknowledged that she had been spared his wrath and expressed empathy for what it must have been like for them. Jane was able to differentiate her experience from that of her brothers.

The client's capacity to express empathy for her brothers is an indication that she has internalized more positive ways of being. The expression of empathy to another is a good indication that clients are able to be more empathic and compassionate toward themselves. Indeed, it was shortly after this that Jane was able to engage in a dialogue with her father and hold him accountable for his mean and brutish behavior toward his children. She was able to state that she deserved better care and that she deserved to be loved and protected.

> Client: I deserved to be protected. We all did. I was a little girl, not someone to terrorize. It wasn't right that you were always angry with me.
>
> Therapist: Yes, you needed protection. Come over [to the other chair]. How does your father respond?
>
> Client: I can see that I hurt you. I didn't mean to cause pain. I never realized I was doing that. I just wanted you all to behave and be quiet. I didn't know how to deal with children.
>
> Therapist: So, you are surprised that she is so hurt? Are you sorry?
>
> Client: Yes, but I did not know how to parent. My father left when I was a baby and then my mother married again and my stepfather was a bully. I wish now that I had known how to do it differently.

Therapist:	Come [back] over [to the opposite chair]. How does it feel when he says he wishes he had been different?
Client:	That feels better. I know he had a hard life. But we needed a parent who was warm and loving . . . not one who punished us and made us feel weak and vulnerable.
Therapist:	Yes, of course you did. You deserved a father who made you feel special and who would have treasured you. What are the tears saying?
Client:	I feel so sad that our childhoods were so hard.

Here the client acknowledged her pain. By accessing protective anger, she was able to assert her needs and begin the process of grieving the absence of love and protection. As she began to grieve her losses, she became more compassionate and less demanding of herself. Her anxiety began to ease as she attended to her organismic experience and found ways to self-soothe herself and be more self-compassionate and self-protective.

The example of Jane was a severe case of GAD because of the harshness of the abuse and the lack of love and support from caretakers. In more severe cases, clients may have internalized very negative ways of treating themselves (e.g., extreme self-rejection). It is often these states of intense self-rejection that the worrier is trying to avoid. In these cases, the therapist needs to work with the client to build more positive, accepting, and nurturing ways of treating the self. In part, this can be accomplished as the client internalizes acceptance, concern, and empathy from the therapist. The therapist becomes the nonjudgmental, accepting, and empathic other that validates the client's pain and provides an antidote to the shame. Impossibly high standards to which clients feel they must live up to ensure that they are safe are challenged as clients learn to allow their vulnerability and relinquish sole responsibility for ensuring that they are not rejected and made to feel disposable. Through the empty-chair task we are able to see clients' capacity for empathy and acceptance grow, as well as their capacity to stand up to the other and assert their previously denied needs for support, care, and protection.

Differentiating and Claiming Space

The silencing of the self and the close alignment with the needs of the other to ensure emotional and or physical safety lead to emotional fusion (Bowen, 1976; Erikson, 1959; Perls, 1969). As a result, some clients may not have processed their inner and outer experiences adequately, nor have they had their emotional needs met. An important aspect of empty-chair work is to facilitate clients' differentiation of the self and others (J. Watson, 2011). The empty-chair task in EFT provides clients with the opportunity to give full expression to the impact of events as well as others' behavior. The full symbolization and expression of what the other did and how the other behaved toward them allows them to see the other more clearly. Clients are able to recognize the longer term impact and begin to apprehend what they needed in the past and what they will need in the future. This new understanding serves as a guide to develop ways of realizing and meeting their needs in ways that are more satisfying. As they rework their relationships with others, clients become more differentiated, developing a better understanding of what they need in relationship as well as what they need to do for themselves. Self-assertive behaviors become consolidated and generalize to their interactions with others. We can see this in the case example of Alex, which was first discussed in Chapter 5.

Alex needed to set boundaries with his mother, who had been anxious and intrusive throughout his life. As he began to develop more confidence, he was able to engage in an empty-chair dialogue with her.

Therapist: Can you imagine your mother in the chair, what do you want to say to her?

Client: You need to keep quiet. I know you are worried but I am a big boy now. So please stop telling me to be careful. You need to trust me.

Therapist: You need her to back off. You need her to trust you. Come over [to the other chair]. How does she respond?

Client: I am only trying to protect you. I do not want you to come to any harm. You know that after you were born you were very sick. I had to watch you constantly to make sure you gained weight. It was very hard for us and I was so worried.

Therapist: So, she says that she was worried after you were born and that she is trying to protect you. What do you say to that?

Alex: You did a good job. Now you have to trust that I will look after myself. You need to stop focusing all your attention on me and what I'm doing. It's not helpful any longer.

Therapist: Yes, you need to reassure her and tell her it's enough. She did a good job.

Here Alex established limits with his mother. He was assertive but also was able to see her as separate from him with her own fears and concerns. He reassured her by saying he can care for himself in an attempt to relieve her of the responsibility to keep him alive. Just as clients need to learn how to reassure and soothe themselves, the capacity to reassure anxious others can be helpful in setting boundaries.

In their dialogues with their others, clients are encouraged to give full voice and expression to their experience, to provide relief as well as to provide insight into how they were impacted and the toll it has taken. As they express their pain, clients are able to clearly identify the legacy of the interaction patterns and see their responses more clearly, as well as how these patterns play out in other arenas. Once clients have a clearer appreciation of their needs and longings with regard to the other and these needs have been expressed, clients are encouraged to respond as the other. In this process, they are representing their internalized sense of the other. In cases where it has been mixed with some positive and some negative, clients often access the positive and are capable of empathizing with the pain that has been expressed. This usually results in a redistribution of responsibility as the other assumes responsibility for the pain and seeks forgiveness. However, in the absence of any positive behaviors from the other, clients need to internalize the therapist's attitudes of acceptance, empathy, and prizing.

DIFFICULTIES WITH EMPTY-CHAIR DIALOGUES

Sometimes clients will have difficulty accessing and expressing painful emotions in the empty chair. In other cases, clients may not be able to accept that life was difficult and hard for them. It can take time for them to accept and come to terms with reality as they begin to construct their narratives. The tendency at first is to deny and dismiss how painful it was as they continue to cope using old established behaviors. Some clients may be so enmeshed with the other that to view the world through their own lens is seen as betraying the other. These clients have to feel strong to stand alone and view the world differently and see the other clearly. The EFT therapist accepts that clients may not be ready to do that at various times in the therapy. When this happens and clients express reluctance or are unable and unwilling to engage, the therapist facilitates clients' disengagement from the dialogue for a time. They continue to respond with empathic reflections, psychoeducation, and work with clients to process their stories as well as their feelings.

Later in therapy, when markers reappear, the therapist can suggest they engage in a dialogue again and see how far clients are able to go. In this way, each stage of the empty-chair dialogue also serves as an indicator of clients' readiness for change and an indication of whether they have acquired the necessary skills and capacity to process their pain and respond in positive self-protective and self-compassionate ways. The EFT therapist does not view clients' refusal to do a task or complete a particular stage in a task as resistance. Rather, when the task stalls, this is viewed as a prognostic indicator of clients' progress—whether they are able to access and symbolize their feelings; whether they feel entitled to and deserving of their feelings and needs to assert and express them to the other, or whether they have sufficient self-compassion and are able to protect themselves. Each time clients stall while engaging in a dialogue the therapist is informed about the work that clients still need to do to resolve these tasks effectively. In this way, the EFT therapist remains empathically attuned, accepting, prizing, and congruent with their clients and their experience, trusting that they are the experts in terms of the timing and their readiness to confront their pain and engage in the specific tasks of therapy.

Resolving pain through empty-chair work is a powerful emotional task that can transform the self. Clients develop new responses to situations, creating relief from years of painful feelings and distress. Empty-chair work facilitates the learning of emotional processing skills as well as different ways of treating the self and being with others. It is hugely healing and empowering as clients develop the capacity to protect themselves or alternatively take the perspective of the other, as they provide self-compassion, self-soothing, and self-empathy. In the next chapter, we look at how to work with clients to engender greater self-soothing and self-compassion.

9

EMOTIONAL TRANSFORMATION AND COMPASSIONATE SELF-SOOTHING IN GENERALIZED ANXIETY DISORDER

Emotional transformation in emotion-focused therapy (EFT) for generalized anxiety disorder (GAD) grows out of improved emotional processing capacities and a strengthened sense of self. As we described in Chapter 5, clients develop self-compassion and self-acceptance in relationship with their therapist. These new attitudes and ways of being toward themselves contribute to clients' capacity to self-soothe and reassure themselves on the basis of a greater sense of resilience and confidence. In previous chapters we described how clients with GAD can be rejecting of themselves and their experience, interrupting and ignoring their feelings out of a fear that they will drown in their anguish and distress. This often prevents clients from feeling they deserve to have their needs met. As they work on the blocks to feeling deserving through two-chair and empty-chair work, clients are able to assert themselves, access empowering anger, and process their sadness and grief. One of the important outcomes of the transformation of GAD is that clients find alternative ways to deal with their painful feelings of fear, sadness, and

http://dx.doi.org/10.1037/0000018-010
Emotion-Focused Therapy for Generalized Anxiety, by J. C. Watson and L. S. Greenberg

shame. This primarily involves self-soothing as they attend to their painful emotions, identify their needs, and find alternative ways of meeting them.

BUILDING SELF-SOOTHING: COPING AND TRANSFORMATIONAL

Self-soothing in EFT refers to a process in which clients are tender, caring, and comforting to themselves during a state of emotional suffering or anguish, which helps to undo their negative feelings (Goldman, Greenberg, & Angus, 2006; Greenberg, 2011; Pascual-Leone & Greenberg, 2007; J. Watson, 2006, 2012). It is a way of people being with and treating themselves that is compassionate to their own suffering and fulfills their own needs for care and comfort. This eases their pain when others aren't there to do it for them. This type of intervention is most applicable when clients are suffering emotionally, are feeling painfully alone in their anguish, and are unable to be self-compassionate. If, at times of distress, clients are able to experience the positive emotions of compassion, tenderness, and caring and comfort themselves, they are engaging in self-soothing and showing evidence of more positive ways of treating the self. If the soothing is successful in undoing the negative emotion, they reduce fear of their painful feelings and have tools to assuage fear, shame, and sadness and overcome anxiety and distress. This, in turn, contributes to a sense of internal security and greater resilience and confidence that they can cope with painful feelings.

An important goal of EFT, therefore, is to facilitate an increase in clients' capacity to self-soothe states of emotional suffering and pain felt as a result of their needs not being met. This is achieved by internalizing the soothing received from others, including their therapist, so that clients are able to be compassionate and self-soothe from an adult-like self-organization. The capacity to self-soothe that is so central to producing change in clients with GAD is facilitated by an empathically attuned relationship with an accepting, warm, and sincere therapist. This type of relationship helps clients regulate their overwhelming and disorganizing painful emotions by providing interpersonal soothing through the therapist's acceptance, empathy, prizing, and genuineness. In relationship with their therapist, clients develop emotion regulation capacities and greater resilience to life's challenges, as well as positive views and beliefs about themselves. Over time the interpersonal regulation of affect becomes internalized into self-soothing and the capacity to regulate inner states (Stern, 1985). When a connection is made with an empathic and accepting therapist, the emotional processing centers in the brain are affected and new possibilities open up. Self-compassion and self-empathy are seen as emerging from the internalization of the soothing aspects of empathy and affect attunement from an accepting, warm, and empathic therapist.

The internalization of the therapist's positive attitudes, however, may take a number of years in therapy. Clients who have a positive foundation and have internalized self-compassion from others will be able to respond quickly and access more positive ways of being with the self and others. For other clients, who have not internalized positive ways of being with the self and whose affect regulation and self-organizations have been compromised more severely, the internalization of positive ways of being with the self and regulating their affective states may take longer. In these cases, in addition to providing the positive therapeutic attitudes of empathy, acceptance, and warmth, the therapist may suggest interventions designed explicitly to facilitate self-soothing. In these dialogues, clients are guided in their imagination or in a chair dialogue to soothe their vulnerable self. These tasks can help to build and intensify the relational process of self-compassion and self-soothing being acquired in therapy.

Self-soothing can be developed in two different ways. The first, referred to as *coping self-soothing*, is for improved emotion regulation of symptomatic secondary anxiety. These types of coping strategies actively target physiological responses. Thus, when levels of anxiety become unmanageable, coping self-soothing is helpful to manage the intensity of the feelings. The second, more central, way in EFT is referred to as *transformational self-soothing*. It involves ways of being with the self, derived from the internalization of self-compassion and self-acceptance received from others that moderates core pain. It is rooted in clients' inner resources to self-soothe when confronting their core painful primary maladaptive emotions, enabling them to transform their pain and sense of self. In GAD, the core pain generally comes from the primary maladaptive emotions of sadness, fear, and shame and the unmet needs for connection and support. These two different forms of self-soothing, coping and transformational, are described in more detail next, along with the markers for initiating self-soothing tasks.

MARKERS FOR SELF-SOOTHING TASKS

There are two different markers of self-soothing, one for each type. For coping self-soothing, which down-regulates a secondary symptomatic experience (e.g., panic, fear, anger) through breathing, distraction, and feelings of safety, the marker is dysregulation in the moment. Transformational self-soothing, which attempts to change core primary feelings by experiencing another emotion, is marked by clients' accessing previously disclaimed anguish and emotional suffering (Goldman & Greenberg, 2014; Ito, Greenberg, Iwakabe, & Pascual-Leone, 2010).

Coping self-soothing, therefore, is used for dysregulated symptomatic distress to help down-regulate the intensity of the emotions being experienced in the session. The focus is on soothing secondary emotional reactions and physiological responses. The anxious reaction is a response to the threat of experiencing underlying core primary emotions. Clients with GAD begin to worry, get anxious, and feel overwhelmed by tightness and pressure in the chest and knots in the stomach. In contrast, the marker for transformational self-soothing is the experience of emotional suffering or anguish (Goldman & Greenberg, 2014; Ito et al., 2010). Primary core painful emotions (e.g., fear of being alone, sadness of being disconnected, shame of being rejected) are activated, along with a basic insecurity and belief that clients cannot survive alone. Often this is accompanied by despair that clients' needs were never met and might never be met. Typically, the anguish occurs in the face of powerful interpersonal needs (e.g., love, validation, protection) that were not met by others and that clients may have avoided recognizing as a way of coping with their painful feelings.

These unmet needs, along with the basic sense of anxious insecurity that clients will disintegrate and will not survive alone, are at the base of GAD. Previously unmet needs and the anguish about never being able to get their needs met is evoked in therapy to access clients' painful emotions and make them amenable to transformation. Unmet needs often emerge through therapeutic work during empty-chair or two-chair dialogues. Clients' anguish, rooted in unfinished business with a significant other, often arises in empty-chair dialogues, in which painful primary emotions and needs are expressed, but the other is unresponsive to them. The lack of response from the imagined other results in feelings of painful loneliness and despair. This despair emerges as clients access their primary feelings of fear and sadness and feel that they cannot bear the pain alone.

In two-chair dialogues, anguish arises after clients express a need in the *self* chair which is not acknowledged or responded to with compassion and care. An indicator for self-soothing in the context of self-critical two-chair work is when the critical self is extremely annihilating and the experiencing self shows no resilience. Typically, in response to this form of criticism, the self collapses into deep despair and anguish and begins to disintegrate. There is little capacity to stand up for the experiencing self's needs. This is a clear indication that clients lack empathy and compassion for the self. This is also evident when the critical self is relentless, intransigent, or intractable. When this occurs, it is unlikely that clients will be able to be compassionate and kind to themselves, and thus "softening" seems out of reach. Often in these situations, clients report that they cannot remember prior experiences in which anyone was kind or gentle to them. The therapist can then assume the role of the soothing, empathic other to help clients down-regulate the intensity of their feelings and provide a model of empathic, accepting, and validating ways of being with the self. Here the therapist, as the empathic and accepting other, provides a corrective emotional and relational experience. In addition, the therapist can teach clients more explicitly about self-compassion using self-soothing dialogues.

COPING SELF-SOOTHING

Coping self-soothing is used in the presence of overwhelming anxiety or negative affect, and high physiological arousal when clients are having difficulty coping with overwhelming feelings. These overwhelming feelings are often signaled by clients saying things like, "I can't stand this, I need to get out." The first step in facilitating emotion regulation is the provision of a safe, calming, validating, and empathic environment. This type of interaction helps soothe underregulated distress (Bohart & Greenberg, 1997; J. Watson, 2002, 2015) and strengthens the self. In addition, this process can be supported by teaching emotion regulation and distress tolerance skills (Linehan, 1993), including identifying and avoiding triggers, identifying and labeling emotions, allowing and tolerating emotions, establishing a working distance, increasing positive emotions, consciously regulating breathing, and engaging in distraction (Greenberg & Paivio, 1997; Kennedy-Moore & Watson, 1999; J. Watson, 2006). Forms of meditative practice and self-acceptance can also be helpful in achieving a working distance from overwhelming emotions. The ability to regulate breathing and observe emotions, to let them come and go, are important processes to help regulate emotional distress.

Physiological Soothing

The intensity of emotion can be down-regulated by soothing at different levels of self-processing, including physiological and psychological. Examples of self-processing include self-talk and imagery exercises. Physiological soothing involves activation of the parasympathetic nervous system to regulate heart rate, breathing, and other sympathetic functions that speed up under stress. When clients feel overwhelmed or emotionally flooded in the session, the therapist can guide them to engage in regulatory self-soothing strategies. These may include suggesting that they attend to their breathing, put their feet on the ground and become aware of what is happening around them, feel themselves in their chair, or look at their therapist and describe what they see (J. Watson, 2006). Alternatively, the therapist might also suggest clients reassure their anxious self by saying, "It's okay if you're feeling anxious now, we will get through this." Relaxation exercises and relaxation tapes can be useful to teach clients these skills. These activities to support and encourage relaxation, grounding, and self-comforting can help clients to regulate their distress in the moment.

Imagining a Safe Place

In addition to these strategies, the therapist can guide clients more explicitly to access self-soothing in the session. Promoting clients' abilities to regulate and achieve a working distance from their emerging painful emotional experience is an important step toward tolerating emotion and self-soothing. A key strategy to promote self-soothing of this type is to suggest to clients in high distress that they imagine a safe place. Once they have this image, they are asked to experience what it would be like to be there (Elliott, Watson, Goldman, & Greenberg, 2004; Gendlin, 1996; J. Watson, 2006). The therapist may say, for example,

> Imagine taking your inner, wounded child somewhere safe where you can care for her and protect her? Where is this place? Can you describe what you see around you? What do you want to say to her to make her feel safe?

Alternatively, the therapist can encourage clients to "clear a space" (Elliott et al., 2004). In this exercise, clients are asked to imagine going to a safe place where they can list their concerns and set them out in front of them or imagine placing them in different containers. In this way clients are encouraged to relieve the tension and press of their concerns and anxiety in the moment. It gives them a sense that they can create some distance from their anxiety and that they can regulate it to feel more relaxed and calm.

These imagery exercises teach clients that they are capable of imagining and providing a safe place for themselves. They are used as a means of soothing high symptomatic distress in the session and as homework to cope with high levels of distress experienced outside the sessions. This explicit teaching of how to access a safe place and down-regulate their emotions helps clients build the skills that enable them, when in a distressed state, to shift into a more soothing stance toward themselves and achieve a calm state. Coping self-soothing is a deliberate skill that can be taught and cultivated to handle immediate feelings of anxiety in specific situations. The intention of these interventions is to help clients build the capacity to calm and reassure themselves that will automatically emerge when they feel distressed.

The following is a case example of how coping self-soothing can be used. A client, who was extremely anxious about work, was dealing with her feelings of intense anxiety about giving a presentation to her superiors the following day. Together with the therapist, she worked to articulate some of the negative things she said to herself that exacerbated her anxiety, such as, "I'm never going to have the presentation ready on time; I'm going to embarrass myself; I should have done more preparation." The client would often worry that her presentations would be a disaster because she did not feel prepared and as a result had difficulty falling asleep. In order to self-soothe, she first focused on breathing more regularly and then tried to access a safe place by imagining herself going into the bedroom she had as a child. There she imagined the pictures of the monkey, Curious George, on the wall and soft music playing. She would relax and say to herself, "It's going to be okay; you've done this before; you've got something important to say; just breathe." This exercise made her feel better. The feeling was reinforced as she imagined a soft blanket around herself. After learning these techniques to soothe herself, she was able to regulate herself physiologically. In this example, we see that the client was able to access memories of a safe place where she could seek refuge. However, some clients may be unable to call up a safe place and alternative ways of soothing the self may need to be built over the course of treatment.

Identifying Comforting Experiences

Other ways of teaching clients self-soothing is to direct their attention to experiences that feel comforting. When clients are unable to call up a safe place or respond with self-compassion when distressed, the EFT therapist focuses them on their feelings of distress and encourages them to articulate and identify their needs for comfort. Once she or he has done this, the therapist can ask clients what experiences are comforting and soothing. For some clients, this may be a good meal, a warm bath, curling up under a blanket with a book, sitting with a hot cup of coffee, listening to music, playing an instrument, or watching a movie. For example, one client would buy herself a special magazine, just as she had done as a child and go home and read it to soothe her distress as she was processing her sadness and anger at a parent's abuse.

These are just a few ways clients have identified as helpful as they try to comfort and soothe themselves when distressed (J. Watson, 2006). The important thing is for them to come up with ways that they personally find comforting and soothing. Some have difficulty knowing what is comforting. They have not experienced or attended to times when they experienced comfort, nor have they been able to provide it for themselves. It is important to encourage these clients to experiment and try to attend to those experiences in their day-to-day lives that they find comforting. As they do this, they slowly begin to build up strategies and ways of caring for themselves when feeling distressed, anxious, and alone. In tandem with these interventions, the therapist continue to work to build clients' self-compassion using self-soothing dialogues as well as clients' greater self-acceptance and new ways of treating themselves and their emotional experience.

TRANSFORMATIONAL SELF-SOOTHING

Being able to self-soothe and develop optimal self-regulation of emotion develops initially with the internalization of the soothing functions of the protective other (Sroufe, 1996; Stern, 1985), including self-empathy and self-compassion. Over time the behavior and attitudes of the protective other, their soothing and acceptance, are internalized and clients develop self-compassion and the capacity to soothe and regulate their painful feelings automatically without deliberate effort. Interventions to enhance the development of this type of self-soothing include the therapist's ongoing empathic reflections showing acceptance, prizing, and understanding of clients' emotions. In addition, the therapist can teach self-soothing more explicitly by drawing on clients' experience and understanding of care, compassion, and soothing. This is done by asking clients to imagine a scene of deprivation or invalidation when there was no one available to provide soothing and to try to soothe and comfort themselves. This intervention can be suggested when a client is in anguish, is expressing a lot of self-condemnation or self-contempt, feels lonely and unsupported, or is suffering emotionally and appears unable to access any self-soothing capacities.

Clients' soothing capacity can be activated in two main ways: (a) having them imagine their current adult selves in a memory of when they were wounded as child and providing a reparative response; and (b) asking clients, in a chair dialogue, if they or some other compassionate figure could soothe themselves as a wounded child. The goal is to evoke compassion for the self (cf. Gilbert, 2012). This intervention is a more active way, over and above the relationship with the therapist, to directly facilitate self-soothing by suggesting to clients that they, as adults, offer compassion to the suffering self. This can supplement the empathic therapeutic relationship and potentially speed up the process of developing the capacity for self-soothing by making it more explicit. It also serves to give therapist and client a read in terms of whether the latter is developing and internalizing self-compassion and self-care.

Dialoguing With the Vulnerable Self

The therapist introduces this task when she or he observes that clients have difficulty being self-compassionate and accepting of themselves or when they have arrived at previously disclaimed painful experience. To facilitate the evocation of self-compassion, the therapist can suggest to clients when they are in a state of emotional suffering or anguish that they engage in a dialogue with an imagined vulnerable self and soothe and care for that self (Ito et al., 2010). Clients are encouraged to be tender, caring, and comforting of themselves.

Compassion toward the self transforms negative emotion with positive emotion, thereby undoing negative feelings (Greenberg, 2011; Tugade & Frederickson, 2004).

Dialoguing With an Imaginary Child

If clients are unable to imagine themselves in an empty-chair dialogue, the therapist may ask them to imagine themselves as a child sitting in the opposite chair. To evoke the child's plight, the therapist might describe the most poignant details of the client's history and ask, "What would you say to that child? What do you feel toward that child?" This can evoke a compassionate response for the child and the child's circumstances, as well as recognition of what the child needs. Research has shown that one of the moderating factors in activating empathy is seeing someone in need of care and protection. For example, the therapist introduced this dialogue to Lisa, a client who was having difficulty being compassionate to herself:

> Client: My mother was too sick to be there when I got home from school, and my father was emotionally weak and leaned on me. I was so lonely and scared. I couldn't manage by myself. I was overwhelmed.
>
> Therapist: You were just so alone. There was no one there to help you or support you?
>
> Client: No, I was a just a child and there were no adults. That's just how it was.

To activate compassion, the therapist continued:

> Therapist: Can you imagine an 8-year-old sitting here? Her mother isn't there, she's sick in bed, and is unable to talk to her [daughter]. Her father looks to [his daughter] for love and companionship. What do you imagine it's like for her? What would you say to her if she were your child?
>
> Client: I know she felt very alone with no one to care for her; she was so overburdened. Looking at her now, I think she deserved to have someone who could take care of her more.
>
> Therapist: So, she needs more care. What do you feel toward her?
>
> Client: I feel concern; compassion for what she must have felt.
>
> Therapist: Tell her. Can you give her some of what she needs?

Once the client recognized the child's needs and responded in a caring, soothing manner, the therapist asked the client if she could respond to her own wounded child in that same way. In EFT, the therapist works with the metaphor of clients' wounded or inner child because the distress is rooted in experiences that clients endured when they were young. Often this self-organization manifests in empty-chair and two-chair dialogues, with the internally organized vulnerable child state being evoked in the session. It is important to note that we are not assuming there is a child within, but rather a self-state of vulnerability experienced at an earlier time or a sense of wound-edness experienced as a child is evoked, which in turn activates the emotions clients experienced at the time of the injury. It can be highly poignant to clients to have the hurt they experienced as a child soothed and comforted by their adult selves to provide the affective attunement and caring that was never received.

WORKING WITH BLOCKS TO SELF-SOOTHING

Timing the Intervention

The timing of this intervention is important, particularly for the questions regarding how clients feel toward the younger self who was wounded. It cannot be asked too soon in therapy, as this can lead the client to feel invalidated or overburdened. When clients have been overburdened and responsible for caring for themselves, they need a period of time where they can lay down the burden and relax, confident that someone else will be there to respond to them with empathy, compassion, and acceptance. Clients need someone else to provide the care and support that was missing before they once again assume the mantle of self-care. Of course, when clients take it up again, it is in a different way—one that acknowledges their feelings and needs and supports them to find better ways to meet those needs in the present.

To soothe themselves in the session, clients may need to be somewhat differentiated from the childhood feelings of anguish and despair. It can be helpful if they have shown or provided examples of times when they have been empathic to others. It is the capacity to be empathic and caring of another in need that the therapist tries to build on and make clients more aware of so that they can access it in the service of self-soothing. If the feelings of vulnerability have not been validated sufficiently for clients to feel more resilient, if their feelings are still too entangled and confusing, if they are still distraught about their behavior and feel ashamed, or if they have not yet begun to differentiate from an unresponsive parent, they may not be able to offer solace and comfort to the distressed self. This may also occur if they still feel weak and vulnerable and are unable to access any sense of confidence that they can cope. If they are still afraid that they will be overwhelmed and unable to cope with their pain, they may not be ready to explore or access feelings of compassion toward themselves. Sometimes clients may feel angry and betrayed by significant others who did not provide for them, and this can also hinder their desire to assume the mantle of self-care. However, as therapy progresses, clients come to accept that they need to do this for their own protection and well-being, if they are to heal and thrive.

Imagining a Universal Child

If clients are reluctant or struggling to be empathic toward their own experience, it can be helpful to start with a universal child, instead of having clients imagining themselves as a child. When the self-soothing dialogue is introduced to clients who are not sufficiently differentiated from the hostile negative caretaker and they are asked to start with their own child self, the contempt or destructive reaction of the other may be evoked. It is precisely this type of negative reaction that needs to be transformed over the course of treatment. In cases like this, it can be difficult, initially, for clients to feel compassionate toward themselves as a wounded child. Instead, they invalidate their own vulnerability. At these times, it is better not to ask clients to see themselves as a child in the other chair or to imagine the part of the self that needs soothing, as this may evoke negative feelings or condemnation of the child or the vulnerable self. Instead, it may be more helpful to symbolize the anguish as being that of a universal child or a close friend who has experienced the same things and that are the source of their anguish. Even though people understand the implication of what they are being asked to do by being compassionate to a universal child in similar circumstances, they may be able to soothe this universal child more easily than themselves as a child, as the latter may automatically evoke self-contempt. But once compassion has occurred in relation to a child in need, it is easier to transfer this feeling to the self.

Providing Protection

Sometimes the adult self may feel overwhelmed by seeing a hurt, damaged child as they do not yet have a sense that they can protect themselves effectively or they may fear that they will disintegrate and drown in their pain. At these times, the therapist can become a surrogate protector. For example, when a client is overwhelmed or frightened by the pain they see in themselves as a young child, therapist and client can work together to confront the abusive or neglectful other. Clients can feel safer in their therapist's presence, drawing strength from it. They can be encouraged to imagine the therapist right behind them, or even in front of them, telling the abusive other to stop. In empty-chair dialogues, the therapist can help clients put their needs into words. For example, she or he might help a client tell an overly protective other to back off:

Therapist: What do you need from him? Do you need him stop?

Client: Yes.

Therapist: Can you say this? [Can you say,] "Stop, you are hurting me. It makes me feel scared and alone."

Client: Yes—stop! It hurts when you criticize me. You make me feel stupid and incompetent. I can do this by myself. Stop pushing me!

There are a number of variations in the way a self-soothing dialogue can be done, but essentially the therapist needs to support and encourage the client to express compassion, kindness, and warmth toward the part of him- or herself that is distressed and vulnerable. The intervention is best introduced when clients are suffering emotionally. The general steps in the intervention involve encouraging clients to be a soothing figure and guiding them to become the wounded self and receive compassion. The comforting agent is represented either as a strong, nurturing aspect of the self, as an idealized parental figure, or as some other positive force. In the *vulnerable* chair, clients can imagine a number of different personages, including a universal child, a known child, their own inner child, or their vulnerable self.

After suggesting that the client play an idealized other expressing compassion and care to the self, the therapist might ask, "Can you be yourself now as an adult entering the scene, and respond to yourself as a child? What do you want to say to her?" If the client is expressing compassion to a known child, the therapist might say, "I know that you really try to be there for your niece." Here the therapist tries to evoke familiar feelings of compassion that the client has demonstrated or shared previously. She or he might ask clients how they would respond to the other: "What would you say to your daughter/niece/friend if she was going through this? Can you see her there and tell her?"

Alternatively, if the client is imagining a universal child, the therapist can ask questions like, "How do you feel toward that child over there? She looks so sad and alone? Tell her what you are feeling toward her." This helps to evoke compassion in the client for the wounded other. If the client does not seem compassionate and empathic, the therapist can try to activate previously experienced positive feelings of compassion by asking, "What would you say to your daughter/niece/friend if she was feeling that way?" After the client expresses concern, the therapist can then ask, "Can you imagine having this same caring feeling and attitude toward yourself?" In order to explore difficulties in being compassionate to the self, the therapist might ask, "What stops you from giving this to yourself?" This can help clients begin to explore what is standing in the way of their being compassionate and reassuring to themselves.

Other ways that the therapist can try to activate compassion is to ask clients to imagine how a soothing other might respond, for example, "How would this imagined other respond to a friend who was going through that?" It can be helpful to have clients recall times when they were soothed or comforted by others. In this case the self-soothing dialogue might involve the therapist saying, "Can you imagine what your grandmother would say to you if she knew how you were suffering?" "Can you be the mother or father of your dreams, what would they say? What did you need to hear?" or "Is there anyone in your past whom you recall as being there for you, giving you care and compassion? What would they say to you?" This imagined other can be an actual person, a grandparent, teacher, spiritual figure, or a collective structure such as a tribe or an agency that provided security.

TRANSFORMATION: EMOTIONAL AND INTERPERSONAL

Emotional Transformation

After clients have expressed some compassion or concern for the self, the therapist asks them to take the child position and encourages them to express their needs and wants from the child state. The therapist might ask, "What do you need from [your adult self/compassionate other] to feel loved? What do you need to hear to feel that you are okay?" He or she also might ask, "How does it feel to hear your mother or your adult self expressing care and concern toward you?" The therapist works with the experience of clients' child state and facilitates recognition of the positive feelings of being soothed. To do this, the therapist helps clients as the child to articulate in language the quality of the soothed feeling. Resolution in this task involves not only feeling compassion toward the self but also supporting the self to access their unmet needs, and potentially grieve the pain and loss that their needs for love, protection, and validation were never met.

Grieving Loss

This process involves clients' moving from anguish, through the main steps of accessing painful primary maladaptive emotions toward a statement of unmet needs and the sadness of grief at not having had these needs met (Ito et al., 2010). At times there may be fear followed by an interruption of emotion and protest about having to soothe the self that must be worked through before clients can access their primary painful emotions. It appears that it is not simply enacting compassion for the self that leads to resolution but also accessing the unmet need and grieving its loss that are important in activating feelings of compassion for the pain of the loss and to provide the missing compassion and responsiveness that is so healing. As clients go through this process with a supportive and empathic therapist, they develop feelings of compassion for themselves for what was lost. Over time, doing this in conjunction with receiving empathic soothing and acceptance from the therapist, who is emotionally attuned, clients eventually develop the capacity to soothe themselves and transform their painful emotions.

Enacting Imaginary Transformations

Imagery can be used in a variety of ways to evoke clients' anguish and transformative compassion. The visual system is highly related to emotion (Lang et al., 1998), so imagination can be used to evoke unresolved painful emotions, to enact dialogues in imagination, to experience the new emotion of compassion, or to imagine adding comforting people or resources to situations or scenes to help clients experience different scenes in new ways. Thus, to access clients' core emotions, the therapist can ask them to imagine a scene in which they were being bullied or neglected. These painful feelings can be transformed as clients express what is needed or by imagining having a protector with them in a childhood scene. In this latter scenario, clients are encouraged to imagine a protector (e.g., a policeman, the therapist) who can offer the protection that was missing. Alternatively, other aids to empower or protect clients can be imagined (e.g., locking the door to secure their room, having the feared person in a cage). This imaginary exercise can help generate new emotions of assertive anger and positive feelings toward the self to change the old maladaptive emotions of fear, shame, and sadness.

In this type of imaginary transformation, the therapist might say,

> Try closing your eyes and remember your experience in this situation. Get a concrete image if you can. Go into it. Be your child in this scene. Please tell me what is happening. What do you see, smell, hear in the situation? What do you feel in your body and what is going through your mind?

After a while, the therapist can ask clients to shift perspective by saying,

> Now I would like you to view the scene as an adult. What do you see, feel, and think? Do you see the look on the child's face? What do you want to say or do? Can you do this? How can you intervene? Can you try to do this now in your imagination?

Changing perspectives again the therapist can ask clients to become the child by asking the following questions:

What do you as the child feel and think? What do you need from the adult? Can you ask for what you need or wish? What does the adult do? What else do you need? Can you ask for it? Is there someone else you would like to come in to help? Can you receive the care and protection offered?

This intervention concludes with the therapist asking,

Check how you feel inside right now. What does all this mean to you, about you, and about what you needed? Can you come back to the present, to yourself as an adult now here with me? How do you feel? Can you say goodbye to the child for now?

These are powerful ways of engendering self-compassion, which many clients lack, and they directly counter self-contempt, guilt, and self-reproach. Engendering self-compassion can also be very eye opening, as clients realize how little compassion they have felt toward themselves or were inclined to feel toward themselves as a child in the beginning. Thus, the maladaptive primary insecurity, sadness, and fear at the core of GAD can be transformed into security and assertive anger to protect and soothe the self to meet needs for comfort and succor.

CASE EXAMPLE: ROSLYN

The process of helping clients develop and access self-compassion and self-soothing is illustrated in the following case example. Here the self-soothing occurred in the context of a two-chair dialogue in which the client, Roslyn, expressed an intransigent critical voice:

Client: I need you to support me, to be there as a friend, not a foe.

Therapist: Switch chairs [and hear that as the critical self]. "I need to know that you support me." What do you say back?

Client: You don't deserve support. You haven't done a thing to deserve support. Nothing. You're weak, pathetic, just worthless.

Deep vulnerability and anguish emerged as the client said this, so the therapist introduced a self-soothing dialogue in an attempt to facilitate compassion for the self that seems so despised:

Therapist: So, this [self] is very contemptuous. Can you imagine a child over there who feels this deep pain? She feels invalidated, just as you did as a child. What would you say to this child?

Client: That's the whole problem. I can't do that. I've never done that; no one has ever done that for me; I simply don't know how. I'm a lost cause.

Therapist: So, it's hard and it feels like you cannot do that for yourself.

The client observed that she did not know how to show compassion because no one had been kind or compassionate to her. The therapist suggested she imagine or think of another child:

Therapist: I wonder what would it be like if you had a child who really needed some support and was kind of saying, "I need to know that you've got my back"? A little while ago you mentioned your father and how even though he was not always available when you were a kid, he used to take you to the circus or the amusement park. I don't know what that was like for you or what you felt, but I imagine you might have felt loved, pretty special. So does it make sense to imagine being him or perhaps someone else, who could be caring to her? Can you try? Can you come over here and maybe tell her, "It's okay, I got your back"?

Client: Well, I could be my father. It's hard for me to remember him but I do have a fond feeling. I could try as I am now, and seeing her so little and say, "Don't worry, I'm here with you."

Therapist: Okay, good. So you can say that to her?

Client: Yeah, I'm here. I'm going to be here for you. You don't have to worry. I'm behind you. You do deserve to be loved and I'm here to give you that.

The client was able to access some compassion for herself and was willing to support and protect herself in her child state. Next, the therapist switched to have the client in her child state focus on what it felt like to be cared for by another:

Therapist: Good, can you switch back to this other chair. Tell her what it's like, from inside of you to hear that.

Client: I really needed to hear that. I feel really good hearing that.

Therapist: You really need to get that love you so deserved. Tell her what it's like to get it.

Client: I just feel kind of warm inside—it's like a blanket around me.

Therapist: So, that is what you need to hear—"you're okay." Tell her.

Client: I needed to hear that. It feels good to hear it. I feel stronger hearing that.

Another example of self-soothing is given next. In this example the general procedure of self-soothing was done without the explicit use of chair work or wounded child imagery. Roslyn talked about her worry, mainly her family, and the dreaded feeling that she had become more aware of through therapy. Her therapist asked her to focus on this feeling.

Therapist: Would it be okay if we kind of tried to go to this vulnerable place [and] bring it into the room and kind of see what it has to say now? Does that sound okay?

For the next few minutes, the client first talked around the feeling without getting into it, and then she observed that she had this feeling currently in the session with respect to her son and his future.

Client: I don't know. I think [this is] just me. It's in me just to do it. [By] trying to help him and because I'm so worried about him, it feels that way.

Therapist: Well, can you try? Almost as if you could turn your eyes inwards and try to actually touch a place, not in your head thinking, but actually go into your body and try to touch that place. I mean almost try to get a feeling for it, not just thinking about it, but try to get a feeling for that spot.

The therapist asked the client to focus on her feeling and to try to symbolize it. The client did this and began to differentiate it.

Client: Yeah, it's that I felt a little bit of emptiness and it's a little bit of sadness too.

Therapist: And what do you want to say if you just [get at that feeling].

Client: I just want to push my stomach like that. It just seems like I felt comfort.

Therapist: So, [you] like to hold it?

Client: Yeah, sometimes I forget about it and I just grab a pillow at night and place it against me. My husband sometimes [asks] what [I am] doing?

The client held her stomach and accessed a sensation of comfort and support. Subsequently, she recalled a memory from the previous week when she was able to comfort herself and instead of turning away from her distress, she was able to focus and attend to it. The therapist reflected how she was able to comfort herself:

Therapist: So, [you're] soothing [yourself] a little and that's so natural to do that. It's almost like that place. [You] didn't get the hugs, support, [or] love, and you know as an adult [you] can do that, in that space. You know you hug and you soothe. What's that feel like when you do that when you comfort [yourself]?

Client:	It feels comfortable, [I feel] more comfortable.
Therapist:	Can you speak to yourself? If you can be in that space [and] tell yourself what it feels like when you as an adult, hug, soothe, and comfort yourself. What does it feel like in that space?
Client:	It feels . . .
Therapist:	Can you say "I" as if you're speaking from the place?
Client:	I feel like I'm like I've been taken care of.
Therapist:	[You] feel like [you're] being taken care of.
Client:	Like I'm going to have to leave [therapy] because now I'm okay.
Therapist:	Like, [you're] doing okay now and maybe [you] can leave [therapy] because [you] got that comfort.
Client:	Right. That's the word: comfort.
Therapist:	Comfort. Can you say more about what that feels like, that, maybe [you] can leave [therapy]? Can [you] say more about that?
Client:	Well, it feels good to be comforted. As the feeling I've been having to make [me] feel what's going on.

Here the client comforted herself. She was able to hug herself and provide an experience of care and support. She and the therapist went on to explore the function of the anxiety and how the client had coped previously.

Therapist:	So I've been informing you of that, and you're just starting to hear me. And it's so important that you started to hear me.
Client:	Yeah, but [this only] happened a couple of times I told you about last week. Before that, I wouldn't let it happen. I was just thinking that it's here and I'd better get a cup of tea or turn [on] the TV [or] read. I would talk to my husband about something because I don't like to feel like that [way]. But this time I didn't do that. This time I remembered the pillow and I felt better because then I thought about it. I thought about what caused that bad empty feeling and what this feeling was and I felt there were solutions.

The client recalled that she was able to comfort herself the previous week. She observed that previously she would have tried to distract herself or seek out her husband to comfort her. However, here she was able to draw on her growing capacity to self-soothe and take care of her pain. The client began to see the value of attending to her painful, distressing emotions. She realized that she can find solutions and that it can be helpful to attend to her feelings. She recalled that the empty feeling was associated with a severe medical condition that she had endured and the fear that she would be disabled, without money or support.

> *Therapist:* So, is this feeling kind of saying that you heard me? You allowed me to be there and then you heard what I had to say.
>
> *Client:* Yeah, well, maybe I needed you. Maybe I needed this feeling.

The therapist then asked the client to engage in a dialogue with the empty feeling.

> *Therapist:* Can you come over [to this other chair]? This is the other [self], right? Can you speak to the empty feeling as if that place is there, that hole is there: "I needed you."
>
> *Client:* I needed you because in that way I would just start thinking in a different way and not feel so sorry for myself, because in a way, I always felt like a victim. But that's not really the way it is. Although I have problems with my eyes, and my husband [has] problems with his legs, we are still productive people. We can still do things.
>
> *Therapist:* Of course, [you are] still young.
>
> *Client:* Yeah, we're still fairly young and we're not ready to [be thrown out with the trash].

Here the client accessed a sense of resilience and confidence in herself. There was a change in her self-organization as she felt able to cope with the future and acknowledged her resources. The therapist encouraged her to look at what the anxiety was saying.

> *Therapist:* No, but maybe "you did something for me." Can you say a little about that?
>
> *Client:* You give me some opportunity of thinking of my problem and try to look for a solution.
>
> *Therapist:* And you've been there for so long it's kind of like no wonder you were trying to tell [yourself] something. Since talking about it, you see that this feeling has a message for you. And that's kind of like the part that protected you is now saying, "I'm starting to hear your message." And it's like you know and then hug [yourself]. So what are you doing when you when you hug [yourself] and you're almost holding yourself with your arms. What do you want to do to that feeling of "I want to soothe you."
>
> *Client:* Yeah, I just want to soothe you.

Therapist: "I want to care for you."

Client: Yeah, in a way, I just want to do it and then I can be better at solving some problems. But I'm thinking that at least there's a hope.

At this point the client accessed some compassion. She began to feel more optimistic.

Therapist: Right, right, so there's hope and what [is that like]? From this side you're saying "we can work together." If [you] work together, you're trying to give [yourself] a message about what's wrong and trying to find solutions. Maybe [you] can, come together on the same thing?

Client: We can come together and maybe [the empty feeling] can just can go and not come back, because I even if I think about things that have been wrong in my life, it was too much.

Therapist: You felt you didn't have control.

Client: Yeah, but maybe I do.

Therapist: That's a big thing.

Client: It is because there are still things that need to be taken care of but I can do it; I can soothe myself.

Therapist: "I'll do it for myself." That's really fantastic to be able to do it for [yourself] because we are going to end [therapy]. There [are] only two more sessions after this and I would imagine that it would give you some feeling of control and a little bit more of strength because [you] can do this for [yourself].

The therapist suggested that the client can do this for herself moving forward, that she had new tools to address her feelings of anxiety and ways of soothing herself. The client agreed:

Client: I might not feel so worried anymore. Because if I see that there are solutions, even though they might not happen, I know that we're not going to fall into a black hole. That [was] the way I felt at the beginning [of therapy]. But now, after so many sessions and talking about these things, it doesn't seem anymore like I'm going to fall into a black hole. [I'm] going to be able to come out of it and find something or [the children] will find something. I mean, I'm not going to find anything for them.

Therapist: No, because it's their choice.

Client:	I can realize that things can be solved and if I can help, I will.
Therapist:	"I'll do the best I can, as I always have."
Client:	Oh, yeah!
Therapist:	But it's not this helplessness or hopelessness?
Client:	It's giving me a little bit of hope that my husband is going to be normal again.
Therapist:	Yeah, so, maybe [you're] both going to be okay?
Client:	He's not that well, and not that I don't have my problem with my eye, but that's okay, I can handle it and its okay.

In this example, the client offered comfort and support to a part of herself that feared being disabled. She was able to soothe herself and begin to problem solve as she recognized that she and her husband, although they have medical conditions, are still able to look after themselves. They would find a way to manage. In order to be reassured and soothe themselves effectively, some clients may need to be released from the responsibility of caring for others' pain, other clients may need to be released from silencing themselves so that people will stay around, and yet other clients may need to allow themselves to be weak and helpless and in need of care and protection and not reject their needs because they were viewed as despicable, ridiculed, and ultimately punished. With clients whose anxiety emanates from the maxims and ways of coping that originated in earlier developmental stages, the capacity to soothe and care for themselves in a gentle, compassionate and, fair manner can take time. It is tied to clients' developing confidence and trust in themselves as well as confidence and trust in their interactions with others.

EMOTIONAL TRANSFORMATION

As clients learn to soothe and care for themselves, they are able to process their emotions more effectively, meet their needs, and make changes in their relationships with others. These changes require them to trust that they can cope with what happens and effectively regulate their emotions and trust that others can respond appropriately to their needs. Gaining trust in the self and others requires clients to rebalance their social contracts and to request that others fulfill their obligations to provide care, protection, support, and succor. In addition to accessing more self-compassion, clients become more self-protective, requiring that others act responsibly; cause no harm, injury, or neglect; and otherwise try their best to ensure clients' well-being. These changes are truly transformative of GAD.

CASE EXAMPLE: SOPHIE

The transformation of GAD can be illustrated through the case example of Sophie, a client dealing with GAD for many years. Sophie had a difficult childhood. Her mother had been very ill after Sophie was born, and her father was away from home for long periods of time because of his job. Her parents were immigrants and had no support of extended family. As a result, Sophie's mother had to rely on neighbors to attend to her infant child and to nurse Sophie when Sophie's mother became ill. Sophie recalled that her mother was emotionally fragile and given to extreme mood swings. She would fly into rages and unpredictably withdraw her love and support. Sophie felt that her mother resented her and was overburdened by caring for her. Her mother prized order, neatness, and cleanliness so Sophie had numerous memories of being scolded and punished for being messy. She felt like a pest that was constantly chastised, ignored, and dismissed.

Sophie realized early on that her mother was very unhappy. There was conflict between her parents. When they quarreled, she recalled trying to get between them and pleading with them to stop. Their outbursts made her very scared as a child. It felt like her whole world was collapsing. After her mother gave birth to a second child, Sophie overheard her mother telling her father that she was unhappy and could not manage with the children. She said she wanted to take an apartment by herself and leave the two girls with him. Sophie recalled how frightened she felt when she heard this. She ran to her mother pleading with her not to leave. From then on Sophie stayed close to her mother, seldom venturing out except to go to school. She worked hard to please her mother, following her around, helping with the care of her sister, and preparing food. She remained alert to her mother's every whim and mood, and sided with her mother against her father. Although her mother remained with the family, during Sophie's childhood and adolescence, she threatened repeatedly to leave, saying she could not manage. These threats culminated when her mother attempted suicide when Sophie was 14.

Sophie came to therapy after a particularly stressful period at work when there was conflict among her colleagues. In therapy, as she explored a problematic reaction with her therapist, she came to see that she had internalized a need to be responsible, to fix things, and to make things better for people she cared about. She realized that the pain she was experiencing at work had its roots in her childhood. She recalled how sad she had been as a little girl. How scared and confused when her parents were quarreling. She recalled how she had wished constantly for a calm, happy home. A place where she could feel safe and secure, sure in the knowledge that people loved each other and would care for each other. As she continued to process her feelings and her memories of her childhood, she realized that she had never let herself play for fear of being chastised and neglecting her mother.

Recognizing how painful her experience had been as a little girl, accepting and allowing the experience to form and be expressed was very important in Sophie's healing. She had not had the opportunity to reflect on her childhood experiences. As she explored her experience with her therapist, she began to see her parents differently. She realized how patient her father had been even though he was not a strong presence in her life. She began to appreciate how difficult her mother had been and see that her father was not to blame for her mother's moods and unpredictable behavior. As a child she had been sworn to secrecy, so she had been unable to share what was going on at home with others and seek support. She and her therapist agreed that she needed to work on her self-silencing and, to redistribute responsibility, to develop a coherent narrative of what happened.

To address her worry, Sophie and her therapist engaged in worry dialogues. During these tasks, it became clear that Sophie dismissed her pain and would tell herself that she was responsible and that she must not be selfish. She recognized that her anxiety was built on the maxim that she must attend to others and ensure they are happy to ensure that they will stay around. It took Sophie some time to internalize her therapist's concern and acceptance. As Sophie began to feel stronger, her therapist suggested two-chair dialogues to change her negative self-treatment, including the expectation and demand that she be responsible and take care of everyone and her tendency to dismiss and silence her feelings and needs. Slowly, she became more compassionate and more self-accepting of her limits. Sophie became more attentive to her feelings and needs and stopped castigating herself for being selfish.

She processed her deep sadness and loneliness as well as her fear of being so alone and so responsible. With the therapist's support, Sophie began to feel deserving of her unmet need for nurture and validation and experienced her anger at having been so deprived and her sadness at all she had so longed for and had missed. Once Sophie began attending to her feelings and acknowledged the pain she had experienced as a child, her therapist suggested they do some empty-chair dialogues with her parents. She was able to access protective anger, telling them how unfair and irresponsible they had been. She told her mother how scared she had felt—how she constantly worried that her mother would desert her. Sophie also told them how sad and lonely she had felt as a child, never being allowed to play. Her one outlet had been reading—escaping into books had provided relief and solace. As she continued to work through her relational injuries in empty-chair work, she told her parents that as a child she needed them to be responsible, that it was unfair to have burdened her with their problems and the care of her mother. Sophie told them that she had forfeited her own needs and did not know who she was and what she wanted.

She asserted that they should have sought help so that they could take better care of her and her sister. She told them that she deserved protection and love as well as a home where she could feel safe and secure.

As therapy progressed, Sophie learned to soothe and comfort herself as a little girl and tell herself that she no longer had to be responsible for the adults. An important step in her healing was when she addressed her wounded child in an empty-chair dialogue and told her that she was acceptable and lovable just as she was and that she did not need to be different or look after others. Hearing this, Sophie began weeping softly as she took in the words. At the end of this dialogue, she seemed relieved and lighter. In one of the last two-chair dialogues, she told herself to "go and play and leave the adults to their own devices." She reassured herself that everything would be all right and reminded herself that she was not responsible. Rather, it was the adults' responsibility to take care of themselves. After uttering these words in the session, she visibly relaxed and began breathing more regularly. Her therapist had observed that Sophie often held her breath in the session and had suggested breathing exercises as well as relaxation tapes to help her regulate her physiological responses.

Hearing the words "you are not responsible" and experiencing the sense of relief and relaxation in the session was a final transformative step for Sophie. The words spoke directly to her anxiety and relieved her tension. These words were important for Sophie because they enabled her to soothe and calm herself. Subsequently, she would invoke that phrase whenever she found herself becoming rattled at work or in other situations that were stressful. Instead of leaping in to fix things or assuming responsibility, she started to step back and say, "It's not my responsibility—other people can take care of it." This would immediately lower her anxiety and stress levels so that she was able to stay calm.

Sophie learned to distance herself from other people's conflict a little more, to look the other way, and to reassure herself that she was not responsible for others' pain. By the end of therapy, Sophie had become more accepting of her own feelings, allowing sadness and irritation, and paid more attention to her needs. Recognizing that her workplace was very stressful, she changed her job. Sophie learned to actively regulate herself physiologically. She became more conscious of her breathing and would take a few minutes throughout the day to monitor and regulate it. She would also use her breathing exercises to regulate her reactions at night if she woke up worried. She actively sought out relaxing and soothing activities and environments to help her stay calm. One of these was yoga, which helped her to stay in the moment, slowed her down, and taught her the technique of breathing out negative emotions.

One of the biggest changes Sophie made was allowing herself to play. For so long she had reined herself in so that she did not easily and freely allow herself to be silly, waste time, or recreate. Her therapist actively supported her to let go, explore, and allow herself to make a mess. She began to play more and to engage in fun and relaxing activities. She took up pottery, enjoying the feel of the clay in her hands, joined a sailing club, and took dancing lessons. Most important, she started reaching out to family and friends more, letting them know she wanted connection. As her friendships grew and she became closer with her sister, from whom she had been estranged, Sophie felt less vulnerable. She began to feel more grounded and connected with the people around her, feeling valued and accepted and more secure in her place in the world.

CONCLUSION

The internalization of self-compassion and the development of self-soothing are the capstones in the treatment of GAD. Once clients have achieved this, they are well on their way to overcoming and transforming their anxiety. As their deep pain comes into view, they see how the worry and anxiety are based on maxims and ways of coping they developed early on to handle painful situations and emotions. As it becomes clear how they have been trying to protect themselves from experiencing similar pain in the present and from being reminded of the earlier pain that has not been attended to in the past, they are able to address their anxiety and core pain in a different manner. In EFT, clients become more aware of their worry dialogues; develop a stronger sense of self, including an improved capacity to process their emotional experience and form new emotion schemes; develop greater trust in their senses and perceptions; transform the negative ways that they relate to their experience; access protective anger to hold others accountable and assert their needs; and, finally, acquire the capacity to self-soothe on the basis of greater self-acceptance and self-compassion. Through this process of transformation, clients are able to assuage their anxiety and begin to care for and comfort themselves in new ways that are more optimal for their well-being. Buoyed by greater self-confidence and trust in their ability to cope with pain and the challenges of living, they can move forward in the world calmer, lighter, and happier. Free of anxiety, they are able to thrive and live more joyously in the moment, experiencing greater freedom to explore their worlds and seek support from others as they master the challenges of living.

REFERENCES

Ackerman, S. J., & Hilsenroth, M. J. (2003). A review of therapist characteristics and techniques positively impacting the therapeutic alliance. *Clinical Psychology Review, 23*(1), 1–33. http://dx.doi.org/10.1016/S0272-7358(02)00146-0

American Psychiatric Association. (2013). *Diagnostic and statistical manual of mental disorders* (5th ed.). Arlington, VA: Author.

Andlin-Sobocki, P., & Wittchen, H. U. (2005). Cost of anxiety disorders in Europe. *European Journal of Neurology, 12*, 39–44.

Angus, L., Watson, J. C., Elliott, R., Schneider, K., & Timulak, L. (2015). Humanistic psychotherapy research 1990–2015: From methodological innovation to evidence-supported treatment outcomes and beyond. *Psychotherapy Research, 25*, 330–347. http://dx.doi.org/10.1080/10503307.2014.989290

Angus, L. E., & Greenberg, L. S. (2011). *Working with narrative in emotion-focused therapy: Changing stories, healing lives.* Washington, DC: American Psychological Association. http://dx.doi.org/10.1037/12325-000

Bachelor, A. (1988). How clients perceive therapist empathy: A content analysis of "received" empathy. *Psychotherapy: Theory, Research, Practice, Training, 25*, 227–240. http://dx.doi.org/10.1037/h0085337

Bakan, D. (1966). *The duality of human existence: An essay on psychology and religion.* Oxford, England: Rand McNally.

Baljon, M., & Pool, G. (2013). Hedgehogs in therapy: Empathy and insecure attachment in emotion-focused therapy. *Person-Centered & Experiential Psychotherapies, 12*, 112–125.

Barlow, D. H. (2000). Unraveling the mysteries of anxiety and its disorders from the perspective of emotion theory. *American Psychologist, 55*, 1247–1263. http://dx.doi.org/10.1037/0003-066X.55.11.1247

Barlow, D. H. (2002). *Anxiety and its disorders: The nature and treatment of anxiety and panic* (2nd ed.). New York, NY: Guilford Press.

Barrett-Lennard, G. T. (1993). The phases and focus of empathy. *British Journal of Medical Psychology, 66*, 3–14. http://dx.doi.org/10.1111/j.2044-8341.1993.tb01722.x

Barrett-Lennard, G. T. (1997). The recovery of empathy-toward others and self. In A. C. Bohart & L. S. Greenberg (Eds.), *Empathy reconsidered: New directions in theory research & practice* (pp. 103–121). Washington, DC: American Psychological Association. http://dx.doi.org/10.1037/10226-004

Bartz, J., Simeon, D., Hamilton, H., Kim, S., Crystal, S., Braun, A., . . . Hollander, E. (2011). Oxytocin can hinder trust and cooperation in borderline personality disorder. *SCAN, 6*, 556–563. http://dx.doi.org/10.1093/scan/nsq085

Beck, A. T., Emery, G., & Greenberg, R. L. (1985). *Anxiety disorders and phobias: A cognitive perspective.* New York, NY: Basic Books.

Benjamin, L. S. (1974). Structural analysis of social behavior. *Psychological Review, 81*, 392–425. http://dx.doi.org/10.1037/h0037024

Benjamin, L. S. (1979). Use of structural analysis of social behavior (SASB) and Markov chains to study dyadic interactions. *Journal of Abnormal Psychology, 88*, 303–319. http://dx.doi.org/10.1037/0021-843X.88.3.303

Benjamin, L. S. (1993). *Interpersonal diagnosis and treatment of personality disorders.* New York, NY: Guilford Press.

Benjamin, L. S. (1996). An interpersonal theory of personality disorders. In J. F. Clarkin (Ed.), *Major theories of personality disorder* (pp. 141–220). New York, NY: Guilford Press.

Benjamin, L. S. (2003). *Interpersonal reconstructive therapy: Promoting change in nonresponders.* New York, NY: Guilford Press.

Berg, A. L., Sandell, R., & Sandahl, C. (2009). Affect-focused body psychotherapy in patients with generalized anxiety disorder: Evaluation of an integrative method. *Journal of Psychotherapy Integration, 19*, 67–85. http://dx.doi.org/10.1037/a0015324

Bernholtz, B., & Watson, J. C. (2011, June). *Client vocal quality in CBT and PET treatment of depression.* Paper presented to 41st Annual Meeting of the International Society for Psychotherapy Research, Bern, Switzerland.

Blatt, S. J., Zuroff, D. C., Hawley, L. L., & Auerbach, J. S. (2010). Predictors of sustained therapeutic change. *Psychotherapy Research, 20*(1), 37–54. http://dx.doi.org/10.1080/10503300903121080

Bohart, A. C. (2012). Can you be integrative and a person-centered therapist at the same time? *Person-Centered & Experiential Psychotherapies, 11*, 1–13. http://dx.doi.org/10.1080/14779757.2011.639461

Bohart, A. C., & Greenberg, L. S. (1997). Empathy: Where are we and where do we go from here? In A. C. Bohart & L. S. Greenberg (Eds.), *Empathy reconsidered: New directions in psychotherapy* (pp. 419–449). Washington, DC: American Psychological Association. http://dx.doi.org/10.1037/10226-031

Bohart, A. C., & Tallman, K. (1999). *How clients make therapy work: The process of active self-healing.* http://dx.doi.org/10.1037/10323-000

Bolger, E. A. (1999). Grounded theory analysis of emotional pain. *Psychotherapy Research, 9*(3), 342–362. http://dx.doi.org/10.1080/10503309912331332801

Bordin, E. S. (1979). The generalizability of the psychoanalytic concept of the working alliance. *Psychotherapy: Theory, Research, Practice, Training, 16*, 252–260. http://dx.doi.org/10.1037/h0085885

Borkovec, T. D. (1994). The nature, functions, and origins of worry. In G. C. L. Davey & F. Tallis (Eds.), *Worrying: Perspectives on theory, assessment and treatment* (pp. 5–33). Oxford, England: John Wiley & Sons.

Borkovec, T. D., Alcaine, O. M., & Behar, E. (2004). Avoidance theory of worry and generalized anxiety disorder. In R. Heimberg, C. Turk, & D. Mennin (Eds.),

Generalized anxiety disorder: Advances in research and practice (pp. 77–108). New York, NY: Guilford Press.

Borkovec, T. D., & Inz, J. (1990). The nature of worry in generalized anxiety disorder: A predominance of thought activity. *Behaviour Research and Therapy, 28*, 153–158. http://dx.doi.org/10.1016/0005-7967(90)90027-G

Borkovec, T. D., Newman, M. G., Pincus, A. L., & Lytle, R. (2002). A component analysis of cognitive–behavioral therapy for generalized anxiety disorder and the role of interpersonal problems. *Journal of Consulting and Clinical Psychology, 70*, 288–298. http://dx.doi.org/10.1037/0022-006X.70.2.288

Borkovec, T. D., Ray, W. J., & Stöber, J. (1998). Worry: A cognitive phenomenon intimately linked to affective, physiological, and interpersonal behavioral processes. *Cognitive Therapy and Research, 22*, 561–576. http://dx.doi.org/10.1023/A:1018790003416

Borkovec, T. D., & Ruscio, A. M. (2001). Psychotherapy for generalized anxiety disorder. *Journal of Clinical Psychiatry, 62*(Suppl. 11), 37–42.

Bowen, M. (1976). Theory in the practice of psychotherapy. In P. J. Guerin, Jr. (Ed.), *Family therapy: Theory and practice* (pp. 42–90). New York, NY: Gardner Press.

Bowen, M. (1978). *Family therapy in clinical practice.* New York, NY: Aronson.

Bowlby, J. (1973). *Attachment and loss: Vol. 2. Separation: Anxiety and anger.* New York, NY: Basic Books.

Bowlby, J. (1988). *A secure base: Parent–child attachment and healthy human development.* New York, NY: Basic Books.

Bozarth, J. (2001). Client-centered unconditional positive regard: A historical perspective. In J. Bozarth & P. Wilkens (Eds.), *Unconditional positive regard* (pp. 5–18). London, England: PCCS Books.

Breitholtz, E., Johansson, B., & Öst, L.-G. (1999). Cognitions in generalized anxiety disorder and panic disorder patients. A prospective approach. *Behaviour Research and Therapy, 37*, 533–544. http://dx.doi.org/10.1016/S0005-7967(98)00147-8

Brown, T. A., O'Leary, T. A., & Barlow, D. H. (2001). Generalized anxiety disorder. In T. A. Brown (Ed.), *Clinical handbook of psychological disorders: A step-by-step treatment manual* (3rd ed., pp. 154–208). New York, NY: Guilford Press.

Buber, M. (1957). *I and thou.* New York, NY: Charles Scribner's Sons. (Original work published 1937)

Carter, R. M., Wittchen, H. U., Pfister, H., & Kessler, R. C. (2001). One-year prevalence of subthreshold and threshold DSM–IV generalized anxiety disorder in a nationally representative sample. *Depression and Anxiety, 13*, 78–88.

Cassidy, J., Lichtenstein-Phelps, J., Sibrava, N. J., Thomas, C. L., Jr., & Borkovec, T. D. (2009). Generalized anxiety disorder: Connections with self-reported attachment. *Behavior Therapy, 40*(1), 23–38. http://dx.doi.org/10.1016/j.beth.2007.12.004

Craske, M. G., & Waters, A. M. (2005). Panic disorder, phobias, and generalized anxiety disorder. *Annual Review of Clinical Psychology, 1*(1), 197–225. http://dx.doi.org/10.1146/annurev.clinpsy.1.102803.143857

Crits-Christoph, P., Crits-Christoph, K., Wolf-Palacio, D., Fichter, M., & Rudick, D. (1995). Brief supportive-expressive psychodynamic therapy for generalized anxiety disorder. In J. P. Barber & P. Crits-Christoph (Eds.), *Dynamic therapies for psychiatric disorders* (pp. 43–83). New York, NY: Basic Books.

Damasio, A. R. (1994). *Descartes' error: Emotion, reason, and the human brain.* New York, NY: Putnam & Sons.

Damasio, A. R. (1999). *The feeling of what happens: Body and emotion in the making of consciousness.* New York, NY: Harcourt Brace.

Davidson, R. J. (2000a). Affective style, psychopathology, and resilience: Brain mechanisms and plasticity. *American Psychologist, 55,* 1196–1214. http://dx.doi.org/10.1037/0003-066X.55.11.1196

Davidson, R. J. (2000b). *Cognitive neuroscience of emotion.* New York, NY: Oxford University Press.

Decety, J., & Jackson, P. L. (2004). The functional architecture of human empathy. *Behavioral and Cognitive Neuroscience Reviews, 3*(2), 71–100. http://dx.doi.org/10.1177/1534582304267187

DeSteno, D., Gross, J. J., & Kubzansky, L. (2013). Affective science and health: The importance of emotion and emotion regulation. *Health Psychology, 32,* 474–486. http://dx.doi.org/10.1037/a0030259

de Vignemont, F., & Singer, T. (2006). The empathic brain: How, when and why? *Trends in Cognitive Sciences, 10,* 435–441. http://dx.doi.org/10.1016/j.tics.2006.08.008

Dugas, M. J., Buhr, K., & Ladouceur, R. (2004). The role of intolerance of uncertainty in etiology and maintenance. In R. G. Heimberg, C. L. Turk, & D. S. Mennin (Eds.), *Generalized anxiety disorder: Advances in research and practice* (pp. 143–163). New York: Guilford Press.

Dugas, M. J., & Robichaud, M. (2007). *Cognitive-behavioral treatment for generalized anxiety disorder: From science to practice.* New York, NY: Routledge.

Elliott, R. (2013). Person-centered/experiential psychotherapy for anxiety difficulties: Theory, research and practice. *Person-Centered & Experiential Psychotherapies, 12*(1), 16–32. http://dx.doi.org/10.1080/14779757.2013.767750

Elliott, R., Bohart, A. C., Watson, J. C., & Greenberg, L. S. (2011). Empathy. *Psychotherapy: Theory, Research, Practice, Training, 48*(1), 43–49. http://dx.doi.org/10.1037/a0022187

Elliott, R., & Freire, E. (2010). The effectiveness of person-centered and experiential therapies: A review of the meta-analyses. In M. Cooper, J. C. Watson, & D. Hölldampf (Eds.), *Person-centered and experiential therapies work: A review of the research on counselling, psychotherapy and related practices* (pp. 1–15). Ross-on-Wye, England: PCCS Books.

Elliott, R., Greenberg, L. S., Watson, J. C., Timulak, L., & Freire, E. (2013). Humanistic-experiential psychotherapies. In M. J. Lambert (Ed.), *Bergin & Garfield's handbook of psychotherapy research and behaviour change* (6th ed., pp. 495–538). New York, NY: Wiley.

Elliott, R., Watson, J. C., Goldman, R. N., & Greenberg, L. S. (2004). *Learning emotion-focused therapy: The process-experiential approach to change.* http://dx.doi.org/10.1037/10725-000

Erikson, E. H. (1959). *Identity and the life cycle: Selected papers* (Vol. 1). New York, NY: W. W. Norton.

Fairbairn, W. R. (1952). *Psychoanalytic studies of the personality.* Oxford, England: Routledge & Kegan Paul.

Farber, B. A., & Doolin, E. M. (2011). Positive regard. *Psychotherapy: Theory, Research, Practice, Training, 48*(1), 58–64. http://dx.doi.org/10.1037/a0022141

Ferrari, P. F., Gallese, V., Rizzolatti, G., & Fogassi, L. (2003). Mirror neurons responding to the observation of ingestive and communicative mouth actions in the monkey ventral premotor cortex. *European Journal of Neuroscience, 17,* 1703–1714. http://dx.doi.org/10.1046/j.1460-9568.2003.02601.x

Feshbach, N. D. (1997). Empathy: The formative years—Implications for clinical practice. In A. C. Bohart & L. S. Greenberg (Eds.), *Empathy reconsidered: New directions in psychotherapy* (pp. 33–59). http://dx.doi.org/10.1037/10226-001

Foa, E. B., & Jaycox, L. H. (1999). Cognitive-behavioural theory and treatment of posttraumatic stress disorder. In D. Spiegel (Ed.), *Efficacy and cost-effectiveness of psychotherapy* (pp. 23–61). Arlington, VA: American Psychiatric Publishing.

Fosha, D. (2000). *The transforming power of affect: A model of accelerated change.* New York, NY: Basic Books.

Freud, S. (1924). *Collected papers* (Vol. 1). London, England: Hogarth Press.

Freud, S. (1961). *Beyond the pleasure principle* (C. J. M. Hubback, Trans.). New York, NY: W. W. Norton. (Original work published 1922)

Frijda, N. H. (1986). *The emotions.* Cambridge, England: Cambridge University Press.

Gallese, V. (2005). "Being like me": Self-other identity, mirror neurons, and empathy. In S. Hurley & N. Chater (Eds.), *Perspectives on imitation: From neuroscience to social science: Vol. 1. Mechanisms of imitation and imitation in animals* (pp. 101–118). Cambridge, MA: MIT Press.

Geller, S. M., & Greenberg, L. S. (2002). Therapeutic presence: Therapists' experience of presence in the psychotherapy encounter. *Person-Centered & Experiential Psychotherapies, 1*(1-2), 71–86. http://dx.doi.org/10.1080/14779757.2002.9688279

Geller, S. M., & Greenberg, L. S. (2012). *Therapeutic presence: A mindful approach to effective therapy.* http://dx.doi.org/10.1037/13485-000

Geller, S. M., Greenberg, L. S., & Watson, J. C. (2010). Therapist and client perceptions of therapeutic presence: The development of a measure. *Psychotherapy Research, 20,* 599–610. http://dx.doi.org/10.1080/10503307.2010.495957

Gendlin, E. T. (1978). *Focusing.* http://dx.doi.org/10.1037/h0088716

Gendlin, E. T. (1996). *Focusing-oriented psychotherapy: A manual of the experiential method.* New York, NY: Guilford Press.

Gilbert, P. (2012). Compassion focused therapy. In W. Dryden (Ed.), *Cognitive behaviour therapy* (pp. 140–165). London, England: Sage. http://dx.doi.org/10.4135/9781446288368.n7

Goldfried, M. R., & Davidson, G. C. (1994). *Clinical behavior therapy.* Oxford, England: John Wiley & Sons.

Goldman, R. N., & Greenberg, L. S. (2014). *Case formulation in emotion-focused therapy: Co-creating clinical maps for change.* Washington, DC: American Psychological Association.

Goldman, R. N., Greenberg, L. S., & Angus, L. (2006). The effects of adding emotion-focused interventions to the client-centered relationship conditions in the treatment of depression. *Psychotherapy Research, 16,* 537–546. http://dx.doi.org/10.1080/10503300600589456

Goldman, R. N., Greenberg, L. S., & Pos, A. E. (2005). Depth of emotional experience and outcome. *Psychotherapy Research, 15,* 248–260. http://dx.doi.org/10.1080/10503300512331385188

Gottman, J. M., & DeClaire, J. (1997). *The heart of parenting: How to raise an emotionally intelligent child.* New York, NY: Simon & Schuster.

Greenberg, L. (1979). Resolving splits: Use of the two chair technique. *Psychotherapy: Theory Into Practice, 16,* 310–318.

Greenberg, L. (1984). Task analysis of intrapersonal conflict. In L. Rice & L. Greenberg (Eds.), *Patterns of change: Intensive analysis of psychotherapy* (pp. 67–123). New York, NY: Guilford Press.

Greenberg, L. S. (2002). *Emotion-focused therapy: Coaching clients to work through their feelings.* Washington, DC: American Psychological Association. http://dx.doi.org/10.1037/10447-000

Greenberg, L. S. (2011). *Emotion-focused therapy.* Washington, DC: American Psychological Association.

Greenberg, L. S. (2015). *Emotion-focused therapy: Coaching clients to work through their feelings* (2nd ed.). Washington, DC: American Psychological Association. http://dx.doi.org/10.1037/14692-000

Greenberg, L. S., & Angus, L. E. (2004). The contributions of emotion processes to narrative change in psychotherapy: A dialectical constructivist approach. In L. E. Angus & J. McLeod (Eds.), *The handbook of narrative and psychotherapy: Practice, theory, and research* (pp. 330–349). Thousand Oaks, CA: Sage. http://dx.doi.org/10.4135/9781412973496.d25

Greenberg, L. S., & Bolger, E. (2001). An emotion-focused approach to the overregulation of emotion and emotional pain. *Journal of Clinical Psychology, 57*(2), 197–211. http://dx.doi.org/10.1002/1097-4679(200102)57:2<197::AID-JCLP6>3.0.CO;2-O

Greenberg, L. S., & Dompierre, L. (1981). The specific effects of Gestalt two-chair dialogue on intrapsychic conflict in counselling. *Journal of Counseling Psychology, 28,* 288–294. http://dx.doi.org/10.1037/0022-0167.28.4.288

Greenberg, L. S., & Elliott, R. (1997). Varieties of empathic responding. In A. C. Bohart & L. S. Greenberg (Eds.), *Empathy reconsidered: New directions in psychotherapy* (pp. 167–186). Washington, DC: American Psychological Association. http://dx.doi.org/10.1037/10226-007

Greenberg, L. S., & Geller, S. (2001). Congruence and therapeutic presence. In G. Wyatt & P. Saunders (Eds.), *Rogers' therapeutic conditions: Evolution, theory and practice: Vol. 1. Congruence* (pp. 131–149). Ross-on-Wye, England: PCCS Books.

Greenberg, L. S., & Goldman, R. N. (2008). *Emotion-focused couples therapy: The dynamics of emotion, love, and power.* Washington, DC: American Psychological Association. http://dx.doi.org/10.1037/11750-000

Greenberg, L. S., & Johnson, S. M. (1988). *Emotionally focused therapy for couples.* New York, NY: Guilford Press.

Greenberg, L. S., & Malcolm, W. (2002). Resolving unfinished business: Relating process to outcome. *Journal of Consulting and Clinical Psychology, 70,* 406–416. http://dx.doi.org/10.1037/0022-006X.70.2.406

Greenberg, L. S., & Paivio, S. C. (1997). *Working with emotions in psychotherapy.* New York, NY: Guilford Press.

Greenberg, L. S., & Pascual-Leone, J. (1995). A dialectical constructivist approach to experiential change. In R. A. Neimeyer & M. J. Mahoney (Eds.), *Constructivism in psychotherapy* (pp. 169–191). Washington, DC: American Psychological Association. http://dx.doi.org/10.1037/10170-008

Greenberg, L. S., & Pascual-Leone, J. (1997). Emotion in the creation of meaning. In M. Power & C. R. Brewin (Eds.), *The transformation of meaning in psychological therapies: Integrating theory and practice* (pp. 157–173). Hoboken, NJ: John Wiley & Sons.

Greenberg, L. S., & Pascual-Leone, J. (2001). A dialectical constructivist view of the creation of personal meaning. *Journal of Constructivist Psychology, 14*(3), 165–186. http://dx.doi.org/10.1080/10720530151143539

Greenberg, L. S., Rice, L. N., & Elliott, R. K. (1993). *Facilitating emotional change: The moment-by-moment process.* New York, NY: Guilford Press.

Greenberg, L. S., & Rushanski-Rosenberg, R. (2002). Therapist's experience of empathy. In J. C. Watson, R. N. Goldman, & M. S. Warner (Eds.), *Client-centered and experiential psychotherapy in the 21st century: Advances in theory, research and practice* (pp. 168–181). Ross-on-Wye, England: PCCS Books.

Greenberg, L. S., & Safran, J. D. (1987). *Emotion in psychotherapy: Affect, cognition, and the process of change.* New York, NY: Guilford Press.

Greenberg, L. S., & van Balen, R. (1998). *The theory of experience-centered therapies.* New York, NY: Guilford Press.

Greenberg, L. S., & Watson, J. C. (1998). Experiential therapy of depression: Differential effects of client-centered relationship conditions and process experiential interventions. *Psychotherapy Research, 8*, 210–224. http://dx.doi.org/10.1080/10503309812331332317

Greenberg, L. S., & Watson, J. C. (2006). *Emotion-focused therapy for depression.* http://dx.doi.org/10.1037/11286-000

Griffin, D., & Bartholomew, K. (1994). The metaphysics of measurement: The case of adult attachment. In K. Bartholomew & D. Perlman (Eds.), *Attachment processes in adulthood* (Vol. 5, pp. 17–52). London, England: Jessica Kingsley.

Hanrahan, F., Field, A. P., Jones, F. W., & Davey, G. C. (2013). A meta-analysis of cognitive therapy for worry in generalized anxiety disorder. *Clinical Psychology Review, 33*, 120–132.

Hazan, C., & Shaver, P. (1987). Romantic love conceptualized as an attachment process. *Journal of Personality and Social Psychology, 52*, 511–524.

Henry, W., Schacht, T. E., & Strupp, H. (1990). Patient and therapist introject, interpersonal process, and differential psychotherapy outcome. *Journal of Consulting and Clinical Psychology, 58*, 768–774.

Hettema, J. M., Neale, M. C., & Kendler, K. S. (2001). A review and meta-analysis of the genetic epidemiology of anxiety disorders. *American Journal of Psychiatry, 158*, 1568–1578. http://dx.doi.org/10.1176/appi.ajp.158.10.1568

Hoffman, D. L., Dukes, E. M., & Wittchen, H. U. (2008). Human and economic burden of generalized anxiety disorder. *Depression and Anxiety, 25*, 72–90.

Hofmann, S. G., & Smits, J. A. J. (2008). Cognitive-behavioral therapy for adult anxiety disorders: A meta-analysis of randomized placebo-controlled trials. *Journal of Clinical Psychiatry, 69*, 621–632. http://dx.doi.org/10.4088/JCP.v69n0415

Horvath, A. O., Del Re, A. C., Flückiger, C., & Symonds, D. (2011). Alliance in individual psychotherapy. *Psychotherapy: Theory, Research, Practice, Training, 48*(1), 9–16. http://dx.doi.org/10.1037/a0022186

Horvath, A. O., & Greenberg, L. S. (1989). Development and validation of the working alliance inventory. *Journal of Counseling Psychology, 36*, 223–233. http://dx.doi.org/10.1037/0022-0167.36.2.223

Hughes, S. (2013). *Transforming emotional injury with a developmentally significant other through a series of unfinished business dialogues in clients with generalised anxiety disorder: A task analytic approach* (Unpublished doctoral dissertation), Trinity College, Dublin, Ireland.

Hughes, S., Timulak, L., & McElvaney, J. (2013, June). *Transforming emotional injury with a developmentally significant other through a series of unfinished business dialogues in clients with generalized anxiety disorder: A task analytic approach.* Paper presented at the Annual Conference of the Society of Psychotherapy Research, Copenhagen, Denmark.

Ito, M., Greenberg, L. S., Iwakabe, S., & Pascual-Leone, A. (2010, June). *Compassionate emotion regulation: A task analytic approach to studying the process of self-soothing in therapy session*. Paper presented at the World Congress of Behavioral and Cognitive Therapies (WCBCT) Boston, MA.

Jackson, P. L., Brunet, E., Meltzoff, A. N., & Decety, J. (2006). Empathy examined through the neural mechanisms involved in imagining how I feel versus how you feel pain. *Neuropsychologia, 44*, 752–761. http://dx.doi.org/10.1016/j.neuropsychologia.2005.07.015

Johnson, S. M. (2004). *Emotionally focused couples therapy*. Boston, MA: Allyn & Bacon.

Judd, L. L., Kessler, R. C., Paulus, M. P., Zeller, P. V., Wittchen, H. U., & Kunovac, J. L. (1998). Comorbidity as a fundamental feature of generalized anxiety disorders: Results from the National Comorbidity Study (NCS). *Acta Psychiatrica Scandinavica, 98*(393), 6–11.

Keil, W. (1996). Hermeneutic empathy in client-centered therapy. In U. Esser, H. Pabst, & G. Speirer (Eds.), *The power of the person-centered approach: New challenges, perspectives and answers* (pp. 65–80). Cologne, Germany: GwG-Verlag.

Kennedy-Moore, E., & Watson, J. C. (1999). *Expressing emotion: Myths, realities and therapeutic strategies*. New York, NY: Guilford Press.

Kennedy-Moore, E., & Watson, J. C. (2001). How and when does emotional expression help? *Review of General Psychology, 5*, 187–212.

Kessler, R. C., Ruscio, A. M., Shear, K., & Wittchen, H. U. (2009). Epidemiology of anxiety disorders. In M. B. Stein & T. Steckler (Eds.), *Behavioral neurobiology of anxiety and its treatment* (pp. 22–35). Berlin, Germany: Springer.

King, J. L., & Mallinckrodt, B. (2000). Family environment and alexithymia in clients and non-clients. *Psychotherapy Research, 10*(1), 78–86. http://dx.doi.org/10.1080/713663595

Klein, M. H., Mathieu-Coughlan, P. L., & Kiesler, D. J. (1986). The experiencing scales. In L. S. Greenberg & W. M. Pinsof (Eds.), *The psychotherapeutic process: A research handbook* (pp. 21–71). New York, NY: Guilford Press.

Kohut, H. (1984). *How does analysis cure?* http://dx.doi.org/10.7208/chicago/9780226006147.001.0001

Kolden, G. G., Klein, M. H., Wang, C. C., & Austin, S. B. (2011). Congruence/genuineness. *Psychotherapy: Theory, Research, Practice, Training, 48*(1), 65–71. http://dx.doi.org/10.1037/a0022064

Korte, S. M., Koolhaas, J. M., Wingfield, J. C., & McEwen, B. S. (2005). The Darwinian concept of stress: Benefits of allostasis and costs of allostatic load and the trade-offs in health and disease. *Neuroscience and Biobehavioral Reviews, 29*(1), 3–38. http://dx.doi.org/10.1016/j.neubiorev.2004.08.009

Kwan, K., Watson, J. C., & Stermac, L. (2000, June). *An examination of the relationship between clients' social experience of psychotherapy, the working alliance and psychotherapy outcome*. Paper presented at the 31st Annual Meeting of the Society for Psychotherapy Research Conference, Chicago, IL.

Lamagna, J., & Gleiser, K. A. (2007). Building a secure internal attachment: An intrarelational approach to ego strengthening and emotional processing with chronically traumatized clients. *Journal of Trauma & Dissociation, 8,* 25–52.

Lang, P. J., Bradley, M. M., Fitzsimmons, J. R., Cuthbert, B. N., Scott, J. D., Moulder, B., & Nangia, V. (1998). Emotional arousal and activation of the visual cortex: An fMRI analysis. *Psychophysiology, 35,* 199–210. http://dx.doi.org/10.1111/1469-8986.3520199

Lecce, S. (2008). *Attachment and subjective well-being: The mediating role of emotional processing and regulation* (Order No. NR39774). Available from ProQuest Dissertations & Theses Global (304370385).

Lecce, S., & Watson, J. C. (2007, June). *Attachment and affect regulation.* Paper presented at the 37th Annual Conference for the International Society of Psychotherapy Research, Madison, WI.

LeDoux, J. E. (1996). *The emotional brain.* New York, NY: Simon and Schuster.

Legerstee, M. (2013). The developing social brain: Social connections and social bonds, social loss, and jealousy in infancy. In M. Legerstee, D. W. Haley, & M. H. Bornstein (Eds.), *The infant mind: Origins of the social brain* (pp. 223–247). New York, NY: Guilford Press.

Legerstee, M., Markova, G., & Fisher, T. (2007). The role of maternal affect attunement in dyadic and triadic communication. *Infant Behavior & Development, 30,* 296–306. http://dx.doi.org/10.1016/j.infbeh.2006.10.003

Lieberman, M. D., Eisenberger, N. I., Crockett, M. J., Tom, S. M., Pfeifer, J. H., & Way, B. M. (2007). Putting feelings into words: Affect labeling disrupts amygdala activity in response to affective stimuli. *Psychological Science, 18,* 421–428. http://dx.doi.org/10.1111/j.1467-9280.2007.01916.x

Lietaer, G. (1993). Authenticity, congruence, and transparency. In D. Brazier (Ed.), *Beyond Carl Rogers: Towards a psychotherapy for the twenty-first century* (pp. 17–47). London, England: Constable.

Linehan, M. M. (1993). *Cognitive-behavioral treatment of borderline personality disorder.* New York, NY: Guilford Press.

Luborsky, L., & Mark, D. (1991). Short-term supportive-expressive psychoanalytic psychotherapy. In P. Crits-Christoph & J. P. Barber (Eds.), *Handbook of short-term dynamic psychotherapy* (pp. 110–136). New York, NY: Basic Books.

Malin, A. J., & Pos, A. E. (2015). The impact of early empathy on alliance building, emotional processing, and outcome during experiential treatment of depression. *Psychotherapy Research, 25,* 445–459. http://dx.doi.org/10.1080/10503307.2014.901572

Marganska, A., Gallagher, M., & Miranda, R. (2013). Adult attachment, emotion dysregulation, and symptoms of depression and generalized anxiety disorder. *American Journal of Orthopsychiatry, 83*(1), 131–141.

Mauri, M., Sarno, N., Rossi, V. M., Armani, A., Zambotto, S., Cassano, G. B., & Akiskal, H. S. (1992). Personality disorders associated with generalized anxiety, panic, and recurrent depressive disorders. *Journal of Personality Disorders, 6,* 162–167.

McCann, I. L., & Pearlman, L. A. (1990). *Psychological trauma and the adult survivor: Theory, therapy, and transformation.* New York, NY: Psychology Press.

McGaugh, J. L. (2002). Memory consolidation and the amygdala: A systems perspective. *Trends in Neurosciences, 25,* 456–461. http://dx.doi.org/10.1016/S0166-2236(02)02211-7

McGaugh, J. L., & Roozendaal, B. (2002). Role of adrenal stress hormones in forming lasting memories in the brain. *Current Opinion in Neurobiology, 12,* 205–210. http://dx.doi.org/10.1016/S0959-4388(02)00306-9

McMullen, E. J., & Watson, J. C. (2011, June). *Clients' productive processing in cognitive-behavioural therapy and emotion-focused therapy for depression.* Paper presented to 30th Annual Meeting of the Society for Psychotherapy Research, Bern, Switzerland.

McMullen, E. J., & Watson, J. C. (2015, June). *Does therapists' empathy contribute to changes in clients' self-criticism and neediness?* Paper presented at the Society for Psychotherapy Research Conference, Philadelphia, PA.

McMullen, E. J., Watson, J. C., & Watson, N. (2014, June). *The relationship between attachment style, affect dysregulation, and anxiety to wellbeing.* Paper presented at the Society for Psychotherapy Research Conference, Copenhagen, Denmark.

Mennin, D. S. (2004). Emotion regulation therapy for generalized anxiety disorder. *Clinical Psychology & Psychotherapy, 11*(1), 17–29. http://dx.doi.org/10.1002/cpp.389

Mennin, D. S., Heimberg, R. G., Turk, C. L., & Fresco, D. M. (2002). Applying an emotion regulation framework to integrative approaches to generalized anxiety disorder. *Clinical Psychology: Science and Practice, 9*(1), 85–90. http://dx.doi.org/10.1093/clipsy.9.1.85

Mennin, D. S., Heimberg, R. G., Turk, C. L., & Fresco, D. M. (2005). Preliminary evidence for an emotion dysregulation model of generalized anxiety disorder. *Behaviour Research and Therapy, 43,* 1281–1310. http://dx.doi.org/10.1016/j.brat.2004.08.008

Mineka, S. (1985). Animal models of anxiety-based disorders: Their usefulness and limitations. In A. H. Tuma & J. D. Maser (Eds.), *Anxiety and the anxiety disorders* (pp. 199–244). Hillsdale, NJ: Erlbaum.

Mineka, S. (2004). The positive and negative consequences of worry in the etiology of generalized anxiety disorder: A learning theory perspective. In J. Yiend (Ed.), *Cognition, emotion and psychopathology: Theoretical, empirical and clinical directions* (pp. 29–48). New York, NY: Cambridge University Press. http://dx.doi.org/10.1017/CBO9780511521263.003

Mineka, S., Yovel, I., & Pineles, S. L. (2002). Toward a psychological model of the etiology of generalized anxiety disorder. In D. Nutt, K. Rickels, & D. Stein (Eds.), *Generalized anxiety disorder: Symptomatology, pathogenesis and management* (pp. 41–55). London, England: Martin Dunitz.

Mineka, S., & Zinbarg, R. (1996). Conditioning and ethological models of anxiety disorders stress-in-dynamic-context anxiety models. In D. A. Hope (Ed.), *Nebraska symposium on motivation, 1995: Perspectives on anxiety, panic, and fear* (pp. 135–210). Lincoln: University of Nebraska Press.

Mlotek, A. (2013). *The contribution of therapist empathy to client engagement and outcome in emotion-focused therapy for complex trauma* (Master's thesis). Available from ProQuest Dissertations & Theses Global. (Order No. MR87379)

Moons, W. G., Eisenberger, N. I., & Taylor, S. E. (2010). Anger and fear responses to stress have different biological profiles. *Brain, Behavior, and Immunity, 24,* 215–219. http://dx.doi.org/10.1016/j.bbi.2009.08.009

Murray, H. A. (1938). *Explorations in personality.* Oxford, England: Oxford University Press.

Nadel, L., Hupbach, A., Gomez, R., & Newman-Smith, K. (2012). Memory formation, consolidation and transformation. *Neuroscience and Biobehavioral Reviews, 36,* 1640–1645. http://dx.doi.org/10.1016/j.neubiorev.2012.03.001

Newman, M. G., & Llera, S. J. (2011). A novel theory of experiential avoidance in generalized anxiety disorder: A review and synthesis of research supporting a contrast avoidance model of worry. *Clinical Psychology Review, 31,* 371–382. http://dx.doi.org/10.1016/j.cpr.2011.01.008

Niles, A. N., Craske, M. G., Lieberman, M. D., & Hur, C. (2015). Affect labeling enhances exposure effectiveness for public speaking anxiety. *Behaviour Research and Therapy, 68,* 27–36. http://dx.doi.org/10.1016/j.brat.2015.03.004

Norcross, J. C., & Wampold, B. E. (2011). Evidence-based therapy relationships: Research conclusions and clinical practices. In J. C. Norcross (Ed.), *Psychotherapy relationships that work: Evidence-based responsiveness* (2nd ed., pp. 423–430). New York, NY: Oxford University Press. http://dx.doi.org/10.1093/acprof:oso/9780199737208.003.0021

Paivio, S. C., & Laurent, C. (2001). Empathy and emotion regulation: Reprocessing memories of childhood abuse. *Journal of Clinical Psychology, 57,* 213–226. http://dx.doi.org/10.1002/1097-4679(200102)57:2<213::AID-JCLP7>3.0.CO;2-B

Paivio, S. C., & Pascual-Leone, A. (2010). *Emotion-focused therapy for complex trauma: An integrative approach.* Washington, DC: American Psychological Association. http://dx.doi.org/10.1037/12077-000

Park, A. (2011, December 5). Two faces of anxiety. *Time Magazine.* Retrieved from http://time.com/741/the-two-faces-of-anxiety/

Pascual-Leone, A., & Greenberg, L. S. (2007). Emotional processing in experiential therapy: Why "the only way out is through." *Journal of Consulting and Clinical Psychology, 75,* 875–887. http://dx.doi.org/10.1037/0022-006X.75.6.875

Pascual-Leone, J. (1987). Organismic processes for neo-Piagetian theories: A dialectical causal account of cognitive development. *International Journal of Psychology, 22,* 531–570. http://dx.doi.org/10.1080/00207598708246795

Pascual-Leone, J. (1991). Emotions, development, and psychotherapy: A dialectical-constructivist perspective. In J. D. Safran & L. S. Greenberg (Eds.), *Emotion, psychotherapy, and change* (pp. 302–335). New York, NY: Guilford Press.

Pennebaker, J. W. (Ed.). (1995). *Emotion, disclosure, and health.* Washington, DC: American Psychological Association. http://dx.doi.org/10.1037/10182-000

Perls, F. S. (1969). *Gestalt therapy verbatim.* Moab, UT: Real People Press.

Piaget, J. (1972). *The child's conception of the world.* Totowa, NJ: Littlefield, Adams, & Co.

Porensky, E. K., Dew, M. A., Karp, J. F., Skidmore, E., Rollman, B. L., Shear, M. K., & Lenze, E. J. (2009). The burden of late-life generalized anxiety disorder: Effects on disability, heath-related quality of life, and healthcare utilization. *American Journal of Geriatric Psychiatry, 17,* 473–482. http://dx.doi.org/10.1097/JGP.0b013e31819b87b2

Porges, S. W. (2011a). Neuroception: A subconscious system for detecting threat and safety. In S. W. Porges (Ed.), *The polyvagal theory: Neurophysiological foundations of emotions, attachment, communication, and self-regulation* (pp. 11–19). New York, NY: W. W. Norton.

Porges, S. W. (2011b). *The polyvagal theory: Neuro-physiological foundations of emotions, attachment, communication, self-regulation.* New York, NY: W. W. Norton.

Pos, A., Geller, S., & Oghene, J. (2011, June). *Therapist presence, empathy, and the working alliance in experiential treatment for depression.* Paper presented at the meeting of the Society for Psychotherapy Research, Bern, Switzerland.

Prigerson, H. G., Shear, M. K., Bierhals, A. J., Zonarich, D. L., & Reynolds, C. F. (1996). Childhood adversity, attachment and personality styles as predictors of anxiety among elderly caregivers. *Anxiety, 2,* 234–241.

Prosser, M. C., & Watson, J. C. (2007). *Beyond rapport: How therapist empathy contributes to outcome in the treatment of depression.* Paper presented at the Society for Psychotherapy Research Conference, Madison, WI.

Pynoos, R. S., Steinberg, A. M., & Piacentini, J. C. (1999). A developmental psychopathology model of childhood traumatic stress and intersection with anxiety disorders. *Biological Psychiatry, 46,* 1542–1554.

Rankin, K. P., Gorno-Tempini, M. L., Allison, S. C., Stanley, C. M., Glenn, S., Weiner, M. W., & Miller, B. L. (2006). Structural anatomy of empathy in neurodegenerative disease. *Brain: A Journal of Neurology, 129,* 2945–2956. http://dx.doi.org/10.1093/brain/awl254

Rapee, R. M. (2001). The development of generalized anxiety. In M. W. Vasey & M. R. Dadds (Eds.), *The developmental psychopathology of anxiety* (pp. 481–504). http://dx.doi.org/10.1093/med:psych/9780195123630.003.0021

Rennie, D. L. (1994). Clients' deference in psychotherapy. *Journal of Counseling Psychology, 41,* 427–437. http://dx.doi.org/10.1037/0022-0167.41.4.427

Revicki, D. A., Travers, K., Wyrwich, K. W., Svedsäter, H., Locklear, J., Mattera, M. S., . . . Montgomery, S. (2012). Humanistic and economic burden of generalized anxiety disorder in North America and Europe. *Journal of Affective Disorders, 140,* 103–112. http://dx.doi.org/10.1016/j.jad.2011.11.014

Rice, L. N. (1965). Therapist's style of participation and case outcome. *Journal of Consulting Psychology, 29,* 155–160. http://dx.doi.org/10.1037/h0021926

Rice, L. N. (1974). The evocation function of the therapist. In D. Wexler & L. N. Rice (Eds.), *Innovations in client-centered therapy* (pp. 289–311). New York, NY: Wiley Interscience.

Rice, L. N., & Kerr, G. P. (1986). Measures of client and therapist vocal quality. In L. S. Greenberg & W. M. Pinsof (Eds.), *The psychotherapeutic process: A research handbook* (pp. 73–105). New York, NY: Guilford Press.

Rice, L. N., & Saperia, E. (1984). Task analysis and the resolution of problematic reactions. In L. N. Rice & L. S. Greenberg (Eds.), *Patterns of change: Intensive analysis of psychotherapy process* (pp. 29–66). New York, NY: Guilford Press.

Rizzolatti, G. (2005). The mirror neuron system and imitation. In S. Hurley & N. Chater (Eds.), *Perspectives on imitation: From neuroscience to social science: Vol. 1. Mechanisms of imitation and imitation in animals* (pp. 55–76). Cambridge, MA: MIT Press.

Rodrigues, A. (2016). *Exploring the relationships among attachment, emotion regulation, differentiation of self, negative problem orientation, self-esteem, worry, and generalized anxiety.* (Unpublished doctoral dissertation). University of Toronto, Toronto, Ontario, Canada.

Rodrigues, A., & Watson, J. C. (2015, August). *Attachment in worry and generalized anxiety.* Paper presented at the Annual Conference for the American Psychological Association, Toronto, Canada.

Roemer, L., Molina, S., & Borkovec, T. D. (1997). An investigation of worry content among generally anxious individuals. *Journal of Nervous and Mental Disease, 185,* 314–319. http://dx.doi.org/10.1097/00005053-199705000-00005

Roemer, L., & Orsillo, S. M. (2002). Expanding our conceptualization of and treatment for generalized anxiety disorder: Integrating mindfulness/acceptance-based approaches with existing cognitive-behavioral models. *Clinical Psychology: Science and Practice, 9,* 54–68. http://dx.doi.org/10.1093/clipsy.9.1.54

Roemer, L., Orsillo, S. M., & Barlow, D. H. (2002). Generalized anxiety disorder. In D. Barlow (Ed.), *Anxiety and its disorders: The nature and treatment of anxiety and panic* (2nd ed.; pp. 477–515). New York, NY: Guilford Press.

Rogers, C. R. (1951). *Client-centered therapy: Its current practice, implications, and theory.* Oxford, England: Houghton Mifflin.

Rogers, C. R. (1957). The necessary and sufficient conditions of therapeutic personality change. *Journal of Consulting Psychology, 21,* 95–103. http://dx.doi.org/10.1037/h0045357

Rogers, C. R. (1959). A theory of therapy, personality, and interpersonal relationships, as developed in the client-centered framework. In S. Koch (Ed.), *Psychology: A study of a science: Vol. II. Formulations of the person and the social context* (pp. 184–256). New York, NY: McGraw-Hill.

Rogers, C. R. (1961). *On becoming a person.* Boston, MA: Houghton Mifflin.

Rogers, C. R. (Ed.). (1967). *The therapeutic relationship and its impact: A program of research in psychotherapy with schizophrenics.* Madison: University of Wisconsin Press.

Rogers, C. R. (1975). Empathic: An unappreciated way of being. *The Counseling Psychologist, 5*(2), 2–10. http://dx.doi.org/10.1177/001100007500500202

Rogers, C. R., & Truax, C. B. (1967). The therapeutic conditions antecedent to change: A theoretical view. In C. R. Rogers, E. T. Gendlin, D. J. Kiesler, & C. B. Truax (Eds.), *The therapeutic relationship and its impact: A study of psychotherapy with schizophrenics* (pp. 97–108). Madison: University of Wisconsin Press.

Saedi-Chekan, S. S., & Watson, J. C. (2015, October). *Comparing two clients in emotion-focused therapy for generalized anxiety disorder across four dimensions of negative emotions, positive emotions, negative treatment-of-self, and positive treatment-of-self.* Poster presented at the meeting of the Ontario Psychological Association, Toronto, Ontario, Canada.

Safran, J. D., & Muran, J. C. (2000). *Negotiating the therapeutic alliance: A relational treatment guide.* New York, NY: Guilford Press.

Salzman, C., & Lebowitz, B. (1991). *Anxiety in the elderly: Treatment and research.* New York, NY: Springer.

Schore, A. N. (1994). *Affect regulation and the origin of the self: The neurobiology of emotional development.* Hillsdale, NJ: Erlbaum.

Schore, A. N. (2003). *Affect dysregulation and disorders of the self.* New York, NY: W. W. Norton.

Shahar, B. (2014). Emotion-focused therapy for the treatment of social anxiety: An overview of the model and a case description. *Clinical Psychology & Psychotherapy, 21,* 536–547.

Siegel, D. J. (2012). *The developing mind: How relationships and the brain interact to shape who we are* (2nd ed.). New York, NY: Guilford Press.

Spinoza, B. (1967). *Éthique.* Paris, France: Gallimard.

Sroufe, L. A. (1996). *Emotional development: The organization of emotional life in the early years.* http://dx.doi.org/10.1017/CBO9780511527661

Staal, M. A. (2004). *Stress, cognition, and human performance: A literature review and conceptual framework.* Hanover, MD: National Aeronautics & Space Administration.

Stern, D. N. (1985). *The interpersonal world of the infant: A view from psychoanalysis and developmental psychology.* New York, NY: Basic Books.

Sullivan, H. S. (1953). *The interpersonal theory of psychiatry.* New York, NY: W. W. Norton.

Timulak, L., & McElvaney, J. (2015). Emotion-focused therapy for generalized anxiety disorder: An overview of the model. *Journal of Contemporary Psychotherapy.* Advance online publication.

Tugade, M. M., & Fredrickson, B. L. (2004). Resilient individuals use positive emotions to bounce back from negative emotional experiences. *Journal of Personality and Social Psychology, 86,* 320.

Ulvenes, P. G., Berggraf, L., Wampold, B. E., Hoffart, A., Stiles, T., & McCullough, L. (2014). Orienting patient to affect, sense of self, and the activation of affect over the course of psychotherapy with cluster C patients. *Journal of Counseling Psychology, 61,* 315–324. http://dx.doi.org/10.1037/cou0000028

van der Kolk, B. A. (1994). The body keeps the score: Memory and the evolving psychobiology of posttraumatic stress. *Harvard Review of Psychiatry, 1,* 253–265. http://dx.doi.org/10.3109/10673229409017088

van der Kolk, B. A. (1996). The body keeps the score: Approaches to the psychobiology of posttraumatic stress disorder. In B. A. van der Kolk, A. C. McFarlane, & L. Weisaeth (Eds.), *Traumatic stress: The effects of overwhelming experience on mind, body and society* (pp. 214–241). New York, NY: Guilford Press.

van der Kolk, B. A. (2005). Developmental trauma disorder: Toward a rational diagnosis for children with complex trauma histories. *Psychiatric Annals, 35,* 401–408.

van Deurzen, E. (2012). *Existential counseling and psychotherapy in practice* (3rd ed.). Thousand Oaks, CA: Sage.

Vygotsky, L. S. (1978). *Mind in society: The development of higher psychological processes.* London, England: Harvard University Press.

Warwar, S., & Greenberg, L. S. (1999, June). *Emotional processing and therapeutic change.* Paper presented at the annual meeting of the International Society for Psychotherapy Research, Braga, Portugal.

Watson, J. C. (1996). The relationship between vivid description, emotional arousal, and in-session resolution of problematic reactions. *Journal of Consulting and Clinical Psychology, 64,* 459–464. http://dx.doi.org/10.1037/0022-006X.64.3.459

Watson, J. C. (2002). Re-visioning empathy. In D. J. Cain & J. Seeman (Eds.), *Humanistic psychotherapies: Handbook of research and practice* (pp. 445–471). Washington, DC: American Psychological Association. http://dx.doi.org/10.1037/10439-014

Watson, J. C. (2006). Resolving trauma in process-experiential therapy. In G. Striker (Ed.), *Case studies in psychotherapy integration* (pp. 89–106). Washington, DC: American Psychological Association. http://dx.doi.org/10.1037/11436-008

Watson, J. C. (2007). Facilitating empathy. *European Psychotherapy, 7*(1), 59–65.

Watson, J. C. (2011). The process of growth and transformation: Extending the process model. *Person-Centered & Experiential Psychotherapies, 10*(1), 11–27. http://dx.doi.org/10.1080/14779757.2011.564760

Watson, J. C. (2012, July). *Working with self-soothing for anxiety in EFT.* Paper presented at the 10th Conference of the World Association for Person Centered and Experiential Psychotherapy and Counselling, Antwerp, Belgium.

Watson, J. C. (2015, June). *Mapping patterns of change: Implications for theory, research, practice and training.* 46th Annual Meeting of the Society for Psychotherapy Research, University of Pennsylvania, Philadelphia, PA.

Watson, J. C., & Bohart, A. (2001). Integrative humanistic therapy in an era of managed care. In K. Schneider, J. F. T. Bugenthal, & F. Pierson (Eds.), *The handbook of humanistic psychology* (pp. 503–520). Thousand Oaks, CA: Sage.

Watson, J. C., & Geller, S. M. (2005). The relation among the relationship conditions, working alliance, and outcome in both process-experiential and cognitive-behavioral psychotherapy. *Psychotherapy Research, 15*(1-2), 25–33. http://dx.doi.org/10.1080/10503300512331327010

Watson, J. C., Goldman, R., & Vanaerschot, G. (1998). Empathic: A postmodern way of being? In L. S. Greenberg, J. C. Watson, & G. Lietaer (Eds.), *Handbook of experiential psychotherapy* (pp. 61–81). New York, NY: Guilford Press.

Watson, J. C., Goldman, R. N., & Greenberg, L. S. (2007). *Case studies in emotion-focused treatment of depression: A comparison of good and poor outcome.* Washington, DC: American Psychological Association. http://dx.doi.org/10.1037/11586-000

Watson, J. C., Gordon, L. B., Stermac, L., Kalogerakos, F., & Steckley, P. (2003). Comparing the effectiveness of process-experiential with cognitive-behavioral psychotherapy in the treatment of depression. *Journal of Consulting and Clinical Psychology, 71*, 773–781. http://dx.doi.org/10.1037/0022-006X.71.4.773

Watson, J. C., & Greenberg, L. S. (1994). The working alliance in experiential therapy: Enacting the relationship conditions. In A. Horvath & L. Greenberg (Eds.), *The working alliance: Theory, research and practice* (pp. 153–172). New York, NY: Wiley.

Watson, J. C., & Greenberg, L. S. (1996). Emotion and cognition in experiential therapy: A dialectical-constructivist position. In H. Rosen & K. Kuelwein (Eds.), *Constructing realities: Meaning-making perspectives for psychotherapists* (pp. 253–276). San Francisco, CA: Jossey-Bass.

Watson, J. C., & Greenberg, L. (1998). The alliance in short term experiential therapy. In J. Safran & C. Muran (Eds.), *The therapeutic alliance in brief psychotherapy* (pp. 123–145). http://dx.doi.org/10.1037/10306-005

Watson, J. C., & Greenberg, L. S. (2009). Empathic resonance: A neuroscience perspective. In J. Decety & W. Ickes (Eds.), *The social neuroscience of empathy* (pp. 125–138). http://dx.doi.org/10.7551/mitpress/9780262012973.003.0011

Watson, J. C., & Kalogerakos, F. (2010). The therapeutic alliance in humanistic psychotherapy. In J. C. Muran & J. P. Barber (Eds.), *The therapeutic alliance: An evidence-based guide to practice* (pp. 191–209). New York, NY: Guilford Press.

Watson, J. C., & Lilova, S. (2009). Testing the reliability and validity of the scales for experiencing emotion with a Canadian sample. *Person-Centered & Experiential Psychotherapies, 8*, 189–207. http://dx.doi.org/10.1080/14779757.2009.9688488

Watson, J. C., McMullen, E. J., Prosser, M. C., & Bedard, D. L. (2011). An examination of the relationships among clients' affect regulation, in-session emotional processing, the working alliance, and outcome. *Psychotherapy Research, 21*(1), 86–96. http://dx.doi.org/10.1080/10503307.2010.518637

Watson, J. C., McMullen, E. J., & Watson, N. (2014, June). *The role of early life experiences in the subjective experience of well-being.* Paper presented at the Society for Psychotherapy Research Conference, Copenhagen, Denmark.

Watson, J. C., & Prosser, M. (2002). Development of an observer rated measure of therapist empathy. In J. C. Watson, R. Goldman, & M. Warner (Eds.), *Client-centered and experiential psychotherapy in the 21st century: Advances in theory, research and practice* (pp. 303–314). Ross-on-Wye, England: PCCS Books.

Watson, J. C., & Rennie, D. L. (1994). Qualitative-analysis of clients' subjective experience of significant moments during the exploration of problematic reactions. *Journal of Counseling Psychology, 41,* 500–509. http://dx.doi.org/10.1037/0022-0167.41.4.500

Watson, J. C., & Schneider, K. (2016). Humanistic and experiential psychotherapy. In J. C. Norcross, G. R. VandenBos, & D. K. Freedheim (Eds.), *APA handbook of clinical psychology: Vol. 2. Theory and research.* Washington, DC: American Psychological Association.

Watson, J. C., Steckley, P. L., & McMullen, E. J. (2014). The role of empathy in promoting change. *Psychotherapy Research, 24,* 286–298. http://dx.doi.org/10.1080/10503307.2013.802823

Watson, J. C., & Watson, N. (2010). Operationalizing incongruence: Measure of self-discrepancy and affect regulation. In M. Cooper, J. Watson, & D. Hoelldampf (Eds.), *Person centered and experiential therapies work: A review of the research on counselling, psychotherapy and related practices* (pp. 164–187). Ross-on-Wye, England: PCCS Books.

Watson, N., Watson, J. C., & McMullen, E. J. (2014, June). *Criterion validity of self-discrepancy and affect dysregulation measures.* Paper presented at the Society for Psychotherapy Research Conference, Copenhagen, Denmark.

Weinstock, M. (2009). Contributions of early life stress to anxiety disorder. In H. Soreq, A. Friedman, & D. Kaufer (Eds.), *Stress from molecules to behaviour: A comprehensive analysis of the neurobiology of stress responses* (pp. 189–205). http://dx.doi.org/10.1002/9783527628346.ch10

Whelton, W. J., & Greenberg, L. S. (2001). The self as a singular multiplicity: A process-experiential perspective. In J. C. Muran (Ed.), *Self-relations in the psychotherapy process* (pp. 87–110). http://dx.doi.org/10.1037/10391-004

Wilson, M. (2001). The case for sensorimotor coding in working memory. *Psychonomic Bulletin & Review, 8*(1), 44–57. http://dx.doi.org/10.3758/BF03196138

Wilson, M., & Knoblich, G. (2005). The case for motor involvement in perceiving conspecifics. *Psychological Bulletin, 131,* 460–473. http://dx.doi.org/10.1037/0033-2909.131.3.460

Wing, E. H., Jr. (2010). *The relationship between therapist empathy, the working alliance, and therapy outcome: A test of a partial mediation model* (Doctoral dissertation). Available from ProQuest Dissertations & Theses Global. (Order No. 3398120)

Wolfe, B. E. (2005). *Understanding and treating anxiety disorders: An integrative approach to healing the wounded self.* Washington, DC: American Psychological Association. http://dx.doi.org/10.1037/11198-000

Wolfe, B. E., & Sigl, P. (1998). Experiential psychotherapy of the anxiety disorders. In L. S. Greenberg, J. C. Watson, & G. Lietaer (Eds.), *Handbook of experiential psychotherapy* (pp. 272–294). New York, NY: Guilford Press.

World Health Organization. (2016). *International statistical classification of diseases and related health problems, clinical modification* (10th ed.). Geneva, Switzerland: Author.

Yalom, I. D. (1980). *Existential psychotherapy*. New York, NY: Basic Books.

Zaretskii, V. K. (2009). The zone of proximal development: What Vygotsky did not have time to write. *Journal of Russian & East European Psychology, 47*(6), 70–93. http://dx.doi.org/10.2753/RPO1061-0405470604

Zinbarg, R., Craske, M., & Barlow, D. H. (1994). *Therapist's guide for the mastery of your anxiety and worry program*. Albany, NY: Graywing.

INDEX

Avoidance of feelings, as emotional
change principle, 53–55
Awareness
and avoidance of feelings, 53–55
as emotional change principle, 52–53
of emotions, 77–78
of emotion schemes, 25
experiential, 44–45
of inner experiences, 45–46
of negative self-treatment, 175
of organismic experience, 125–126
of painful emotions, 68–69
Axis I disorders, 5
Axis II disorders, 5

Barrett-Lennard, G. T., 97, 129
Behaviors of others, naming, 194,
198–201
Benjamin, L. S., 100
Berg, A. L., 39
Blame
and collapsed self, 175
transforming, 160–161
in two-chair dialogues, 79, 168–169
Blame–withdraw cycle, 100
Blocks to self-soothing, 218–221
Bodily experience(s)
awareness of, 6
in awareness of emotions, 54–55
in emotion processing, 121, 122
of emotions, 44–46, 54–55
helping clients access, 161
of psychological and physical pain, 43
of therapist during treatment,
110–111
Body language, 111
Bohart, A. C., 24
Bolger, E. A., 42–43
Bonding, 66
Borkovec, T. D., 21–23
Bowen, M., 20
Bowlby, J., 20
Breathing, for anxiety regulation, 22
Buber, M., 95

Caretaking
abusive, 49
and affect regulation, 33
and expression of needs, 32–33
and self-soothing, 58
and vulnerable sense of self, 31–32

Caring
facilitating expression of, 177–178
in therapeutic relationship, 93
Case formulation, 69–73
Cassidy, J., 21
Catastrophizing, 9, 59, 73, 136, 162
Chair dialogues, 7, 11. *See also* Empty-
chair dialogues; Two-chair
dialogues; Worry dialogues
Change, working at growth edge to
facilitate, 156
Childhood trauma
and development of GAD, 25–26
and GAD in adulthood, 18, 21–22
Choice, 67
Circumplex model, 99, 100, 125, 199
Claiming space, 204–206
Cognitive avoidance theory of worry,
22–23
Cognitive behavioral perspectives,
21–23
Cognitive organizing process, 59–60
Collaboration, in therapeutic
relationship, 105–107
Collapsed self
markers of, 175
working with, 161–163, 170
Comforting experiences, identifying, 215
Comorbidities, 5
Compassion. *See also* Self-compassion
activating, 217–221
facilitating expression of, 177–178
Compassionate self-soothing, 81–82,
155. *See also* Self-soothing
Competence, developing sense of, 58
Comprehensiveness, 98–99
Congruence
in therapeutic relationship, 97–100
through awareness of inner
experiences, 46
Conjectures responses, empathic, 103
Connection
psychological need for, 30
sacrificing needs and feelings for, 130
unmet needs for, 25
Control, fear of being out of, 107
Coping self-soothing, 81, 211, 213–215
identifying comforting experiences,
215
imagining a safe place, 214–215

Expression
of care, 177–178
of compassion, 177–178
of core pain, 171–172
as emotional change principle, 55–56
of feelings, 170–171, 176, 188–194
of impact of worrying, 140–150
of needs, 32–33, 150–153, 170–171, 176
of negative self-treatment, 169–170
of self-compassion, 201–204
of self-protective anger, 201–204
supporting full expression, 188–194
of understanding, 97
of worries, 139–140

Facial expressions, 187, 191
Fairbairn, W. R., 20
Fear, 17, 18, 51
of abusive caretaker, 49
acknowledging, 159–160
anxiety distinguished from, 51
in development of vulnerable sense of self, 30
of disintegration of self, 34, 62–63, 212
of experiencing emotions, 34–35
softening, 159–160
as threat to integrity of self and identity, 27
transforming, 61
triggers of, 46
unconscious, 21
undifferentiated, 122
unresolved, 162
Feelings. *See also* Emotion(s)
accessing, 186
avoidance of, 53–55
expressing, 170–171, 176, 188–194
naming, 52
sacrificing, 130
supporting full expression of, 188–194
Fichter, M., 21
Freedom, as source of anxiety, 24
Freud, S., 30
Freud, Sigmund, 20, 54

GAD. *See* Generalized anxiety disorder
Geller, S. M., 106

Gendlin, E. T., 24
Generalized anxiety disorder (GAD), 5–6. *See also specific topics*
development case example, 27–39
development of, 25–27
as DSM anxiety condition, 18–19
EFT treatment for, 38–40. *See also* Emotion-focused therapy (EFT) for GAD
impact of, 3
intergenerational transmission of, 3
symptoms of, 18
theories of, 19–24
undifferentiated distress in, 4–5
Genetics, 19
Genuineness, 93, 98
Goals, emotions and, 57
Goldman, R. N., 70
Greenberg, L. S., 66–67, 70, 106, 136
Grief
accessing, 75
emotional pain distinguished from, 43
in empty-chair work, 80, 182, 201
as healing, 80
and self-protective anger, 56
self-soothing for, 221–222
in transforming maladaptive emotions, 69, 182
Growth, 67

Health care costs, 3
Helplessness, 30
fear of, 107
"staying with," 161–162
Hermeneutic function of empathic responding, 120
Hoffman, D. L., 3
Hughes, S., 82–84

Identity formation
differentiation in, 130
and vulnerable sense of self, 30–32
Identity injuries, 31, 41, 43
Identity validation, 30
Imaginary child, dialoguing with, 217–218
Imaginary transformations, 222–223
Imagined other, visualizing, 187

Pain. *See also* Core pain
    in achieving goals, 57
    acknowledging, 159–160
    bodily experience of, 43
    emotional, 42–44
    physical, 43
    reluctance to address, 114
    transforming. *See* Empty-chair
        dialogues
Painful emotions
    becoming aware of, 68–69
    difficulty in accessing/expressing,
        206
    empathizing with, 162
    grief distinguished from, 43
    importance of processing, 121–122
    negative ways of responding to, 34
    resolving, 66. *See also* Emotional
        processing
    source of, 74
Physical pain, 43
Physiological response, suppression of,
    23
Physiological soothing, 81, 213–214
Polyvagal theory, 94, 123
Porges, S. W., 54, 94
Presence, therapeutic, 66, 93–95, 105
Primary adaptive emotions, 49
    defined, 12
    in transforming primary maladaptive
        emotions, 60–62
Primary maladaptive emotions, 49–50
    defined, 12
    fear and anxiety, 51
    transforming, 60–62
Productivity loss, 3
Proprioception, 44
Protection, 4
    anger as, 39, 56, 69, 80, 131, 152–153,
        201–204
    anxiety as, 29, 30, 48
    providing, 219–221
    psychological need for, 30
    unmet needs for, 25, 26
    worry as, 29, 30, 74
Proximal zones of development,
    working in, 132–134
Psychodynamic perspectives, 20–21
Psychological needs, 30

Redefining the self, 130–132
Reflection(s)
    in EFT therapy, 101–104
    as emotional change principle, 59–60
    function of, 120
Refocusing responses, empathic, 103–104
Regulation. *See also* Affect regulation
    as emotional change principle,
        56–58
    by organism, 45
    self-, 31
Relational psychodynamics, 20–21
Relationships. *See also* Caretaking;
        Therapeutic relationship
    and development of anxiety, 20
    early, importance of, 23
    rebalancing responsibility in, 130–132
Resilient self-organization, developing,
    159
Resonance, 97
Responsibility in relationships,
    rebalancing, 130–132
Responsiveness, of therapist, 109–113
Rogers, C. R., 24, 54, 96–98
Rudick, D., 21
Ruptures, in therapeutic relationship,
    106, 113–114

Sadness
    acknowledging, 159–160
    in development of vulnerable sense
        of self, 30
    as threat to integrity of self and
        identity, 27
    in transforming maladaptive
        emotions, 68–69
    unconscious, 21
    undifferentiated, 122
    unresolved, 162
Safe place, imagining, 214–215
Safety
    building, 107–109
    neuroception of, 94
    relational context for, 95
Sandahl, C., 39
Sandell, R., 39
Secondary emotions, 12–13, 50
Self
    differentiation of others and, 130–132,
        203–206

as threat to integrity of self and
identity, 27
transforming, 61, 62
Short-term treatments, 6
Sibrava, N. J., 21
Siegel, D. J., 119
Signal anxiety, 20
Sincerity, 97. *See also* Congruence
Small-t trauma, 25, 135
Soothing, 4, 5
Steckley, P. L., 128
Stern, D. N., 31
Stories, 118–119. *See also* Life narratives
Strengthening the self, 77–78, 115–134
case example: impact of an intrusive
other, 132
case example: overburdening the
self, 126–129
changing negative self-treatment
and processing affect, 121–126
defined, 14
fostering more positive
self-organizations, 117–118
rebalancing responsibility in
relationship and redefining
self, 130–132
symbolizing experience, 118–121
working in clients' proximal zones
of development, 132–134
Subjective experience
anxiety disorders as result of, 24
differentiation of, 130, 131
of pain, 42–434
therapist understanding of, 110
Sullivan, H. S., 20
Supportive-expressive psychotherapy, 21
Symbolization of experience, 32, 118–121
and deconstruction of worldviews,
120–121
by developing more coherent
narratives, 118–119
in empty-chair dialogues, 205
and identifying triggers for anxiety,
119–120
inadequate, 35–38

Task(s)
defined, 13
of EFT, 6–7
refusal to do or complete, 206–207

Task collaboration, 67
Task completion, 68
Task-specific work, promoting, 67–69
Theories of generalized anxiety disorder,
19–24
cognitive behavioral, 21–23
experiential, 24
psychodynamic, 20–21
Therapeutic attitudes
clients' experience of, 128–129
expression of, 100–104
in processing pain, 44
Therapeutic presence, 66, 93–95, 105
Therapeutic relationship, 6, 7, 76, 93–114
acceptance and warmth in, 95–97
building trust and safety in, 107–109
and changes in clients, 116–118.
See also Strengthening the self
congruence/sincerity in, 97–100
developing collaboration and
working alliance in, 105–107
developing therapist responsiveness
in, 109–113
empathy in, 97
expression of therapeutic attitudes
in, 100–104
facilitating, 66–67
positive, effects of, 105
ruptures in, 106, 113–114
therapeutic presence in, 94–95
Therapist responsiveness, developing,
109–113
Thomas, C.L., Jr., 21
Timulak, L., 24, 82–84
Transformation(s)
of blame and defensiveness, 160–161
by developing self-soothing, 178–182
from EFT perspective, 52
emotional, self-soothing for, 221, 229
as emotional change principle, 60–62
imaginary, 222–223
of old emotions by new emotions, 56
of pain. *See* Empty-chair dialogues
Transformational self-soothing, 81,
178–182, 221, 229
dialoguing with imaginary child,
217–218
dialoguing with vulnerable self,
216–217
markers for, 211, 212

ABOUT THE AUTHORS

Jeanne C. Watson, PhD, is a professor in the Department of Applied Psychology and Human Development, Ontario Institute for Studies in Education, University of Toronto. As a major exponent of humanistic–experiential psychotherapy, she has contributed to the development of emotion-focused therapy, the process experiential approach. In 2001, she received the Outstanding Early Career Achievement Award from the International Society for Psychotherapy Research and served as president of the International Society for Psychotherapy Research from 2014 through 2015. Dr. Watson has co-authored or coedited seven books on psychotherapy and counseling, including *Learning Emotion-Focused Therapy: The Process Experiential Approach to Change* (2003); *Expressing Emotion: Myths, Realities, and Therapeutic Strategies* (1999); *Client-Centered and Experiential Psychotherapy in the 21st Century: Advances in Theory, Research and Practice* (2002); *Handbook of Experiential Psychotherapy* (1998); *Process-Experiential Psychotherapy in the Treatment of Depression* (2005); and *Case Studies in Emotion Focused Treatment of Depression* (2007), as well as more than 70 articles and chapters. She conducts trainings in emotion-focused therapy in Europe and North America and maintains a part-time private practice in Toronto.

Leslie S. Greenberg, PhD, is a Distinguished Research Professor Emeritus of Psychology at York University in Toronto, Ontario, Canada. He has authored the major texts on emotion-focused approaches to treatment of individuals and couples. These include the original texts *Emotion in Psychotherapy* (1986), *Emotionally Focused Therapy for Couples* (1988), *Facilitating Emotional Change* (1993), and *Emotion Focused Therapy: Coaching Clients to Work Through Their Feelings* (2002); and more recently, *Emotion-Focused Therapy of Depression* (2006), *Emotion-Focused Couples Therapy: The Dynamics of Emotion, Love, and Power* (2008) with Jeanne Watson, and *Case Formulation in Emotion-Focused Therapy* (2015) with Rhonda Goldman, as well as *Emotion-Focused Therapy: Theory and Practice* (2010). He has published extensively on research on the process of change. Dr. Greenberg has received the Distinguished Research Career Award of the International Society for Psychotherapy Research, as well as the Carl Rogers Award and the American Psychological Association Award for Distinguished Professional Contributions to Applied Research. He also has received the Canadian Psychological Association Professional Award for Distinguished Contribution to Psychology as a Profession. He conducts a private practice for individuals and couples and trains people internationally in emotion-focused approaches.